The Book of

Penge, Anerley & Crystal Palace

The Book of Penge, Anerley & Crystal Palace

The Community Past, Present & Future

Peter Abbott

HALSGROVE

First published in Great Britain in 2002

British Library Cataloguing-in-Publication Data
A CIP record for this title is available from the British Library

ISBN 1 84114 210 7

HALSGROVE

Halsgrove House
Lower Moor Way
Tiverton, Devon EX16 6SS
Tel: 01884 243242
Fax: 01884 243325
email: sales@halsgrove.com
website: http://www.halsgrove.com

Frontispiece photograph: *Queen Victoria celebrated many occasions at Crystal Palace.*

Printed and bound in Great Britain by Bookcraft Ltd, Midsomer Norton

CONTENTS

Rural days, rural views. A view of the Palace from the east, taken in the 1930s from the church tower at Beckenham. (LCH)

The Palace grounds, once powerful in attracting the great and the good, are now honoured by dogs on their daily walks. (EP)

Acknowledgements

Considerable help was provided by the following, to whom deep gratitude is felt: Raymond Martin for cataloguing and managing nearly 1,000 illustrations, keeping track of their owners and returning masters; Chris Doran, Andrew and Penny Read, Doris E. Pullen and Aliyi Ekineh for proof-reading the entire text and offering valued suggestions. Grateful acknowledgement is offered for contributions from members of the Anerley Writers Circle and the entire community in and around Penge, Anerley and Crystal Palace, especially the 68 as identified in the text and captions as follows:

Peter Abbott	PA
Amber Valley Gazetteer	AV
Anerley Methodist Church	AMC
Bank of England	BoE
Nicholas Barton	NB
T.M. Baynes	TB
Patrick Beaver	PB
Beckenham Crematorium	BC
Martin Booth	MB
Borough of Bromley, London	LBB
Brenda Brent	BB
John Brown	JB
June Burrows	JBs
Ivan Butler	IB
Croydon Advertiser	CA
Croydon Library	CL
Crystal Palace Campaign	CPC
Crystal Palace Magazine	CPM
Mrs J. Deakins	JD
P.H. Delamotte	PHD
Chris Doran	CD
Neil Everitt	NE
Tarzem Flora	TF
Crystal Palace Foundation	CPF
Nick Grimsdale	NG
John Gwyer	JG
Frederick Hartt	FH
Sidney Hodgson	SH
Eddie Homewood	EAH
Colin Hood	CH
Terence W. Jenkins	TWJ
Sheldon Kosky	SK
Lambeth Libraries	LL
Living Publications Ltd	LP
Local History Centre, Bromley	LHC
Austin Lockwood	AL
Steve McCarthy	SMcC
John McKean	JM
MacMillan's Encyclopaedia	ME
Derek Mark	DM
Raymond Martin	RM
Peter Moyse	PM
New Millennium Exper Co.	NMEC
News Shopper	NS
Ordnance Survey	OS
Penge Congregational Church	PCC
Penge Urban District Council	PUDC
Roy Peskett	RP
Eric Price	EP
John Price	JP
Price & Harrison Collection	P & H
Doris E. Pullen	DP
GVR 'John' Pullen	VRP
Andrew Read	AR
Nicholas Reed	NR
Eddie Richardson	ER
Steven Rose, Prof.	SR
Nigel Sands, Revd	RNS
Ravensbourne Geological Soc.	RGS
Muriel V. Searle	MS
Jan Shorrock	JS
Steve & Jayne Stinton	S & JS
Caroline Stokes	CS
David Tomkin	DT
Biff Vernon	BV
Paul Vernon	PV
George West	GW
Writing Magazine	WM

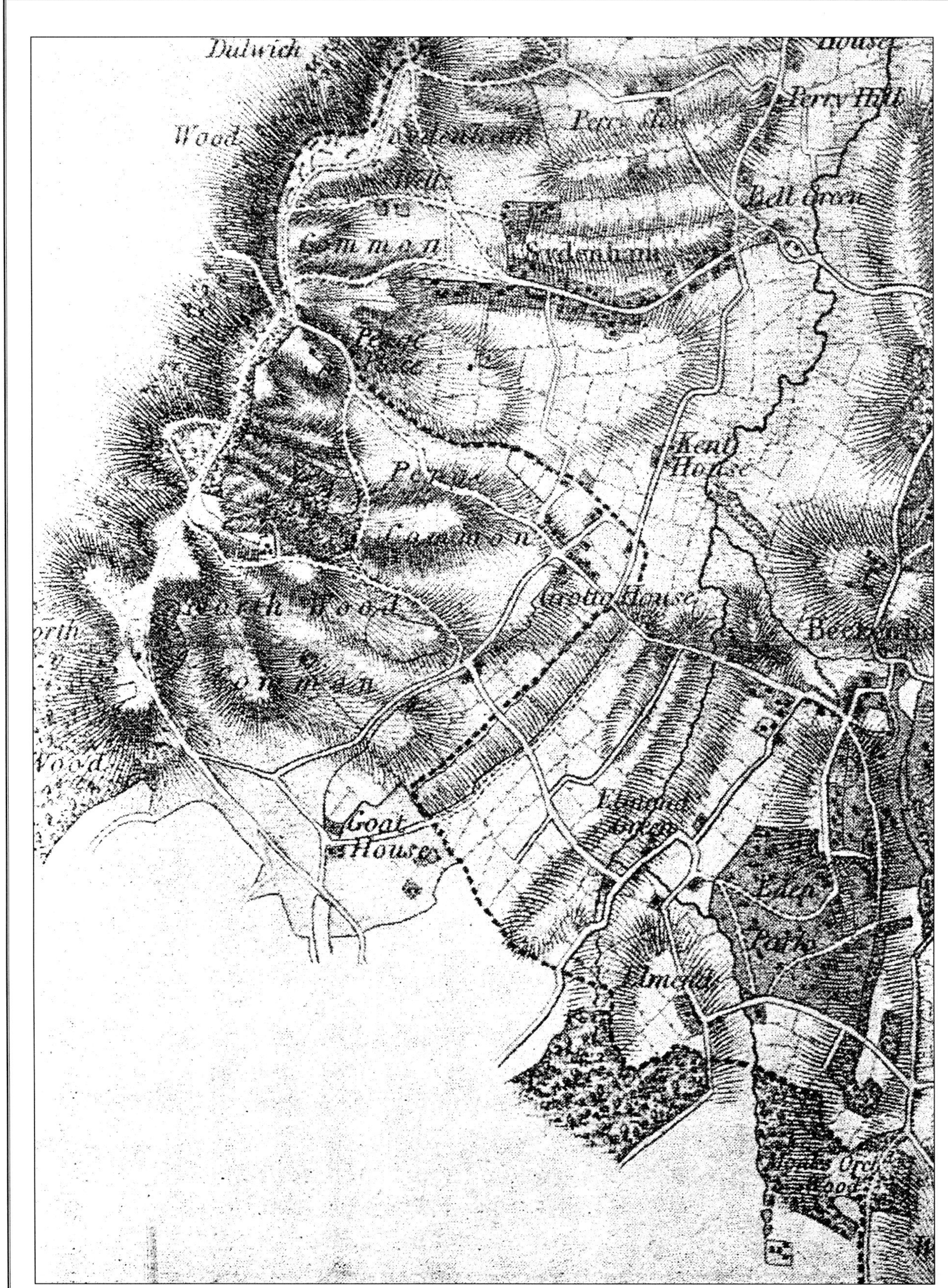

Ordnance Survey Map, 1801. (OS)

INTRODUCTION

Writing this book has been such an exciting project. Sifting through the contacts, the friends of friends, meetings, memories, earlier works, memorabilia, loose ends and muddled recollections, sorting them and knitting them together in some semblance of order has been a maze of a journey. Of course even the story unravelled here is but a microcosm of what happened, and is still happening, in the area. One stands on the shoulders of others, of course, and we have drawn on over 100 sources, many of which are acknowledged.

Sadly, many of the sources are secondary reports of other people's reports. Their accuracy has not always been independently verifiable. Later writers have copied earlier writers. According to Simon Finch, manager of the central library's local studies centre, pretty well all of the official records were recycled in 1941 as part of the war effort.

Defining an area to focus on is never too easy, especially in London. How can one write about Penge without covering Anerley where its town hall stands? And how can one cover both without including Crystal Palace, which has dominated the whole area in so many ways? Then, one might ask, if covering that, should one include Upper Norwood and Sydenham, which played, and still play, influential roles in the area? This is not to mention the GLC who developed Crystal Palace Park, the LCC who ran it and the LBB who does so today. The best that we can do is to draw a thin line around an inner core or community area, within which we cover as much as we can, and from this area we stray whenever and wherever it suits, to paint a fuller and richer picture. This area is defined as that which has been governed by its local authority for just over half a century – Penge Urban District Council, whose reign from 1900 to 1965 did a great deal to forge its character. Thus we refer to this area throughout as the District.

The District of Penge, Anerley and Crystal Palace has had a chequered history – from the authorisation of a canal in 1801 to today, when the Eurostar glides through it; from the arrival of one Crystal Palace to the rejection of its replacement. Clearly, transport has had more than a passing interest, being more or less responsible for the development of the area.

It is clear that we can merely scratch the surface, providing a glimpse of life here; listening to a thousand and one stories and reading others whose fragments have graced the local press over the years. We can only attempt to make our contribution representative, to offer a flavour of what it is really like. Yet at best this can only be a sniff, and a biased one at that. It began as some idle doodling by our chairman. One can hardly be more biased than that. Casting his net around, haphazardly, some dozen or so others came forward to join him. These trawled rather wider to bring in the views – both emotional and visual – of maybe 100 others. Yet how can even that really represent a community of 20,000? All we can say to those of you who seem least represented, is why not play a more active role next time? In particular, we, from the Anerley Writers Circle, set out to explore how life has changed, with a view to crystal-ball gazing into what will happen next. We invite you to enjoy the journey with us.

ANERLEY WRITERS CIRCLE
2002

Contributors

Peter Abbott has lived in or around Penge, Anerley and Crystal Palace since 1948, when his father's job brought the family to the area. He went to school, bought the family's weekly shopping in the Maple Road Market, attended St Anthony's School, played truant in Crystal Palace Park, caught tiddlers in the Pool River and had his first suit handmade at Thorogoods, where the main Post Office now stands. Although, like so many, he has moved on, he still finds it worthwhile returning regularly, not just to maintain lifelong friendships and show visitors the sights of Crystal Palace Park, but also to buy household goods and vegetables at some of the keenest prices and standards in the whole of South London. Peter is an established speaker, the writer of a few hundred articles and author of five books – the first of his series of novels is due out shortly after publication of this volume.

Raymond Martin was born in London in 1940 and moved to the area in 1998. After working for some years in engineering he moved into the publishing sector, mostly producing technical publications for the Ministry of Defence. Then, a few years on, he returned to college to study technical illustration, gaining an Association of Computing qualification in Java programming, before setting himself up as a freelance illustrator. He finds the Internet extremely useful and appreciates its potential for his business. Raymond has a wide knowledge of art, design and architecture and the related disciplines of painting, drawing, photography, printmaking and computer art. For these pages he has built up a library of over 1,000 illustrations, selecting just a selection of those to illustrate stories, and preparing them for publication.

Doris Pullen was born in 1920 in Sydenham, London. Her father, George Lord, was serving in the RAF and after a private school education she travelled to Egypt. Returning to the UK in 1935, Doris married in 1939. Her second marriage took place in 1952 and she brought up three daughters, a son and two stepsons. In 1970 she became a teacher after training at Rachel McMillan's College, Deptford. After working for a while at a private school, she became a tutor for ILEA in Family History and the Monumental Inscription Secretary for the Society of Genealogists, where she worked part-time for 25 years and made a FSG in 1996. Doris has published five local history books and co-edited a sixth; these feature Sydenham, Penge, Forest Hill, Dulwich, war memoirs and Beckenham. Her interests are mainly in local history and social history. She is a member of the Institute of Genealogical Studies, the Lewisham History Society, Bromley Local History Society, North West Family History Society, the National Trust and Crystal Palace Foundation. In Chapter Nine she recalls 80 years of change in Penge.

Peter M. Cooke was born in Nottingham and has lived in Upper Norwood since 1965. A lifelong member of the Salvation Army, he contributed widely to their publications for 40 years, and wrote four books. His interests include music, poetry, theatre, travel and history.

Eric Price, born in 1932 in Thornton Heath, was evacuated to East Devon in 1941, returning home in 1944. He attended Ingram Senior Boys' School, after which he left to start a four-year apprenticeship at a ladies' and gentlemen's hairdresser in Croydon. From 1950–2 he served in the RAF, before taking over a hairdressing business at 84 Anerley Road, SE19, in 1957 and purchasing the property in 1959. He was an active member of the Penge & District Round Table and in the 1960s won an award for the best silent film in a national competition run by the Round Table. He also achieved a Diploma of Merit at the Scottish Amateur Film Festival of 1966 entitled The Integrated Tutorial System. In the 1970s, he and six other enthusiasts and collectors of memorabilia met regularly in the flat over his barber's shop to discuss ways of keeping the memory of Crystal Palace alive. In the spring of 1979 they organised two 'History of Crystal Palace' exhibitions in the National Sports Centre. Such was the response, with over 1,000 visitors attending, that they formed the Crystal Palace Foundation and, after much fund-raising and negotiation, the museum was opened on 17 July 1990 by the Duke of Devonshire in the Anerley Hill building, which had originally housed the Crystal Palace School of Practical Engineering. Many of his local pictures have been used for picture postcards; others adorn his barber's shop and quite a few illustrate many parts of this book. Still practising his hairdressing business today, he is believed to be the longest-serving trader in the district.

Elena Gelpke was born in 1936 and grew up in Holland. She trained in Spain and speaks five European languages. After 35 years in New York, 25 of them with the UN, she retired to the comparative quietness of Brussels to write memoirs of over 80 spells in nearly all of the world's hottest trouble spots. Like our Queen Elizabeth I, she invariably found herself a single woman in a tumultuous sea of 1,000 men, including many men of passion. Being attractive in so many ways, remaining in sole charge of her life was quite a challenge; as she says, 'but I lived to tell the tale'. In Brussels she flung herself into no less than nine local organisations, but none more enthusiastically than Toastmasters International. Here, in just a year she became a Competent Toastmaster, in two years an Advanced Toast-master, and is currently an area governor. A frequent and regular visitor to Anerley, she writes of her experiences in the area movingly, with understanding and with sympathy in Chapter Nine.

Paul Vernon is the second of Brian and Elisabeth Vernon's five children. In his early days, his physics teacher notably asked, 'Vernon, what do you want to be, when you grow up? If you grow up.' First he wanted to be an artist, but learned that this was not a very financially fulfilling career. Then he thought about being an architect, as it combined the arts with the sciences, but he soon felt that this would be too chancy and/or hard work carving out a niche and developing the self-confidence to make a living. So he settled for a career in engineering, moving from design to management and on to consulting, writing about his experiences all the way.

Terence W. Jenkins describes himself as an ex-teacher, traveller, short-story writer, freelance journalist, London Guide and flâneur, and he has lived in the area for the last 17 years.

Chris Doran was born in 1947 just over the border in Beckenham. Like his parents and grandparents, he has lived most of his life in the area, apart from a few years spent in Nottingham where he obtained his doctorate in physics. He attended three of the schools about which he writes: Alexandra Infants and Junior schools, and Penge Grammar School for Boys. He was secretary of Penge Council of Churches from 1978 until its closure in 1991. At the time of writing he holds the same post in Penge Forum, an association for local residents and voluntary organisations. He is also the archivist for Penge Congregational Church.

Andrew Read, born Chesham, Bucks., has lived in Penge with his family since 1988 and works for a major TV company. Fascinated by the First World War since the age of six, and with Penge since moving here, has made Andrew an ideal contributor to Chapter Five on the world wars.

Aliyi Ekineh was born to Anglican parents in 1921, in the island port of Abonnema in the Niger Delta. He converted to Catholicism while at school and began his working life as a school teacher. In 1947 he came to the UK and studied law and political science at the London School of Economics. He was called to the Bar of Lincoln's Inn in 1953, but later returned to Lagos to set up a practice which continues to this day. He was sometime editor of the *Nigerian Bar Journal* and secretary of Liberty, the Nigerian section of the International Commission of Jurists, based in Geneva. He served on various governmental commissions and enjoyed a spell as 'Scholar in Residence' at the University of California, Los Angeles before returning to his practice. He also worked as a freelance journalist for the *Daily Times* and presented discussion programmes on Federal TV. Having now retired, Aliyi lives in Beckenham with his wife Florence, a former ward sister at St James' Hospital, Leeds. They recently celebrated their golden wedding anniversary. Aliyi spends much of his time campaigning for the separation of Southern Nigeria from the rest of the country, which he believes to be ungovernable and 'bogged down in never-ending conflicts rooted in the country's unwieldly number of communities'. He is the author of several books on this subject, as well as two novels. His latest, *Juju Moon*, was published in 2001.

Paula Bookham, an architect's assistant, has lived in the area since the age of eight, a 1960s child born of an evangelically fanatic mother and a stoical LSE-trained father. She studied accountancy and finance at Croydon College before embarking on a career of business management and a private life of writing, painting and a little sculpting, in between raising two strapping lads, one of whom is now raising children of his own. Paula says, 'All I want now is to be read, hung and erected in public.'

Postcard map, 1822. Only Penge Place and the Croydon Canal are new. (CPF)

One

EARLY DAYS

Imagine an expanse of stately mansions, built on a luscious common by a medieval woodland, in front of a curving canal. Now imagine this a short ride from the hub of the greatest empire ever. And then imagine all this raised a few hundred feet above and beyond the smoky stenches of this metropolis and set on the sun-facing slopes of a ridge that curtains those unhealthy lowlands from their panoramic vistas of Kent, the 'Garden of England'. This is the birthright of Penge and Anerley, an area built on foundations of oak. Take the grand old mansions of Anerley Park or the ancient Watermen's Asylum down by Penge's Crooked Billet. All over, the district of Penge and Anerley was being built to last.

Watermen's Asylum on the High Street, Penge, was built 1839. (JP)

Its solidarity began in the soil, a heavy clay laid on chalk and overlaid by millennia of forest remains. It matured in its edifices. It blossomed in its people. And, as in the truest of all human experiences, from soap operas to Shakespearean tragedies, every star character contained a personality flaw. For Penge and Anerley this exploded in the horrendous murder of 1877. Crimes of passion, over in moments, may still be forgiven in some Western-European countries even today, but this was a murder made all the more gruesome in that it took several months to inflict. So far-reaching in its effects was it that it warrants an entire chapter here (see Chapter Three). This brutal murder of the innocent Harriet Staunton by her closest relatives left deep wounds and scars on society's memory, wounds which are still healing today, over a century on.

This guide plots the course of the solidly established quarter of London. It highlights its modern features and points the way to an even better tomorrow. Penge became a suburb largely by chance. For centuries the Beckenham Road merely passed through Penge Common and on to Kent and its ports like Dover. It was such a good road that not until the Crooked Billet was built, or rebuilt in 1827 as a horse-changing hostelry, did people think of pausing here. Croydon was not so lucky. Its road from London passed through lowlands and often got bogged down, congested more than today and in winter could be quite impassable. Croydon traders got three Acts of Parliament passed in 1801, one each for the construction of the Surrey Canal, the Surrey Iron Railway and the Croydon Canal. The illustration *(see overleaf)* shows how the latter followed the local contours as it ran around the hillside where Minden Road now runs; such hillside-hugging canals are called embankment canals as an embankment on one side is all that required digging. The deep London clay underneath readily helped to make it watertight.

The Surrey Canal reached little further than the Surrey Docks, from where the Croydon Canal began. This was opened in 1809, though not completed until 1811 and included a wharf near to where Penge West now stands. Coal, food and other goods could now be readily conveyed via what was then, relatively, a great beauty spot. Penge's population stratosphered. Like so much else in life, these numbers form nature's famous ogee curve, an exponential rocketing followed by an exponential falling away:

Year	Population
1821	228
1841	270
1851	1,196
1861	5,015
1871	13,202
1911	22,330
1965	26,330
1991	25,000

'000
20
10
1800
1900
2000

Croydon Canal, 1809–36, in Penge Wood.

Penge and Anerley's popularity was given a further fillip when the railways took over the canal in 1836. Nearly all of it was drained and the railway was opened in 1839. The Palace provided a third big boost to the locality in 1854.

The 'Toffs' Move In...

The moment the canal was opened, the 'toffs' spotted how it opened the way to the distant vistas, the clean fresh air and the elbow room, all within ready commuting distance of grimy London. They stormed in, in droves, and some of their most elegant mansions remain to this day. A fine sweep of such imposing properties still stands half way down Anerley Park. These houses might have sported ten or more bedrooms, with the main reception rooms situated on an upper ground floor, reached by a number of steps up to and through the huge front door, itself wide enough to readily accommodate the hooped dresses so much the vogue amongst ladies of the mid-nineteenth century. The semi-basement floor would be where the cooks both lived and prepared the meals for the family. The attic floor held the garret rooms for the maids who undertook much of the rest of the family chores, including the daily fetching and carrying of coal to the open fires in each room, and the removal of the ashes therefrom each morning.

Gardeners for the equally spaciously set out gardens, front, rear and to the side, were more often employed on a casual and seasonal basis. Such mansions of course also required the services of a great many other workers, from the 'tinkers, tailors and candlestick makers' through to cab drivers, constables and canal operators. And as happened the world over, as the gentry occupied the drier, healthier higher ground with better views, so the manual workers tended to congregate in the nadir of the lowlands, invariably in far smaller and simpler homes. Here, Anerley represented the former, Penge the latter.

The best houses were set to face south to command the most favourable views over towards the heights of West Wickham and the Shirley Hills. Sadly the canal which dominated the immediate view

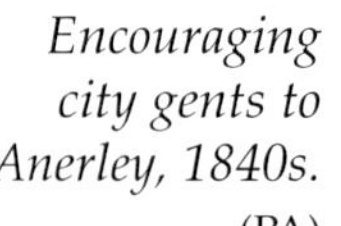

Encouraging city gents to Anerley, 1840s. (PA)

Anerley Park's finest Victorian architecture. In the 1830s this stretch overlooked the canal. (PA)

from Anerley Park is no more. And not-quite-as-smart, yet still spacious, properties have taken its place.

... & The Workers Follow

Hard on the heels of the 'toffs' came the workers. They were needed to make life bearable for their luckier counterparts. First were butlers, maids, servants and nannies – housed in those attics and basements. Next followed traders; the suppliers of daily food, milk, fuel and clothing. Then came a tier of supporters; the gardeners, road builders, chimney sweeps, Uncle Tom Cobbleys and all – each with their cloth caps or smocks, lace-up boots or draping shawls, long shovels or bulging baskets – all picking up crumbs from the 'toffs' who ran the city, country and empire. And as was constantly pointed out in church, all were busy making the world a better place. This was cleverly taught in school and church alike. Society, it was explained, was highly hierarchical. The middle class set an example to the working class by 'civilising' the Empire, and the upper class set examples to the middle classes by inspiring estates, schools and entertainments for themselves at home.

The workers were often not treated so well. Although some complained, many realised they were better off than they had been before. Indeed, their work was less hard, less uncertain and less precarious than that of the navvies and others they succeeded. No sooner had the navvies finished one railway, canal or road, than they'd be laid off into total poverty – unless by chance they heard of more back-breaking work, often many days' walk away. For them 'water was too precious for washing with', but even navvies felt better off than the charcoal burners of Upper Norwood. These grime-ridden humpers of heavy loads foraged a meagre existence for hundreds of years, once London had restricted coal supply. Charcoal-making was highly seasonal and relied on how well the coppices grew. Every drop of water was needed for fire-damping and often there was hardly any left for domestic needs.

What's in a Name?

The contrast between the words Penge and Anerley could hardly be starker. Penge dates from at least AD957, when it was spelt Penceat. Pen meant 'edge', 'end' or 'chief', and 'ceat' was a 'wood'. But Anerley dates only from the nineteenth century. A Scotsman, William Sanderson, built one of the first houses there. He named it after the Scottish word Anerly, meaning 'only' or 'alone'. He then gave land to the railway, with the proviso that they built a station nearby. So naturally they named it after the house. Now the words are sometimes used as different place names, and sometimes interchangeably, one for another. For many years there was just one local authority, Penge Urban District Council, although it operated from Anerley Town Hall. Today it is part of the unitary Bromley. The lower and eastern half is the Penge and Cator ward and the higher western half is the Crystal Palace ward.

Geological Origins

Penge and Anerley run down from the ridge of Sydenham Hill, spanning from Forest Hill to Beulah Heights and encircling much of London's southern side, sweeping down to the plains of Beckenham and Elmers End wherein meander several soggy streams. The ridge itself was most likely thrust up by a process known as the Alpine Orogeny, about ten million years ago. Its origins can be traced back to the breakup of the earth's single supercontinent of Pangea, some 150 million years ago. However, since then, Europe and Africa have moved apart and collided in several tectonic episodes. Of course the Pangea Plate was not named after Penge, or even vice versa, but the coincidence is a handy reminder of how we are all so connected together. Our Ravensbourne Geological Society has given us a permanent reminder of the vastness of geological time, in the form of several 2,000-million-year-old boulders of Lewisian Gneiss. These rocks, a gift from the Highland Council to the people of Bromley, were emplaced outside the Crooked Billet, at the top of Betts Park, and by the Penge Gate Café in Crystal Palace Park to mark the recent millennium year.

Anerley Town Hall in c.1905. Built in 1878, it was known as the Vestry Hall until 1900. (PA)

Anerley Town Hall as extended in 1911. (PA)

The Mayor of Bromley, Councillor David Crowe, unveiling the millennium boulder in Crystal Palace Park; the other boulders are now in Betts Park and by the Crooked Billet. (RGS)

Early Mentions, Early Actions

The Public Record Office, now at Kew, contains a deed written by William the Conqueror in 1067 mentioning Penge, 'Moreover I have also conceded to them [The Abbot of Westminster] all the hunting of the wood Penge' – an early example of the Abbot's dictum, 'To him which hathe shall more be given.' From these times Penge was considered a 'detached' hamlet of Battersea in the county of Surrey and the Domesday Book of 1086 includes mention of a wood here for grazing some 50 hogs in return for which duties were paid to the lord of the manor of Battersea.

In 1203 Richard of Flitch charged Almaric with stealing four pigs, though in his defence Almaric claimed the pigs were straying in Penge Wood and so he placed them in the pound at the corner of the High Street and Kent House Road.

It seems incomers have always found a welcome in Penge; a register of around 1220 included Angle names such as Woderowe, Saxon ones such as Alditha and Albretha, and Norman ones such as Alanus de Bruges and Bataille.

From the mid-twentieth century enough Poles had settled here to make it worthwhile for nearby Beckenham Library to fill an entire bookcase with Polish volumes. And from the late-twentieth century quite a community of Sri Lankans has sprung up who readily found gainful occupation in jobs such as the food and petrol retail trades.

Annie Kingham, answering calls for workers, came here from Dublin in 1946, and married Douglas Fernando, a commissioned Sri Lankan officer in the British Army, in 1947. Nowadays she is to be seen chatting to passers-by in Croydon Road, Anerley. Annie is but one of nine siblings, who like many of her compatriots, spread out from Dublin. She has siblings ranging from councillors in Sheffield to millionaires in Florida, although she lives in most modest quarters, in the basement of a former gentrified Anerley mansion.

But Penge has also helped in keeping other foreigners at bay. In 1568 oaks from what is now Crystal Palace Park were used for the ships of Drake's Armada to help defeat the Spanish navy, a navy increasingly desperate to stop buccaneers such as Sir Walter Raleigh from plundering the gold the Spanish were bringing back from Central and South America.

In 1597 a bitter dispute arose over goat grazing rights between Oliver St John, the lord of the manor of Battersea, and Edmund Style. Later, two goats had to be removed from Penge Common 'at the entreatye of a woman dwelt there.' And on William Kip's 1607 map of Surrey the place is spelt 'Pensgreene' (although local historian Sydney Hodgson believes that Kip, a Dutchman, mistook the letter 'g' for an 's').

Another wave of migrants, gypsies from Eastern Europe, came to settle in the dense woodlands of Penge and Upper Norwood (itself a corruption of Northern Wood) throughout the seventeenth and eighteenth centuries. These people found it harder to assimilate into the local community and were often feared as much as the indigenous highwaymen who found the woods a conveniently covert place in which to melt away. It is believed the Robin Hood pub derived its name from such associations.

Hodgson recounts how, in 1605, 'a most interesting survey described as "The Mete and Bounde of the Hamlet of Penge" was made.' Starting at Rockhills, a

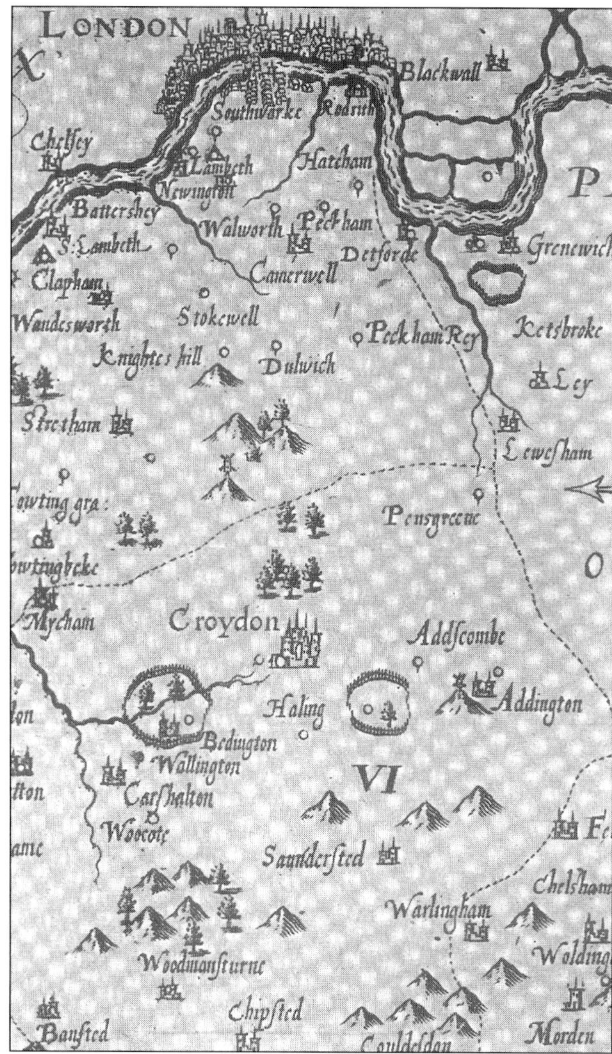

Above: *Kip's 1607 map.* (CPF)

Above right: *Section of Norden's 1595 map, from which the 1607 map was probably crafted.*

Right: *Margaret Finch, Queen of the Gypsies, who died in 1740 apparently aged 108.* (SH)

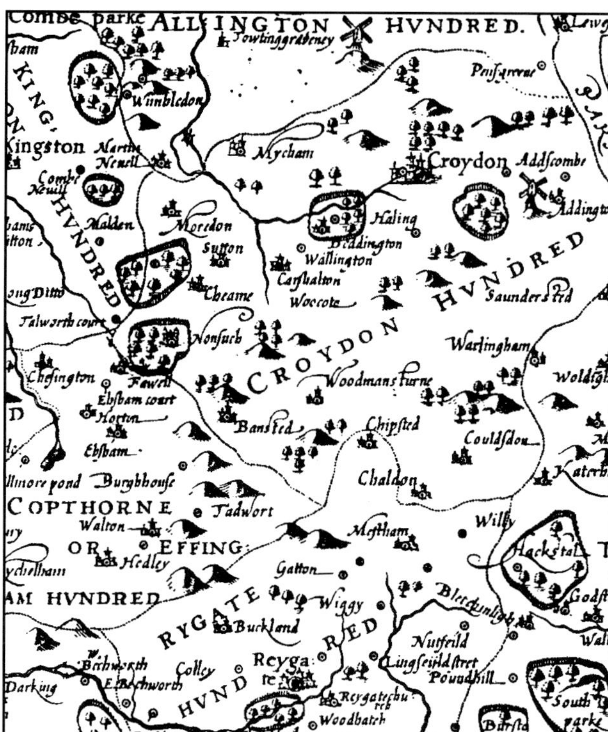

house at the top of Crystal Palace Parade, it proceeded down to Shire Ditch, also known as Boundary Stream, Penge Drain, Penge Brook and the River Willmore, where the High Street meets Kent House Road. Here it turned right, along the Ditch to Selby Road, up Maberley Road to the 'Greate Oake called Vicar's Oake at the partinge of the parishes of Croydon, Lambeth and Camberwell,' and along Crystal Palace Parade again. In 1661 this custom incurred a sum of £3.8s.0d. on the parish of Battersea for the dinner of those involved. By 1733 this item of expenditure had risen to £17.18s.0d., though this may have been due more to inflated participation than to the mere financial inflation.

In 1772 the only large house in the area, Penge Place, was sold by Mr Christie, founder of the Christie's auctioneers. It stood in the park, on Crystal Palace Park Road, near the top. Some 80 years on, and owned by the wealthy speculator Leo Schuster, it was to play a phenomenal role in shaping Penge.

As recently as 1808 Battersea held rights to pasture their animals and collect brushwood on Penge Common. The 1827 Enclosure Acts brought the common to an end, as it generated 'but little profit'. An early benefit of the Act was to require the construction of the district's two main roads; Croydon Road from east to west and Anerley Road from north to south, each 'to be 50 feet wide'.

From Pillar to Post

For centuries the Hamlet of Penge, as it was then called, was paying its tithes and taxes to Battersea, which was in the county of Surrey. But in 1855, in an attempt to overcome the confusion of government throughout London, Penge was transferred to

Above: *Annie Fernando, of Croydon Road, born in 1925 and still keeping a large garden going until 2002.* (PA)

Left: *Highway robbery! The Robin Hood pub was named after the area's reputation for banditry.*

Lewisham, a parish still in Kent. Then an 1888 Act brought Lewisham, including Penge, into London – but this only until 1900, when an Order in Council transferred Penge back into Kent again, setting it up as an Urban District. There were no less than four changes of county in 45 years.

Although it now became an independent authority for the first time, this might have been not so much due to its large population, as an official guide would have it, but more a result of a knock to its reputation following a heinous and calculated murder. A fifth change of county, in 1965, took both Penge and Beckenham Urban District Councils into the newly created London Borough of Bromley. Two further dates, the 1839 coming of the railways and the 1854 coming of the Crystal Palace, are so significant to the area they deserve entire chapters to themselves. As does, sadly, that most notorious murder ever recorded in the area, in 1877. Penge's reputation swung from fame to infamy overnight. The road where the crime was committed was even renamed. Ordinary folk started saying they'd come from Anerley, rather than from Penge. It was like Calder Hall changing its name to Windscale after its first serious nuclear accident, and to Sellafield after a second one. But more of this later.

Football Crazy

Crystal Palace conjures up the image of a great football club to millions of ardent fans across the country and across the world. But in the early days it conjured up a different picture altogether. It was the home of the Football Association's annual Cup Final from 1885 to 1914, after which the ubiquitous Wembley Stadium came into service. In 1904 the Crystal Palace Company which owned the ground proposed forming an FA soccer club, but the FA felt this might lead to a conflict of interests and in 1905 launched its own Crystal Palace Football Club, using the grounds as a tenant until after the First World War, when it moved, via Herne Hill, to Selhurst Park, while still retaining a huge Penginian following.

On the Map

Ask someone like local painter Ron Whellan of Raleigh Road or writer Dai Davis where they come from, and they're likely to say Penge and be rightly proud of it. Ask people like writer and local historian Nicholas Reed of Maple Road, or pet couturier Lynne Moran of Marlow Road and they're likely to emphasise coming from Anerley. Ask others, 'Where's Anerley?' and they'll reply, 'In Penge.' Or if pushed, 'Under the shadow of Crystal Palace.' They see the map as just three sectors, as shown.

Ask Chris Gaster, councillor of the Anerley Ward since 1971, and he says this is a shame, as Penge and Anerley have really blossomed since becoming part of that largest and best-heeled London Borough of Bromley. It's fitting that Bromley calls itself the Green Borough. This greening is a continual task, be it new squares in the High Street, trees along roadsides or the constant replanting that goes on in all the parks. Its largest park, the 300-acre (120-hectare) Crystal Palace Park, snuggling tightly between Penge and Anerley, is constantly being re-shaped to match people's changing interests.

The Ordnance Survey maps of 1861–70 show pretty well every aspect of the Crystal Palace, its park layout and the high- and low-level railway stations in place. Clearly the latter, the shorter tunnel, was there first, as it bore the simpler name of 'Crystal

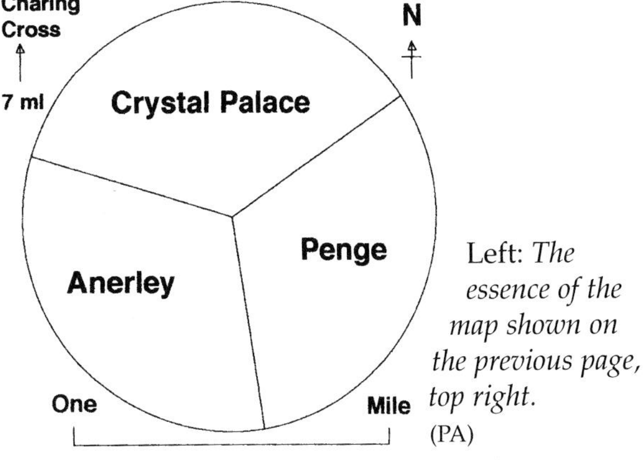

Left: *The essence of the map shown on the previous page, top right.* (PA)

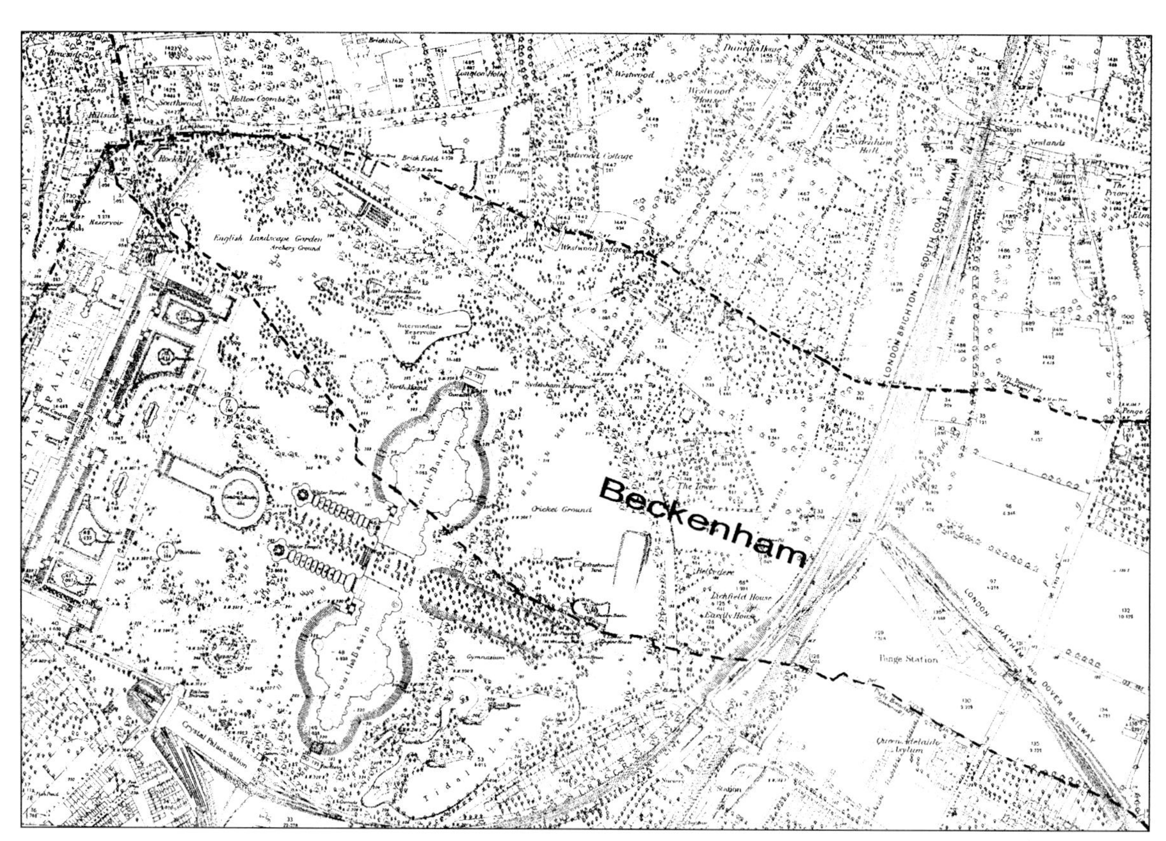

Beckenham's sliver of land up to Sydenham Hill. (PA & OS)

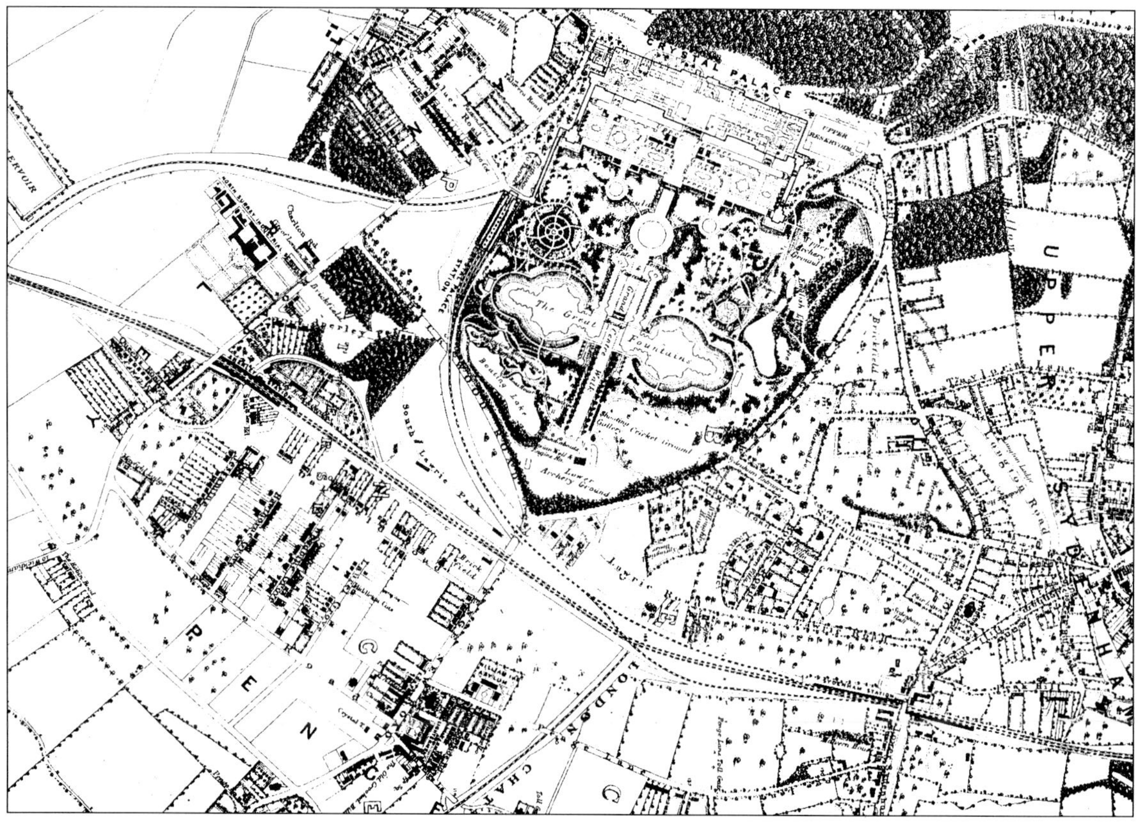

1866: the Palace has landed – the Old Crooked Billet established. (OS)

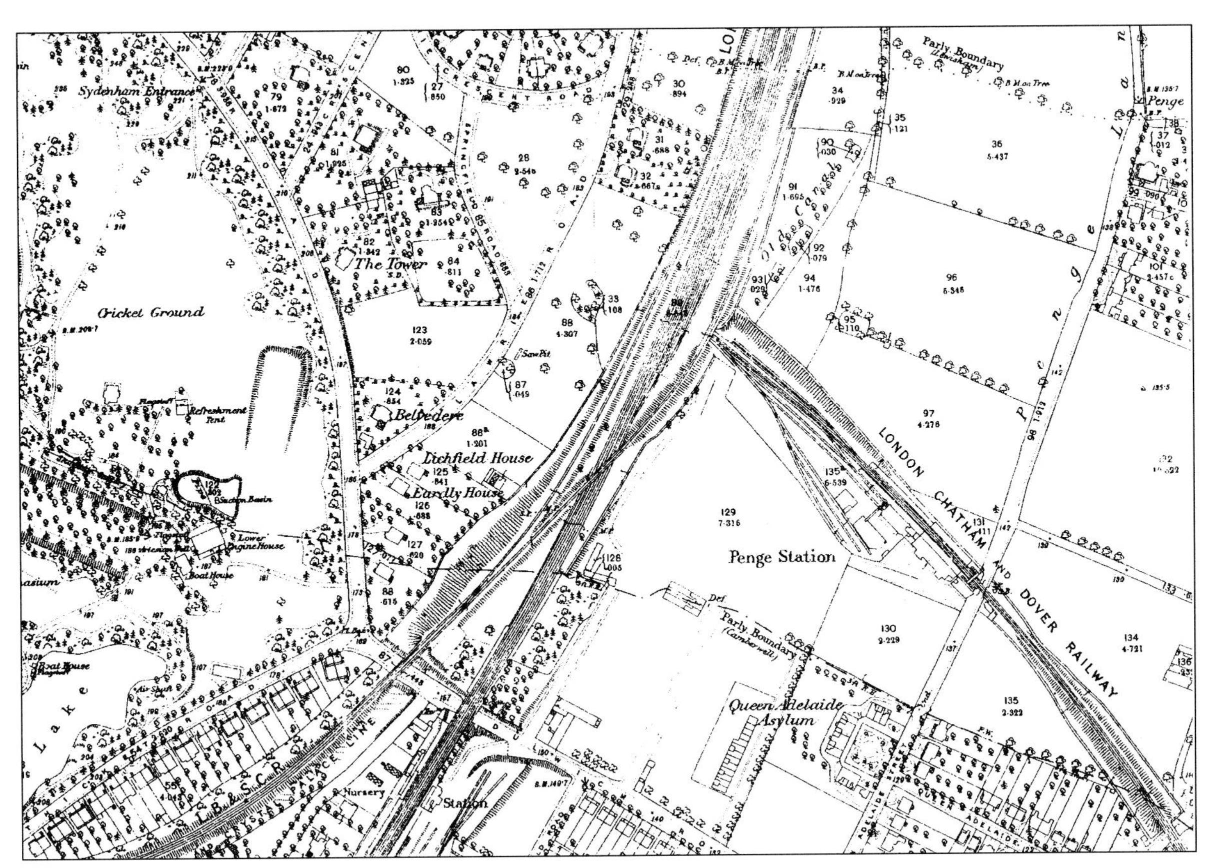

The level crossing from Queen Alexandra Street, now St John's Road, and Penge Lane, now Newlands Park Road, has long since been replaced by a footbridge. (OS)

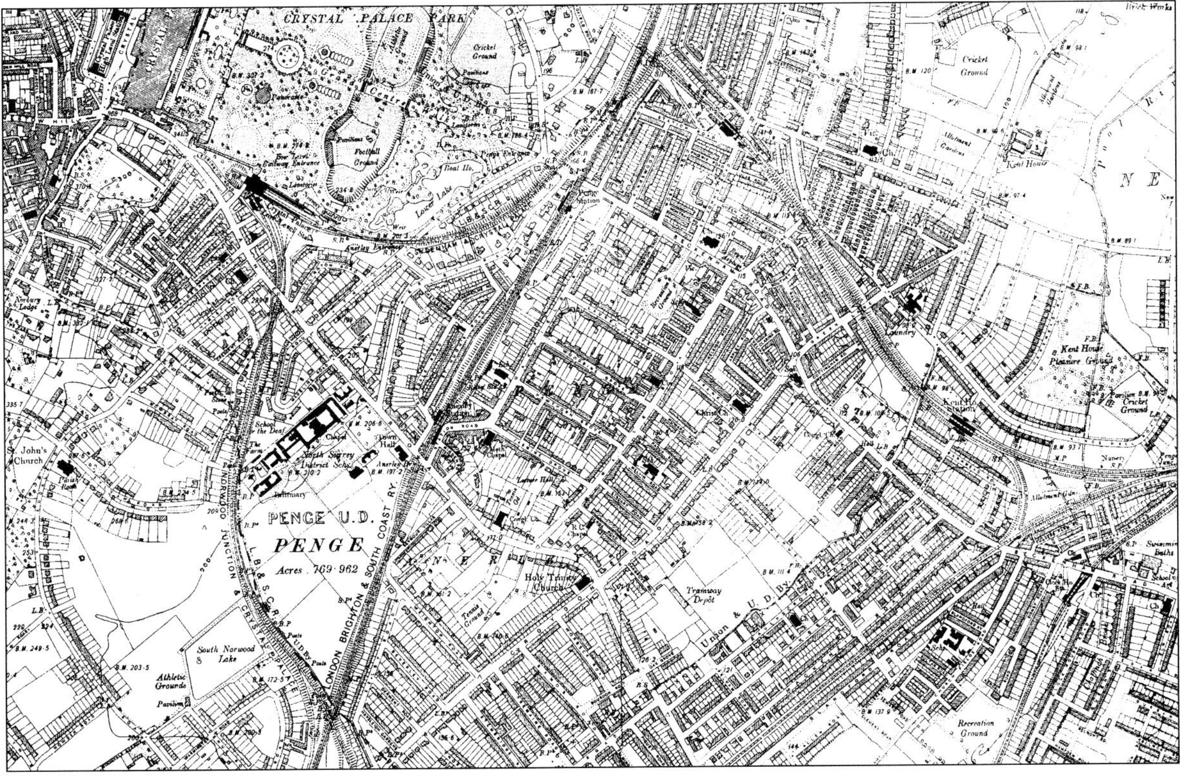

Beckenham overtakes Penge with its new railways, baths and golf courses, 1919. (OS)

Palace Station'. All the roads within a mile or more were named and flanked with large spacious residences as they are today. However, Penge Lane was the name given to what today is called Newlands Park; Maple Road was the name given to what today is Penge Lane; and High Street Penge was then known simply as Dulwich Road.

The maps of this time also show Penge as far more developed and populated than Beckenham, although Beckenham was more spaciously laid out, and its parish church older, larger and more splendid than anything Penge then sported. Penge, Anerley and most of Crystal Palace Park were in the Battersea hundreds, a 'detached' part of Battersea parish.

Beckenham Parish Church, for many years the only one available to Penginians. **(RM)**

Many an interested person has found themselves asking why Beckenham's Kentish boundary follows such a long pencil-thin tranche of land, right up from Kent House Road to a point where Fountain Drive and Sydenham Hill meet Westow Hill – right under the shadow of the BBC's 710ft TV mast, which is equally needle-sharp. Legend has it that an odd thing happened in the 1700s when such boundaries were still rather vague and only just beginning to be defined a little more thoroughly.

A beggar is reputed to have died on the road just at this point. Although it was customary by now for the parish in which someone died to be responsible for burying the said person, no one was at all sure as to whose parish this unfortunate gentleman of the road now belonged. To save further embarrassment, the worthy burghers of Beckenham took pity on the situation, agreed to bury him, and thereby claimed this sliver of land up the side of Sydenham Hill.

The development of the area, from a pig-grazing common, to a vibrant twenty-first-century suburb of a world-ranking capital, can be traced through the maps of 1801, 1822, 1866, 1871, 1919 and 2001. On the first of these, only Penge Place, Penge Grotto and Kent House appear; Beckenham sported considerably more buildings. By 1822, the Croydon Canal had been added. By the 1840s the London, Chatham and Dover Railway had brought Penge, later Penge East, Station to the area and the canal had been replaced by the London [Bridge], Brighton and South Coast Railway (LBSCR), including Penge West and Anerley stations. The arrival of the Crystal Palace removed Penge Place, moved the road it had stood in for many years, changed its name from Dulwich Road to New Penge Road, and brought a single-track spur to the LBSCR to Crystal Palace (Low Level) Station. These in turn encouraged the development of hundreds of buildings throughout scores of residential roads, from workers' hovels to grand hotels like the Queen's Hotel at the top of the hill, to Anerley Hotel (now Anerley Arms) in Ridsdale Road. Indeed, there was so much development that by now Penge and Anerley were far larger than Beckenham. An avalanche was in full flow, and all strata of society were well represented.

The 1871 map shows that Jessamine Grove had changed to Jasmine; the Luton Park pub had become the Royal Oak and the Wesleyan Chapel had joined the Congregational one. The Anerley Hotel had become the Anerley Arms pub and developed some pleasure gardens along the canal, including that popular Victorian distraction, a maze. Also by 1871 the high-level station had arrived, including its Italian subway connection under the Parade. By 1888 Anerley House had become Anerley Lodge, and Beckenham was overtaking the place as a desirable place to live.

By 1919 Beckenham had a larger built-up area and sported swimming baths, three golf courses and seven railway stations. Although Penge and Anerley had three stations, both Penge stations still claimed the same name. But at least, and since 1878, Penge had its own Town Hall, albeit in Anerley. By now Penge, Anerley and Crystal Palace were about as developed as they could be, and some early minutes of the Urban District Council, formed in 1900, record that the Council continued to interest itself 'in everything to assist the material comfort of the residents of Penge.' It had just been authorised to take over from its predecessor long since known as the Penge Vestry.

Maps of much of the twentieth century charted the continued decline, especially with the loss of the Palace – its soccer club as well as its so-called Crystal Palace – and more and more of its major mansions. Trams and trolleybuses came and went, as did the high-level station. Only recently a projected return to Crystal Palace of the tram in the forms of the Croydon Tramlink and the Docklands Light Railway extensions has been planned.

Close inspection of recent maps shows the small-scale improvements taking place since the area's absorption by the London Borough of Bromley, such as the three mini-squares in the High Street, the closure to traffic of more and more residential streets, the slowing down of others by the use of sleeping-policemen, if not total eviction of the car by pedestrianisation. All in all a wide panorama of change brought about by a galaxy of distinguished individuals, as the following chapters attempt to highlight.

Two

The Palace

If anyone suggested something like Canary Wharf be moved to Penge they'd be called mad. If this meant moving a main road to Kent a quarter of a mile east they'd say 'No way ever'. And if anyone suggested this was an enterprise worth investing in, they'd be considered barmy. Yet that's just what happened in Penge in 1852. The 1851 Great Exhibition at Hyde Park had attracted six million visitors to see the wonders of the new and scientific age. But as with anything novel, there was much opposition to the very idea of having this 'Crystal Palace' there. So it had to come down within six months. There was not even time for snow to fall upon it, so the winter scene depicted on page 25 owes more to the imagination of Peter Moyse, the artist, than his reproduction skills. Even though the bridge looks authentic, and even allowing for the differences in viewpoint, it is hard to reconcile the individual trees between the 'summer' and 'winter' views.

The Palace's architect, then Mr, later Sir, Joseph Paxton (see Chapter Eight), was desperate for a home for his masterpiece, and to raise money for its purchase and dismantling. He approached Leo Schuster, a Brighton Railway director and owner of Penge Place, which was described as 'unquestionably the most magnificent site on the outskirts of London.'

Greatest of its Day

By now Paxton had become better connected than ever and raised the money through public subscription, floating a company for the purpose on the Stock Exchange. He bought the Palace for £50,000, equivalent to some £50m at today's prices, spent another £70,000 buying the land and employing 6,400 men to rebuild it. Queen Victoria and Prince Albert even came in 1853 to see the reconstruction progress.

Paxton's ambitions grew in line with those of his directors. The floor area of the Palace was doubled to 13 acres, a second transept was added to the southern end and the structure was given a semicircular roof. At 350 feet it was taller than St Paul's Cathedral. It even required construction of the world's first New Town, at Oxford Road off Central Hill, along with three pubs, for its workers. The gardens were to be grander than those at Versailles. The private Act of Parliament for all this included provision for the moving eastwards of Penge Road, once called Dulwich Road but later renamed again as Crystal Palace Park Road.

Paxton had been the Duke of Devonshire's head gardener and done the Grand Tour of Europe by this time, during which he saw the wonderful gardens of

Bird's-eye view of the park. (JS)

Crystal Palace from the north, from Woodland Hill. (LL)

Above: *Gardens to challenge those at Versailles in France.* (P & H)

Left: *Sir Joseph Paxton, entrepreneur and architect of the Crystal Palace concept. His bust stands on a plinth in the centre of the parks and was used as shown for a campaign poster against the 1990s redevelopment proposal.* (CPC)

The Hyde Park Crystal Palace in summer. (EP)

The Hyde Park Crystal Palace in winter. (EP)

Versailles. Back at the Duke's Chatsworth House, Paxton had also been commissioned to construct the 'greatest fountain ever', and with an abundance of water available in Derbyshire it reached 270 feet. Now Paxton saw his chance to outdo both Versailles and Chatsworth. Soon he was talking his board into developing the grandest water garden and arrangements of fountains.

The main hurdle was a total absence of water, but undeterred Paxton set about digging a well, first 300 feet deep, and then nearly 600 feet, requiring a 300 horsepower steam engine to pump water up. Since vast amounts would be needed during exhibiting hours he had a large lake built at the bottom of the gardens, which soon became known as the Tidal Lake. Today it is known as the Boating Lake. The twin fountains too were to outdo those at Versailles. Paxton's original steel and glass water tower at the north end, plus a matching one for administration to the south, did not provide the pressure to outstrip the Versailles fountains, so within months these were removed and replaced with the more familiar stone and brick ones by Brunel (see Chapter Eight), who was by now also on the board of directors. These fountains easily outdid those at Versailles, sporting six times their flow. Indeed the Niagara Falls themselves claimed only six times as much flow again.

By 1854 the attraction was open to the public. Incorporating a grand Handel organ, all sorts of concerts, shows and exhibitions were staged at the Palace. Soon the magnificent 300 acres of water gardens were also complete. While the whole show was planned to receive a million visitors a month, and workers put in a six-day week to build it, the Lord's Day Observance Society succeeded in keeping it, and its gardens, closed on Sundays. They argued that if the directors of companies were so concerned, philanthropic and interested about the working class being able to visit, they should arrange for workers to have a half day off a week with no loss of pay. But society does not change so dramatically, so quickly. It was to take another century, several wars, the coming of trade unions and numerous other campaigns before that was to occur.

Meanwhile, the £0.25m–£0.5m construction estimates rose to £1.35m by the time of opening, in the commendably short time of under two years. In 1866 the north transept burnt down, in 1911 the owning company went bankrupt and the rest of the Palace sadly burnt down in 1936; even the water towers, which survived these fires, were removed in 1940 and '41 at the behest of the local residents, who were worried that they might guide enemy bombers.

Wild Prehistorics

The history of Crystal Palace models the history of evolution. As always, great chunks of it are hidden. Someone, maybe the young anatomist Richard Owen, Sir Joseph or even Prince Albert, stumbled on the idea of exhibiting life-size prehistoric animals. All we know is that the plan was approved in 1853,

A Victorian postcard of the dinosaurs. (EP)

Part of the dinosaur collection, prior to the restoration in 2002. (CPF)

An aerial view of the park. Note the maze, the BBC TV mast, the National Sports Centre and the daisy-petalled residential skyscraper. (JS)

six years before Darwin published his *Origin of Species* just down the road in Cudham.

In a way it all began a couple of centuries earlier. In 1677 a Revd Robert Plot from Cornwall seems to have found the first prehistoric bone, a 20lb 15ins piece of thigh from a reptile dinosaur, named 150 years later as a Megalosaurus. It made him the first of what we now call palaeontologists.

This new science was progressed considerably in the early 1800s by Baron Georges Cuvier of Paris; he identified a 3ft jawbone from Masstricht – of 1990 Maastricht Treaty fame – as belonging to a large marine reptile. He called it Mosasauros; and some elongated front-leg fingers were identified as being from a flying reptile he called a Pterodactyl.

Taking a chance, he published a theory that some of these extinct animals might have predated man. But in those days Genesis reigned supreme. It taught that all animals, including man, were made at the same time. So this was not just revolutionary, but heretical as well.

As for fossil-hunting, soon everyone was at it. Mary Anning of Lyme Regis was only 11 when she found what was later to be called an Ichthyosaur. She found parts of a Plesiosaurus and then bits of a Pterosaurus. In 1822 a Mary Mantell found a strange rock which her husband, a surgeon, identified as the tooth of an unknown creature, later calling it an Iguanodon. By 1824 a William Buckland had found a fossilised bone he named Megalosaurus and in 1832 bits of another he called Hylaeosaurus. Terry Jenkins of Upper Norwood writes:

In 1825 the surgeon Gideon Mantell had collected enough parts to attempt the first reconstruction of Mary's Iguanodon; only then [did he realise] that it stood a colossal 35 feet high... Later, the collection was so large the British Museum paid £5,000 for it, a princely sum in those days... His tomb may be seen in West Norwood.

By 1841 a Richard Owen noticed that three of these dinosaur finds were land animals, different from Cuvier and Anning's water-based beasts. He supposed they must have lived in a different era; soon there were 15 dinosaurs, grouped into three major eras.

A local sculptor, Benjamin Waterhouse Hawkins, was commissioned to make statues of them and erect them on three specially prepared islands in the new tidal lake. They represent one of the world's earliest applications of reinforced concrete. Completed in 1858, they still stand to this day. The *Illustrated London News* published a photograph of VIPs, scientists, engineers, contractors and sculptors enjoying a formal celebratory dinner inside the mould for the Iguanodon.

Era	*Period*	*Species of dinosaurs*
Palaeozoic (Primary) Era	*Millions of years ago*	Dicynodon
	500	
		Labyrinthodon
	Cambrian *et al*	Plesiosaurus
	300	
		Ichthyosaurus
	Permian	
Mesozoic (Secondary) Era	200	
		Teleosaurus
	Triassic	
	170	
		Megalosaurus
	Jurassic	
		Hylaeosaurus
	140	
		Iguanodon
	Cretaceous	Pterodactyl
		Mosasaurus
Cenozoic (Tertiary) Era	65	
	Palaeocene	
	60	Palaeotherium
	Eocene	
		Anoplotherium
	40	
	Oligocene	
		Megatherium
	30	
	Miocene	
	10	Mastodon
	Paleocene	Dinornis
	0	
	Holocene	Megaloceros

BATTLE OF PENGE

Catherine Marsh, sister-in-law to Beckenham's rector at the time, befriended the navvies who built the Palace. She noted in her diary, 'Wild they might be, and absolutely undisciplined, but they never let me hear a single oath, nor one expression which could in the remotest degree shock or pain me.'

In 1854 Britain and France took up arms to defend Turkey against Russia. Paxton was invited to form a corps of these men to serve as road-builders or trench diggers in the Crimea, but shortly before setting off

The new Penge Gate, replacing the worn-out one. (PA)

some got drunk in Penge. A couple started a friendly boxing bout and others gathered round. Two worried women urged a reluctant policeman to stop them and soon the boxers had turned on him. A second officer arrived, but being heavily outnumbered, the policemen sought shelter in a house. The navvies broke in and the constables were lucky to escape with their lives, but the Penge butcher's shop was wrecked in the process. The rest of the navvies retired to their tents in Crystal Palace Park. However, hearing that two of their colleagues 'had been murdered', another troop of police turned up, began laying into the navvies with truncheons and arrested quite a few.

'A great crowd of navvies bore down to the Penge gates to rescue their comrades and it seemed as if something like slaughter was imminent.' This is how the historian Warwick described it, continuing:

> *Then a remarkable thing happened. An open carriage with two ladies drove in between the navvies and the police, halting among the seething masses. One of them stood up and shouted, 'The first one who throws a stone is my enemy. We will have no more fighting today. Two policemen are nearly killed, and seven of our poor fellows are likely to be hanged if they die.'*

The men recognised her as Catherine Marsh, calmed down, and let her speak on their behalf to get their arrested comrades released. This she did at a hastily convened magistrates' court. The Government redoubled its efforts to get everyone embarked the next morning for the Crimea. Needless to say, Miss Marsh drove to Blackwall Wharf and saw them off amongst great cheering.

A Grand Opening

The Palace was opened by Queen Victoria on 10 June 1854, precisely on time, before an enormous gathering of ambassadors, MPs, dignitaries of every hue, 1,000 musicians and choirs of 1,800 singers. You could hear a pin drop as she hailed:

> *It is my earnest desire that this wonderful structure, and the treasures and art and knowledge it contains; will elevate, instruct and delight the minds of all classes of my people.*

The organ, designed by Handel himself, was one of the largest of its day. A statue called 'Abu Simbel' was also on a magnificent scale. Antonio Canova's 'The Three Graces' in the main aisle proved so popular that concrete models were moulded for the next 100 years and no doubt adorn hundreds of back gardens, as indeed they do in that of Annie Fernando (see Chapter Eight) where they support her much-loved bird bath.

The Palace was the greatest exhibition hall of its day, it grew larger with an extra wing upon moving to Sydenham Hill, was home to concerts, boxing, annual general meetings – pretty well anything popular at the time. Imagine the craze for mazes throughout the nineteenth century; Crystal Palace just couldn't be without one, and indeed it wasn't. Built of hedges and trees, and reinstated by Bromley in the 1980s, it was made to last and is still largely there today.

One of the more popular, never mind visually spectacular, exhibits was Sir Hiram Maxim's 'famous captive flying machine.' Mrs Mark of Norwood Road recalls the many stories which Mr Walter Mark (1863–1910), her grandfather-in-law and owner of a 50-man house-building business, told her about this. When Walter Mark lived here, now thought to be the oldest house in West Norwood, Maxim lived just across the road. Maxim employed Mr Mark as his chief constructor, from around 1900 to 1904, to build a prototype for the machine in his garden. A photograph was taken on 4 March 1904, the day Walter invited 'gentlemen of the press' along, mainly from *The Times*, to view it operating with just four of its ten gondolas in place. His first son, George, born 1887, stands in the foreground looking up, aged 16 when this was taken in 1903. George's grandson Derek Mark still cherishes many huge accounts books relating to many of the houses Walter was responsible for from the 1870s to the first decade of the 1900s.

The Crystal Palace itself hosted no end of special occasions for decade after decade. Baden-Powell's Boy Scouts held many rallies there and on one occasion lots of girls turned up, wanting to join in. Lord Baden-Powell would have none of it, and all he could do was to ask his wife to see what she could manage. This was still a society in which the Suffragette movement was regarded more as a subversive extremist movement. But when Baden's wife organised this spontaneous gathering of girls, the light began to dawn and with his support she launched the (then, Girl Scout) Guide Association as their founder-leader, with growing enthusiasm over the years.

The central fountain. **(EP)**

The flying machine at Crystal Palace.

The secluded Middle Lake, stocked for fishing. **(RM)**

Scouts on one of their many major rallies in the park. **(PB)**

The bottom lake, Crystal Palace Park, 1975. (PA)

Palace Attractions

Below left: *Racing at Crystal Palace was planned before it burned down; indeed the ceremonial cutting of the turf went ahead as planned on the very day after the fire and racing commenced within five months.* (CPF)

The Topsy-Turvy Ride was a favourite among Edwardian visitors. (P & H)

A full-sized replica of the ancient Egyptian temples at Abu Simbel, as seen down the central aisle. (EP)

The Three Graces in the central aisle. (P & H)

The Greatest Fire

Following the nineteenth-century fire when the north transept was lost, a fire station was built alongside the main building. And although it helped with a few minor outbreaks, no one was the slightest prepared for what was to happen in 1936. As Patrick Beaver put it:

At 6pm on 30th November 1936, Sir Henry Buckland, on his way to post a letter, noticed a red glow within the central transept. He found one of the resident firemen and some workmen trying to put out a small fire that had broken out in a staff lavatory. The only others in the building were some rehearsing musicians. Sir Henry sent his daughter to say there was no danger. The rehearsal continued but within a few minutes he hurried back to tell them to run for their lives. Five minutes later their concert room was ablaze... The dry wooden floorboards, walls and sashes burnt like tinder and within half an hour the building was an inferno from end to end.

In all, 89 fire engines with 381 firemen, nearly half London's total force, were called. Huge crowds of sightseers required an army of foot and mounted policemen to keep them safe and force a way through for the firemen. The collapse of the central transept could be heard from five miles away, 'like the thunder of distant cannon'. Residents from all over London, as far as Harrow on the Hill 16 miles away, witnessed the ghoulish spectacle.

Times were lean in those days and the building and its contents were only insured for a 'pathetic' £110,000, which Lloyds paid out just a week later. The sinking of the *Titanic* in 1912 had been considered a 'prophetic symbol' marking the end of the Edwardian period. Beaver notes that the fire:

... portended the end of an age-old system of values, attitudes and morals already being undermined in the 1930s and which was to be swept away finally by the 1939 war.

Beaver concludes:

The eighty-five years of the Palace's existence were, perhaps, the most significant in the history of Europe. During that comparatively short period, Darwin, Freud and Picasso did their best respectively to destroy the old conceptions of God, the soul and art; while, towards the end of it, Hitler and Stalin got well on the way to destroying civilisation altogether as Einstein unwittingly worked on a formula for a future generation to use in the incineration of the world. The aims of the Crystal Palace were creative and pacific and, if it had to go, it is fitting that it went when it did.

Main: ***The beginning of the fire, 30 November 1936.***
Top: ***The aftermath of the fire; Sir Henry Buckland, general manager of the Crystal Palace Company, surveys the devastation of the morning after the fire of 30 November 1936.*** **(P & H)**

The geological seams demonstration by the dinasaur area. (PA)

Some of the 6,000 navvies who erected the Palace – Irish immigrants or local itinerant workers. (LP)

After the Wars

After two world wars and the great fire in between, the park was in a pretty poor state of neglect. Major W.F. Vernon, a London councillor in the 1950s, was charged with reviving the place for the greater benefit of nearby residents. His sports and recreation committee sought to upgrade the motor racing. The country already had excellent Formula One tracks at Silverstone and nearby Brands Hatch and Brooklands. They were big affairs requiring large tracts of land, but there were no comparable facilities for the up-and-coming popularity in Formula Four racing. Using smaller cars the sport gave a greater impression of speed and could readily be shoehorned into a smaller and more densely built-up area such as was on offer at Crystal Palace. It got off, shall we say, to a flying start. The entire park was given over to the sport every bank holiday Monday and its following grew and grew. Before long the roars of the crowds matched that of the engines, and the noise could be heard for miles around. This very success was its Achilles' heel and, some might say inevitably, soon enough the protest movement also grew and grew. Within five years restrictions imposed upon the sport lead to its curtailment and end. At another extreme, fishing was always popular in such turbulent times. Crystal Palace Park offered unrivalled peace in so tumultuous an area. Its middle lake, heavily secluded by large shrubs and many trees, formed a true haven of peace for those aficionados of this sport, and even today it has a waiting list for new members.

Everything was tried around the park. The Caravanners found a nice little niche just down from the top of the hill in what could claim to be the nearest such park to the centre of London. A hollow pit was given over to advanced car driving. A dry ski slope was readily accommodated on one of its many natural slopes. A children's zoo was launched on the opposite side of the park. The country's largest TV transmitter tower found a natural spot right at the top, vastly more dominating than either of the two water towers which had once graced the skyline so majestically. Then came the National Sports Stadium. For the locals this was simultaneously quite an intrusion as well as a first-class benefit. Centrally, the swimming pool and gymnasium housing half a dozen badminton and squash courts proved popular.

The lower lake was soon found ideal for boating, and on warm summer days attracted hundreds of rowers, paddlers and peddlers, aged from eight to eighty and more, all milling around lazily under the very shadows of the mighty dinosaurs. The hinterland behind this lake sports far more than mere dinosaurs. There's an attractively valleyed botanical garden matching anything found at Kew, and even showing off a rich set of geological strata including a coal seam. Durable and colourful notices describe the many species of ducks and other wild fowl to be found there today.

Naturally items of a more pedestrian nature have also abounded in the park. Today, near the bottom, or Penge Gate entrance, is to be found a large café, a children's playground and occasionally a visiting fairground. Considering how every such new facility brings its own share of critics, it says much for the stalwartness of the Penginian spirit that so many and such a diversity of attractions have become so popular. And yet, despite all this, it was not to last.

Post-war revival attempts included Formula Four racing, 1953. (LL)

Crystal Palace Moves to Selhurst Park

Today, to thousands of people across the world, the name 'Palace' means but one thing – soccer, Top Division soccer; not the park, still less the glass exhibition hall, but the mighty club which has been down the road at Selhurst Park since 1919. The Eagles at The Nest, as their rousing fans know them. An earlier Crystal Palace soccer club was formed in 1861 from the staff of the exhibition hall itself, and ten years on was one of the 15 original clubs to form the FA Challenge Cup. Roy Peskett, the leading football writer for the *Daily Mail*, records that 'Scratchings [in the face], defections and refusal to travel and other excuses meant that Crystal Palace reached the semi-final, losing only to the Royal Engineers.' The FA held its cup finals under the shadow of the Palace from 1885 through to 1915. Soon this was drawing crowds of up to 110,000, considerably larger than most such matches today. Indeed, so popular was soccer that in 1904 the Crystal Palace exhibition company proposed forming a new Crystal Palace football club, but the FA resisted this, fearing a possible clash of interests between its landlord and what would then be one of its members.

However, as in so many matters, a compromise was reached and an independent Crystal Palace Football Club was formed in 1905. Their first skipper, John Robson, instilled a determination in his team that they must 'win nearly every Southern League match,' to ensure that they would be invited into its First Division. In this they soon became embattled with Leyton in a race for promotion, during which attendances rocketed from a mere dozen for their opening match to over 4,000 by the end of the season.

By 1907 the Palace had secured an FA quarter final home attendance of 35,000 in just two years since their formation. Advice was sought from Aston Villa, the 'pedigree' club of the day, and their Eddie Goodman was hired as club secretary. At 19 years old he had been one of Villa's most promising players. But then he injured a knee and had to have a leg amputated. Undaunted, Eddie set about his new job with great gusto. Cannily, he searched through the records of the Crystal Palace company, and found that amongst those who bought several cup final tickets was a Mr Sydney Bourne. Contacting him, he floated the idea of starting this local soccer club, and talked him into being its first chairman. Two years later Goodman had sorted out much of the administration and became the club's manager as well, holding both jobs until retiring in 1927. In February 1915 the club, like so many other parts of Britain, faced an especially hard blow. Its ground, along with the Palace itself, was requisitioned by the Admiralty. The club moved to Herne Hill and after the war was determined to find its own more permanent ground. In June 1918 it leased a pitch opposite Selhurst Station called 'The Nest' and applied for membership of and was welcomed into the Southern League. By May 1920 the Football League formed a Third Division and Crystal Palace was one of its founder members.

From their new base Crystal Palace may have lost their first game to Merthyr and drawn their next against Plymouth, but they went on to win their next

The 2001 Crystal Palace 1st team's squad. **(NE)**

six matches, taking them to the top of the division. They were champions in their first season and with it gained promotion to the Second Division.

Entry to watch the matches in those days was one shilling to the grounds and two shillings to the stand, (five and ten pence in today's money), compared with prices of twenty and thirty pounds nowadays.

The Nest turned out to be a disappointment; not only was it a quagmire after winter rains, but smoky fogs from the nearby engine sheds hampered visibility. So by 1922 negotiations had begun for a better site, that of a disused brickworks just up the hill at Selhurst Park. The cutting of the claret and blue ribbons to mark its opening in August 1924 was undertaken by no less a personage than Sir Louis Newton, the Lord Mayor of London.

Even during the lacklustre days of the 1930s and '40s, Crystal Palace often drew crowds of over 20,000, more than double the male populations of Penge and Anerley. Sadly, competition in the Second Division was far tougher, there were as many losses as victories and the Palace only retained a foothold for four seasons. It would be another 39 years before they would be back in the Second Division again. In the meantime, the Palace got through 12 managers in 20 seasons, but by 1958 found themselves in the newly created Fourth Division. Then in 1961 Arthur Rowe saw them up to the Third Division; in 1964 Dick Graham took them up to the Second; and in 1969 they were led to the First Division by Bert Head – for the Palace, glorious '60s indeed! Now they could regularly expect attendances of over 40,000!

Being in the First Division meant not only higher attendances, but also higher turnstile prices, more cup matches and internationals. These all boosted income, but to remain at the top in this highly competitive market, one had to spend big on the best talent available. Crystal Palace had always had a keen nose for the business side of the sport, but now it had to dominate. Players once bought for a few hundred pounds, and paid under ten pounds a week, now exchanged hands for six-figure sums, and later on eight-figure ones with six-figure wages. Such investment is not for the fainthearted, nor for just the enthusiast. It required business astuteness of the highest order to reach and remain in the top division.

Any mixing of business with pleasure ran enormous risks. One was investing not just in the fickle nature of players' muscles, tendons and bones,

Manager Steve Coppell **(left)** *leading out Crystal Palace against manager Alex Ferguson (later Sir) and Manchester United at Wembley for the 1990 FA Cup Final.* **(NE)**

nor even just in their imagination, intuition and inspiration for the 'game'. One was also investing in the potential of 14- to 18-year-olds to develop such skills and abilities long before they'd demonstrated them. One had to attract just those very few specials who could be nurtured into adulthood, motivated until experienced and finally retained with instilled loyalty and rewards for a decade or two or more.

There were few textbooks on the subject. Yet in so many fields of human endeavour Britain led the world with its seat-of-the-pants managerial magic; and magic it remained for far too long. Others were having better luck with different mixes of business and pleasure. Teams were constantly promoted and relegated. For four wonderful seasons the Palace remained in the top division, even though languishing too close to the bottom for comfort, and by the end of the 1972–3 season it was their turn to grace the Second Division once more – and the Third a season later.

Nevertheless, what comes around goes around and after three short seasons in the Third Division they were back in the Second for just two and back in the First for the 1979–80 season, although they were down again by 1981, remaining there until 1989 saw them back into the First.

The Phantom Palace

Good things, they say, come in threes. There was the Palace made of steel and glass. Then there was the Palace made of footballers' blood, sweat and tears. And most recently, 1996–2002, there was the Palace made of dreams, battles and conquests – perhaps forever a phantom palace, the scene of lost dreams, brutal battles and uncanny conquests. In 1990 Bromley Council had a big idea; to replace the Crystal Palace, on the same now derelict site, with something redolent of the original palace, 'to reflect the spirit of the original' yet fitting for the new millennium whose opening it might commemorate. But, like the not-too-far-away other huge millennium commemorative structure, the Dome, it was also doomed. Worse, construction never even began. It remained on the drawing board, a phantom palace, still redolent of its time nonetheless. The Channel Tunnel was only completed after a fourth attempt, 180 years after the first quarter of a mile was dug; the Channel Link will be 10–20 years late; and Heathrow's Terminal Five has only received planning permission 12 years after it was first mooted. These things aren't rushed; indeed, some may not be built for generations. Why? See Chapter Twelve...

Left: *Bromley's choice for a new palace, 2000.*

Below: *The Palace Park grounds where FA Cup Finals were launched in 1895 and CPFC in 1905.* (ER)

Three

Darkening Clouds

The unfortunate Harriet Staunton.

Once people imagined the world always carried on in the same way, but then came to realise that things changed; they noticed trends, and this time believed trends carried on as before. But now we are aware that even trends sometimes go awry. Glance back at the dinosaur time-chart in the last chapter. Twice, at about 450 and again at about 65 million years ago, nearly all species of life were wiped off the face of the earth. These were two of the last three big ice ages. One heralded in the dinosaurs, the other their exit. Sometimes most terrible things happen. Something like a meteor or asteroid hits the earth, maybe even forming the Pacific Ocean.

Certainly the changes illustrated on the chart *(p.28)* showed a bit of a kink. Even today, when most people realise the world around them is changing, they look for trends to predict how it's going to be. For a few hundred years now, ever since science, technology and engineering have been combining to double our life-spans, it has seemed as if everything grew exponentially, like the beginning of our ogee curve in Chapter One. People imagined we were soon going to run out of food, land or both. All sorts of dire predictions were broadcast. Imaginations ran riot. Doom and gloom descended.

But trends change. The arrival of canals, railways and roads in Penge and Anerley all in one generation, not to mention the Palace a mere generation later, caused the population to Yuri-Gagarin into space. But then what happened? Why did it level off? Did the plague set in? Did 'full-up' notices go up, the place go out of fashion? It could have been any one of these, but it wasn't. And no doubt one could think of a whole lot of equally plausible causes. No doubt all sorts of little things did happen and if one added them all up one might exclaim, 'It was the sum of all of these.' But it wasn't.

Determining cause-and-effect scenarios is always hard, and doing it in a social context is the devil's own game. So it's not all that surprising to learn who wrote the limerick: 'A trend is a trend/The question is will it bend?/Will some unseen force/Make it alter its course/And bring it to a premature end?' It was a civil service planner. But what happened in 1876–77 was not foreseen by anyone, especially not by poor Harriet Staunton, aged 35. As Ivan Butler put it in his *Murderers' London*:

> *... though not handsome, she was neat, well-mannered, and, apart from occasional sulky moods and outbursts of bad temper, generally amiable. She was, however, undeniably deficient mentally, could derive no benefit from ordinary education, could write only with great difficulty and could spell only the simplest words.*

Until 1875 Harriet had lived with her mother. Her mother had a nephew, Mr Hincksman who lived near the Elephant & Castle, who in turn had two stepdaughters, Elizabeth and Alice Rhodes. Elizabeth was married to a Patrick Staunton who had a younger brother Louis, aged 23, an auctioneer's clerk, 'perpetually short of money'. 'In this respect', it was noted, 'Harriet, though short on brains, had one notable asset – she was the owner, in possession and reversion, of about £4,000, a sizable fortune in the 1870s.' Very quickly, never mind much against her mother's wishes, Louis wooed and married Harriet and they went to live next door to Patrick and Elizabeth Staunton in Brixton. Some 18 months later, and on hearing of the birth of a baby, Harriet's mother went to visit but found both houses empty.

Louis and Harriet had moved to Gypsy Hill using her inheritance, together with Alice Rhodes. Louis' elder brother Patrick moved with Elizabeth to an isolated house near Cudham in Bromley. It was decided that Harriet's baby should live with them. Here it would be looked after by Clara, an orphan girl of 15 and a cousin of Elizabeth and Alice. In August 1876 Harriet was also transferred to the Cudham house, leaving her husband and Alice in Gypsy Hill. After this Harriet was never seen by any of the many tradesmen who called. She was, in fact, mostly kept locked up in a cupboard under the stairs. Indeed, Louis and Alice were assumed by the outside world to be married and they moved to a farm in

The Staunton brothers Louis and Patrick and the sisters Alice and Elizabeth Rhodes; one a wife, one a lover. (PA)

Cudham, about a mile from their married siblings, Patrick and Elizabeth. Harriet's mother all this while was still chasing around looking in vain for her Harriet. She was sent along false trails to, among other places, Brighton. Meanwhile, the health of both Harriet and her baby deteriorated day by day. The following April, Patrick and Elizabeth took the baby to Guy's Hospital, claiming that it was the child of a fictitious carpenter, Henry. It was in a pathetic state and died the same day. Louis, making himself out to be this Henry, collected the tiny corpse and arranged to have it buried that evening.

Harriet's health was deteriorating fast. On 12 April 1877 Louis, Alice, Patrick and his wife took Harriet by cab to Bromley South, by train to Penge Station, by now called Penge East, and carried her the few hundred yards to 34 Forbes Road. Earlier that day Louis had rented two rooms, 'for an invalid lady,' from landlady Mrs Emma Chalklin. By now Harriet could hardly walk and was quite unable to speak. She was put straight to bed and her relatives left. She was heard to groan much that night and the following morning the landlady's husband immediately called in a Dr Longrigg. He found her in a terribly emaciated state and disgustingly dirty.

Here, alone, at lunchtime that day, Harriet died. The doctor could not get there until the following day, but, on prior advice from Louis, signed a death certificate which stated that she had died of 'apoplexy supervening upon cerebral disease'.

That might well have been that. The value put on human life was far lower then than now, especially among those of the 'lower classes' and most deaths occurred of causes none too readily diagnosable. Legislation certainly was not what it is today; signing a death certificate, and arranging a simple funeral in the nearby Elmers End Cemetery, which hardly anyone attended, were each commonplace occurrences.

Harriet pretty well passed from the face of the earth unnoticed except by the closest members of her family, just as had happened to her infant daughter – closest members, that is, who had a strong vested interest in ensuring that this should be so.

However, the story might well have ended but for a curious twist of fate. As Butler puts it:

... that evening, by sheer chance, a gentleman with the resounding name of Casabianca, was in the Forbes Road Post Office when a stranger entered to enquire where the Registrar of Births and Deaths could be found. On being told, he casually mentioned that it was in connection with the decease of a lady from Cudham. Mr Casabianca pricked up his ears, for he happened to be the husband of Harriet's half-sister and knew a lot about the anxiety among the family over the mysterious events concerning a lady in Cudham. As a result of his enquiries and a visit to Dr Longrigg, the death certificate was withdrawn.

Thwarting another hasty burial, the already overstretched doctor was persuaded to cancel this certificate, there being concern she may have died of starvation. Her $5^1/_2$ stone weight now was just half of what it had formerly been. An inquest was held at the nearby Park Tavern, close to Penge Station. A verdict of wilful murder was returned against Louis, Patrick, Elizabeth Staunton and Alice Rhodes, and later a charge of manslaughter and returned against the first three in respect of the baby.

Suffice it to say that there was an enormous outcry, as we've seen elsewhere in Britain in recent times. Soon an Old Bailey jury found the two brothers and two sisters guilty of Harriet's murder by starvation. They were carted off to Maidstone Gaol to be hanged. What the press had called The Penge Mystery till then now became The Penge Murder. The fact that no one missed Harriet for months says as much about the locals as it does about the evil of the perpetrators. But the newspaper's labelling this as 'The Penge' case was to have the most profound influence for well over 100 years. Soon the national press was to take up this case, following, as it often does, the lead from the local paper. The court proceedings as usual took a while coming to trial, only adding to the public interest and notoriety of the situation.

All hell was let loose. Beckenham, a middle-of-the-road sort of place, was beginning to take off. It wasn't a 'toffs-and-boffs' sort of place as Penge and Anerley were in those days. But it was a larger place to which middle-aged people retired for a quiet life – a gentlemen's place, even a ladies' place. It was the sort of place where reputations were still being established, formed and carefully nurtured. So it was more than usually sensitive to any little hiccuping, never mind a catastrophe like this. Beckenham was where people had time to read a newspaper – and, naturally, gossip about what it said. So as early as 1876 they had their *Beckenham Journal*, long before Penge was to sport its own paper, even though Penge's population was still double that of Beckenham. Like others the paper thrived on feeding folk with 'isn't-life-terrible' sort of gossip and with this terrible debacle, they had had enough.

They were mobile, the Victorian yuppies. They'd only been there a generation or two and they could quit and dash. The grass is always juicier elsewhere. Older ones retired to Beckenham or Bromley.

Younger ones cut to Woodside or West Wickham. In this case, it would be true to say that 'B' was for the better-off, 'W' for the working-their-way-up ones.

They even changed the name of Forbes Road to Mosslea Road in a vain attempt to paper over the cracks. Fashionable shops gave way to utilitarian ones; theatres and music halls gave way to cinemas, cinemas to bingo halls and these to do-it-yourself stores. Food halls gave way to barrow-laden greengrocers which in turn became street market stalls. Those having invested in green-leafed suburbs soon found their investments turning as yellow as the leaves in autumn. Even as late as 1999, while all the world was gearing itself up for Christmas, the new year, the new century and that rarest of all events, the new millennium, Penge and Anerley's local paper was headlining the place as having been 'the most miserable town in London'.

Further Twists & Turns

But Maidstone was not the end of the road for the guilty, never mind the death sentence was still rigidly enforced. The trial had hinged about the prosecution maintaining that Harriet had been killed by neglect; the defence that essentially she died from a disease. The medical profession was somewhat in a state of disarray and after the verdict many of them signed a petition for the guilty to be reprieved. Alice was released and the others given various terms of imprisonment. Patrick died while still in jail while Louis and Elizabeth were released in due course. And, as Butler recalls, the case had some legal importance as it may well have influenced the passing of the Married Women's Property Act of 1882 and the Prisoners' Evidence Act of 1898. Through all the chaos and tragedy, there is invariably some progress. Every cloud, they say, has a silver lining.

Guilt, Irony & Remorse

Only the hard-pressed working class and unemployed were left behind after the area's decline, with fewer and fewer city workers for the trickle-down effect to sustain them. Penge and Anerley's ogee curve drooped, like the heads of its ever-saddening folk. But why? What had they to feel guilty about? Doesn't the odd murder, here and there, now and then, happen anywhere?

As recently as 1975 Bromley's *Official Guide* recorded, 'Penge never recovered from the stigma.' And even more sadly it went on to point out that the stigma was not really deserved by Penge at all. The rogues came from Brixton, committed 99 per cent of their foul deed in Cudham, and never lived in Forbes Road; indeed No. 34 where poor Harriet finally died was in the Beckenham part of the road. But it was the newly launched *Beckenham Journal* which brought all this to the public's attention. So it made for better copy to call it the Penge Mystery. Doling out the bad news is one thing; upsetting the readership quite another. These include the sensitive, the anxious, the guilty-by-association, the guilty-by-neglect and no doubt a few with even something to feel quite remorseful over, although nothing that couldn't be glossed over with a little air-brushed reportage. As Brian Vernon put it: 'We get the news we want.'

Since way before the 1854 Battle of Penge, Penge's crime rate had been no worse than elsewhere. Of course working-class crime was invariably more recorded than middle- or upper-class crime; it was easier to spot, was easier to write about and was more happily gossiped about by those who could afford the papers and the time. And yet many did feel some sort of communal responsibility. If only there'd been more and better church-based rather than pub-based activities; if only jobs were more plentiful; if only the schooling had been better; if only children were brought up better. All such concerns were epitomised by the callous outrage ending so tragically on 13 April 1877. Nine more churches were built in the next 25 years.

There are always darkening clouds threatening to envelop us, lowering our confidence and striking the fear of God into us. One feels it when neighbours tell of the ills they've suffered at the hands of a few mindless locals. One hears it in the replies when one makes the odd remark to passers-by or to youngsters. Their abruptness might have been prompted by one's none-too-perfectly-chosen words; maybe betraying some unintended slight to their sense of respect. It is not only the locals, so often let down in so many ways, who can feel prickly and let it show in front of others. Graffiti is but one tip of this iceberg; the stolen and damaged property, the lack of support in helping run a Scout or Guide unit; the battered wives; the lack of neighbourhood watches – all are symptoms of reactions following nothing more than a few missing 'thank-yous' for unrequited deeds performed over and over in the past.

No. 34 Forbes, now Mosslea, Road. (PA)

Mr Welford, his foremen, dairymen and deliverymen, outside their Anerley Road dairy, sited between Anerley Vale and the Paxton Arms, in the 1920s. Sadly, a VI flying bomb destroyed it in September 1944.

Streets were kept spotless in the mid 1920s. This photograph shows Anerley Hill, with the Paxton Arms in prime condition on the left, and the Palace's southern water tower dominating the whole scene.

Four

Struggles & Strife

The well-known migrations of peoples all over the world are epitomised here in Penge and Anerley, from nomads to settlers, from hunter-gatherers to farmers. The last farmers on Penge Common and Anerley Wood kept pigs here a little over 150 years ago and gypsies roamed the place until yet more recent times. When fear of crop-stealing had abated, with better policing and a judicial system, a reliable food supply could be better secured through crop planting and cattle herding.

Only the fickleness of the weather remained unconquerable. However, the landed gentry, while providing the umbrella of such security, clearly set their own price for this; affluence went mainly towards those with the greatest security. It was a time prescient for what was to follow, the Industrial Revolution. This was to lead our third great migration, from the countryside to the towns and all of the changes which went with this: from primary occupations of tilling the land to secondary ones of forging the machines of industry; from herding pigs into pig pens to forging pig iron into pig pens; from 80 per cent of workers in the country, to 80 per cent in the suburbs like Penge and Anerley; from jobs traditionally never having holidays, to ones where they would become not only essential, but legally required – and all in the few generations of the late 1800s and early 1900s.

Old Betty Saville, Penge Common, c.1825.

It may have meant regular hours, if boring jobs. It may even have meant the security of a regular if modest wage, albeit at the expense of a dehumanising atmosphere of being a mere cypher in the large cogs of industry. It meant better hygiene, if more polluted air from smoke-belching chimneys. As recently as 1959, London smogs were so thick that the author once found himself driving across Anerley's now fast, busy and dangerous Croydon Road, from Selby Road to Cambridge Road, without ever realising he had crossed it, the kerbs being quite lost in smog.

It meant security of income, even at the price of being treated more as a number than as an individual. Although men might have been lathe operators, plumbers, milk roundsmen or whatever, they were barely considered more than just one of many having the same skills. Women, if they were anything, were housewives or, in the terms of press reports, 'wife of Joe Smith' or whomever. The new age meant conformity to not just the law, not just to parental dictates – including whom to marry – but also vast panoplies of extra customs. If others spat in the street, but not on public trams, then so did you. Throughout the Industrial Age, during this mass-migration from country to town, London's 950 villages bulged into towns and merged into contiguous boroughs and then suburbs indistinguishable save for the occasional official locality signs. Even today many locals have differing opinions as to where Penge stops and Anerley starts. It is somewhere along Croydon Road, but where, exactly? Genoa Road? Stoddard Road? Melvin Road? Ward boundaries only provide a general notion, as they are moved from time to time to equalise the number of electors in each.

Other migrations included intra-London moves. Londoners on average move every seven years. They move from inner to outer London, as we saw with the Stauntons in Chapter Three, and they move three to four miles. This masks a reason for moving; increasing affluence found in the larger, outer and greener urbanities – if sometimes at the price of social isolation – leading to upwardly social mobility. The shift is from working class to middle class, from trade to profession, from wage-slave to salaried to leisured-class. As local residents Annie Fernando,

Above: *A trolleybus in Anerley Road, 1950s, registration number DGY 482. Although operationally more flexible than the trams, they were swept away by the late 1950s, as they delayed the cars used by those in charge.* (EP)

Left: *Gridlock, a common occurrence in the High Street.*

Below: *The Croydon Tramlink – coming to Anerley?* (BOTH RM)

Selby and Cambridge Roads meet Croydon Road. (PA)

Mayday Hospital, Penge's nearest. (RM)

Patricia Fenwick and Lorraine Smithson knew so clearly, a community was one in which one knew one's neighbours, their business and whom could be relied on for help when needed. Too often all that was left in a suburb were societies, merely groups where one hardly knew a neighbour's name, and if one took the rare step of asking for help, all one could expect was to be sent to where assistance might be found commercially.

Disasters Public, Disasters Personal

If Crystal Palace was a disaster writ large, and Harriet Staunton a disaster writ small, Penge has always had its series of disasters, over and over, in another area. Penge and Anerley may never have been large enough to warrant a hospital of their own, but for many a year now they have certainly needed a women's refuge. Here in its local sanctuary women can find a place of security, of comfort and of attention when most desperately in need of it, such as they may have dreamt of for years before getting married, only to find less of it within their marriages than before.

The Trial of Trams

The canal, which triggered off the development of Penge and Anerley as a pleasant clean-air hillside retreat for city gents, fell victim to the railway age a decade or so later. Just over a century later the trams were to follow a similar fate. Arriving in Penge High Street and along Croydon Road, through Anerley and on up to Crystal Palace and Croydon in the early-twentieth century, they soon fell victim to the private car. Well, that's how most commentators put it. After all, from the 1930s to the '50s their tracks were torn up all over the country just as abruptly as in Penge and Anerley. Even the tram shed in Oak Grove Road, which survived in a number of guises, was finally demolished in early 2002. It had served as a wholesale cash-and-carry store, a pet-food distribution centre and as a warehouse. For an all too brief intermediate period, from the 1920s to the '30s, trolleybus lines were installed as a compromise between trams and cars, but even this didn't last.

But to blame the petrol-engined automobile, with its greater door-to-door convenience, is merely to point at the first possible excuse. It fails to answer the question, why didn't they disappear from the many similar towns and cities all over the Continent? There were other, more subtle, forces at work, uniquely in Britain and particularly in Penge and Anerley. Never mind that we've boasted about the fineness of our democracy, compared with former times, and compared with other countries, full enfranchisement is still far, far behind that experienced today, say, in the USA.

Local viewpoints were barely sought, much less listened to, as to whether trams should stay or be swept away. What was taken notice of was that, from the 1930s to the '50s, the influential class were the new car owners. Trams got terribly in the way of cars, never mind that even in the fifties many more people travelled by tram than cars. But trams took pride of place in the centre of the road. They took precedence and cars were obliged never to stop in any place where they might delay trams for even a moment. And they stopped every minute or so to set down and pick up passengers who had to be given priority crossing the road twixt kerb and road-centred tram. Trams, to the ruling class, be they politicians, civil servants or local government officers, hindered the free passage of their cars. So they had to go, and go they did.

It was not until the 1980s that the voice of the common man was heard enough for trams to begin to reappear. By now the common man had not only acquired more of a political voice, a generation after they annually travelled to the Continent for their summer holidays, but so many of them had acquired cars that the congestion was becoming increasingly

Above: *Flooding in Beckenham Road, in Penge High Street and here, outside the Salvation Army Citadel, Maple Road, was once a commonplace sight, but with better drainage locally it is hopefully now a thing of the past.* (LHC)

Left: *The 1911 Festival of the Empire, incorporating three-quarter-sized models of leading buildings from across the Commonwealth capitals, with model railways to take the million-plus crowds around the exhibits.* (LHC)

Below: *The widespread damage from the storm of October 1987 will remain etched on many locals' memories for decades to come; the bank closed after this photograph was taken, was replaced by a bookshop, but was once again closed for business.* (LHC)

impossible to live with. A stretch of highway may hold a score of gridlocked cars carrying a couple of dozen people; but the same stretch of track can hold a fast congestion-free tram of 250 passengers. The result is that average rush-hour traffic speeds are down to 15mph in the mornings and 20mph in the afternoons.

So, from the 1980s onwards, from Manchester via the Docklands and now from Wimbledon and Croydon to Elmers End and Birkbeck on the edge of Penge and Anerley, the trams are coming back, in the form of light-rail transits, the local one being called the Croydon Tramlink. This is even planned to extend right through Anerley to Crystal Palace. And now there is also talk of extending the Docklands Light Railway from Lewisham to Crystal Palace.

Sanitation

An unpleasant feature of all growing cities in the Victorian period was the smells from decaying matter due to inadequate sanitation. It wasn't until 1848 that the world's first ever Public Health Act was passed. And even that was only to deal with the smells. The link between contaminated drinking water and outbreaks of disease was made right here in London, by a Dr John Snow; there had been a terrible outbreak of cholera in Soho in September 1884. When he had the water pump padlocked, the disease halted, and the relationship became confirmed.

Penge and Anerley, as we have seen, grew unusually rapidly in the wake of the canal, the railways and the Palace. The demand for land on which to build large houses grew at an unprecedented rate. As authors Inman and Tonkin stated, Beckenham Vestry was compelled to:

> *... introduce a measure of control over the activities of its residents and the disposal of their waste. A sanitary committee had already been set up in 1848 to remove nuisances such as ill-sited pigsties, and ten years later this became a Nuisance Removal Committee with increased powers under an 1855 Act of Parliament.*

Yet it was not until the Acts of 1871 and 1875 that a vast effort was made to improve hygiene, and Elmers End Sewage Works began. This included the introduction of the WC by our own Thomas Crapper (see Chapter Eight). A veritable avalanche of technical, legal and administrative changes followed, although it was not until 1948 that this culminated in the world's first National Health Service.

Fire! Fire!

Every year the fire brigade receives a call from one premises or dwelling for every 100, invariably for some local disaster.

Back in the 1950s John Manthorpe and Martin Blackmore shared a flat, high up in the garret in a grand Victorian house off Lawrie Park Road. On dropping their only set of house keys down a drain they asked the fire brigade if they could suck the drain empty and retrieve their keys. It was a quiet summer's Saturday morning and the lads on the pump machine were game, but they said regulations forbade it unless there was an emergency. 'Do you have a gas cooker in your kitchen?' one asked. 'Er, why's that?' 'And might you possibly've left it on unattended?' 'What? Oh! Yes! Of course! Yes, of course. That'd make it dangerous, wouldn't it?' The keys were retrieved in just a couple of minutes. But of course things are run to a far tighter schedule these days. The technology is far more sophisticated, the dangers far more complex, the training far more rigorous and the operational procedures vastly more comprehensive. Such rule-bending might be less simple.

The Runaway Steam Engine

Anyone whose local memory goes back to the early 1960s cannot fail to recall the sad case of the man whose steam-roller lost its brakes and escaped early one weekday morning at the foot of Crystal Palace Station Road. Its clanking, clattering, hooting and whistling soon attracted everyone's attention from all around. The poor old driver, still aboard, could only steer hard up against the kerb in a valiant attempt to slow it down as it gathered up a ferocious speed down Anerley Hill. Eric Price, who's been running a business here for longer than anyone else as far as we know (the barber's shop on Anerley Hill), clearly remembers how it was to end in a mess just across the road, while its front roller, becoming detached, ended up in a shop window on his side of the road. On its way it clipped a lady's leg and gave her quite a gash. A passing nurse in full uniform took one look at it, removed her own belt, and applied it as a tourniquet until the emergency services turned up.

A Golden Age Remembered

The custom of glorifying a 'golden age' which is no longer with us has a long history. Even back in 1911 a Festival of Empire and Imperial Exhibition cast a nostalgic eye back to the just-over Victorian age. The world-scale exhibition filled the entire area between the palace and the sports arena at Crystal Palace. Much of it comprised three-quarter-sized models of many famous buildings from around the British Empire, while a fairground and circuses provided a kaleidoscopic panorama of entertainment for all. Yet just three years later all such illusions of peace, harmony and self-assuredness were to be bitterly shaken...

Royal West Kent Territorials on manoeuvres. (AR)

The 6th (Liverpool Rifles) Battalion, King's Regiment, on guard duty at Anerley Railway Station, September 1914. (AR)

Five

World Wars

We noted from the start that history was traditionally written by the victors: the kings, princes and their lords – dukes, earls and knights. But things changed more in the twentieth century than any of 500 preceding centuries. In the course of this single century, death tolls of battles changed from comprising 80 per cent soldiers to 80 per cent civilians. War memorials for the common soldier were erected and the common man began to be recognised. In pride of place at the Recreation Ground in Penge High Street stands its earliest war memorial with the names of the First World War dead; leaving only room for an 'also in memory' plaque for the Second World War.

1914: The Early Years

The growing political crisis that enveloped Europe during the summer of 1914 appeared to resign many to the idea that a war in Europe was inevitable. In the August 1914 edition of the *Kenilworth Magazine*, published by Penge Congregational Church, the Revd Ernest Barson reminded his readership that 'A different world has arisen. The great world war that many had striven to prevent has broken out.' The impact on Penge and Anerley was immediate, with many residents serving in the Armed Forces or on the reserve being mobilised at once. Additionally, 100 reservists were called up for active service from the Norwood postal district, including several members of the Norwood Postal Band.

The realities of war soon gripped the district, with military activity reported as early as 3 August 1914, when soldiers were seen patrolling the track in front of the Norwood Junction signal boxes and the Goat House and Tennison Road bridges. Further troop movements were witnessed on 5 August when the Penge and Beckenham Company of the 5th Battalion, Royal West Kent Regiment, left their drill hall in Parish Lane to join the other companies of the battalion returning to their headquarters in Bromley. By the close of the year both territorial battalions associated with the local area, the 4th (Croydon) Battalion, Queens Royal West Surrey Regiment and the 5th (Bromley) Battalion, Royal West Kent Regiment, had volunteered for overseas service, and were serving in the Indian sub-continent.

Perhaps the most significant movement of troops into the district was associated with the requisition made by the Admiralty of the Crystal Palace on 5 September 1914, for use as a training depot for up to 5,000 men of the Royal Naval Volunteer Reserve. The first detachments arrived from Liverpool and Yorkshire on 9 September to commence two months of basic training, after which they were either sent for infantry training at Blandford Camp, Dorset, or transferred to serve aboard ship. During the first months of occupation, the Admiralty still allowed the public access to both house and grounds. However, by December, the Admiralty announced that the grounds and house would be closed to the public, except for Saturday concerts.

'20 Refugees in their Home'

The men of the Royal Naval Division were not the only newcomers to the district during the early months of the war. The first week of September 1914 saw several thousand refugees arrive in Kent from Belgium. Under the direction of the Belgian Legation to Britain, they were placed in a temporary holding camp in Folkestone, with a smaller number in temporary accommodation in London. Mindful of their plight, Mr Barson and several members of Penge Congregational Church took it upon themselves to assist these unfortunate people.

The original plan had been for Mr and Mrs Grose to accommodate up to 20 refugees in their own home. However, hearing of a property becoming available on a three-month let through local estate agents Noye and Howe, Mr and Mrs Grose were persuaded to set up a hostel, to be administered by a 'Refugee Committee'. This local initiative had an inauspicious launch when, due to a mix-up by the Belgian Legation, a group of wealthy Belgians, expecting to be housed in comfortable furnished accommodation arrived at 'Stoneleigh', 206 Anerley Road, to find the place far from luxurious! Nevertheless, the incident was soon resolved and during September numbers in the hostel rose to 35. The scheme was so successful that the committee resolved to open another hostel at

Commodore's inspection, 1914. The background buildings are from the 1911 Festival of Empire. (EP)

Naval ratings 'at ease'. Sadly we know little about who they were or what became of them but if any readers can advise we would love to publish such details on another occasion. (RM)

Sergeant Albert Frank Wixey officiated at the opening ceremony of the First World War memorial in the High Street. (COURTESY BRENDA BRENT, DAUGHTER OF ALBERT WIXEY)

The Parade Ground, Royal Naval Depot, Crystal Palace, 1915. The many plinth statues were removed for safe-keeping during the Second World War, and sold to Americans thereafter. (EP)

Tudor Lodge, 135 Croydon Road, on the corner of Tremaine Road. The scheme was later extended, with a Mr Hautrive opening a third property at 221 Selhurst Road, South Norwood.

To cover the cost of running the hostels, an 'open-house' policy was encouraged, visitors being asked to leave donations. However, the interest in the refugees was so great that open days were eventually restricted to the hours of 3–5p.m., and collection boxes were affixed to the boundary fences of each property. The hospitality of the locals was also such that Mr Grose published a notice in the local papers appealing for local people not to encourage the male residents from the hostel to frequent the local public houses. As news of the scheme travelled, Upper Norwood followed suit and opened up two hostels at 22 Lunham Road and 22 Highfield Road. In addition, many more refugees were housed with local residents with the wealthier refugees able to secure privately-furnished accommodation. By the close of 1914, local inhabitants had found shelter for 285 Belgian refugees, which was a remarkable effort.

Mindful of the public mood, and eager to assist the war effort, Penge Council organised its first public recruiting meeting at Penge Triangle, outside the Crooked Billet, on 15 August 1914. This was in accordance with an appeal by Kent County Council at Maidstone on 10 August to enlist further recruits for the Regular and Territorial Armies. Recruitment meetings continued throughout August and September, with a further appeal by Lord Kitchener for an additional 100,000 men being published in the local press on 4 September. Ironically, this was also the day on which the district's first fatality of the war was reported. Perhaps rather surprisingly, with the British Expeditionary Force involved in heavy engagements at Mons and Le Cateau, the unfortunate individual was a naval rating: Albert G. Allchin of HMS *Laurel*, killed in action at the Grand Fleet's engagement at Heligoland Bight on 28 August 1914. Despite the heavy casualties sustained by the BEF during the first months of the war, recruiting continued undeterred, and by 28 September some 1,014 men had been recruited from the West Kent military district, of which 285 were known to have come from Penge. By 30 November 1914 a Roll of Honour compiled by Penge Council recorded that a total of 714 local men were 'serving with the colours'.

Equally eager to show their patriotism were the many local men who were exempt from military service on the grounds of age or physical disability. Much debate seems to have taken place during the early months of the war as to the role these men could play, although the first local initiative was taken by the vicar of South Norwood. He proposed that a meeting be held at the Parish Hall in Selhurst Road on 17 October for those over the age of 35 interested in taking part in a scheme of military instruction. The outcome of this was the formation of a South Norwood Home Defence Movement. However, some criticism was expressed by local members of Penge Council, due to the unit having no affiliation to a recognised national volunteer movement. In contrast, Councillor F.W.R. Young proposed via the Works Committee of Penge Council on 16 October that a home defence committee should be formed with the objective of raising a local battalion including a veteran section. This would adopt a scheme of military training proposed by the National Volunteer Reserve. In addition, Councillor Grose generously offered the use of a meadow at Chesham Park for drilling or use as a rifle range. This meeting concluded with a recommendation that a public meeting be held on 2 November to discuss the subject. The response on that date was for 200 local men to enlist. But in order to facilitate a scheme of military training it was agreed that drill would take place at Anerley Town Hall and at the Oakfield Road School. In addition, it was proposed that courses in signalling and ambulance work should be offered. The unit was soon in training and the first route march, organised to show off the prowess of the new corps, took place on 28 November 1914.

The realisation that Britain was now a nation at war also focused the local authorities on matters of national security. Mobilisation of reservists and Lord Kitchener's early appeals for men to enlist in the Regular Army, 'for a term of three years or until the conclusion of the war', seriously depleted the ranks of the police. At the same time, the number of 'vital points' requiring patrolling increased. This resulted in the local police commissioner making an appeal at a public recruiting meeting on 15 August 1914 for those exempt or unable to join His Majesty's Forces to enlist as special constables. This appeal resulted in 126 men being sworn in as 'specials' at Penge Police Court by 17 August. However, whilst the 'specials' helped reduce the workload of the regular police by patrolling vital points such as gas works and water towers, there was still a shortage of men to undertake daylight patrols, as the majority of 'specials'

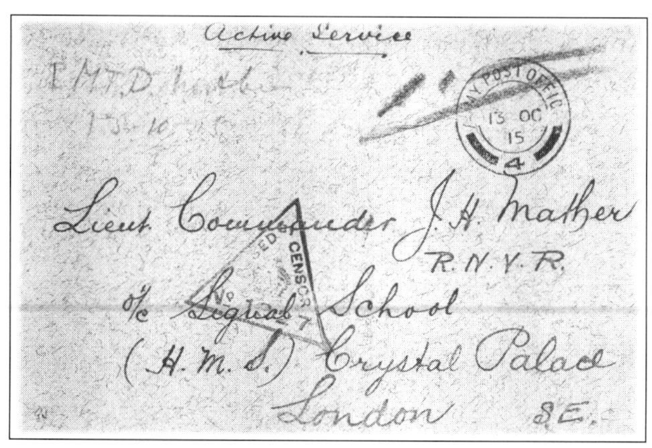

The cover to a letter sent to a lieutenant commander billeted at Crystal Palace, 1915. (SK)

employed were local traders who could only make themselves available outside working hours.

Matters of security were also uppermost in the minds of the general public. Many stories circulated about the existence of spies and saboteurs amongst the population. As a consequence, rumour and accusation were rife. Even Penge councillors were not immune – Councillor F.W. Payne was arrested as a suspected spy at Clapham Junction on 17 August, asd detained until he had proved his innocence. Spy scares reached such a pitch that by mid-August an appeal was made in the local press to deter individuals from sending anonymous letters 'giving information' about alleged anarchists and German nationals. Jingoism and patriotism also fanned the flames of anti-German feeling, forcing some individuals to publicly proclaim their innocence. For instance, one Croydon jeweller was forced to place a copy of his birth certificate in his shop window to correct a rumour that he was German.

Mobilisation of Britain's regular Armed Forces and the declaration of many 'territorials' to make themselves available for 'foreign service' began to focus the minds of the public on matters of fundraising and the sending of comforts to 'our boys' at the Front. Various initiatives were developed which reflected both individual and collective efforts. Many formed groups affiliated to larger national initiatives such as the Queen Mary's Needlework Guild, which provided clothing for soldiers and their families, as well as hospital 'necessities', or the National Relief Fund, of which the Prince of Wales was patron. Others included Mr M.V. Fosdick, a Penge stationer, who took it upon himself to organise the dispatch of comforts from Penge and Anerley residents for those serving at the Front with the Royal West Kents. The shop bearing his name is there to this day. In addition, many individual concerts, recitals and garden parties were organised by patriotic residents in order to raise money for relief work or comforts.

The economic cost was also keenly felt. Within weeks of Britain's declaration of war, many local businesses found their horses requisitioned by Government officials who felt that the Army's needs came first. Trade with certain countries ceased and fear of shortages plus escalating prices reduced the availability of certain provisions such as bacon, butter, sugar and tea. Government notices limited more individual liberties with the closing down of all amateur and experimental wireless telegraphy installations and, in order to save energy stocks, the dimming of gas lighting. Public services and retail traders were further hit by the manpower shortage caused by the mobilisation of reservists and 'territorials', together with those who were now eager to join the ranks of Kitchener's 'New Army'. The hardest hit were the bus, tram and railway companies. The sudden absence of manpower meant, in the short-term, some radical solutions. These included reduced train timetables and, in the case of the Norwood Postal District, collections being cut from seven to four a day.

1915–17: Years of Uncertainty

After a surge in recruitment at the beginning of 1915, possibly due to individuals requiring release from employers and those with businesses having to put their affairs in order, the number of men volunteering gradually fell. Although Penge Council estimated by April 1915 that the number of local men in the Armed Forces exceeded 1,000, they believed the total number of men eligible for military service was as high as 7,000. This almost certainly prompted the local recruiting committee to suspend the regular recruiting meetings at Penge Triangle and replace them with ad-hoc meetings held in response to specific appeals. For example, on 5 June 1915, a meeting was organised by Mr R.S. Johnson, JP, at the Triangle, in response to an appeal by the vice-lieutenant of Kent to raise a further battalion of the Royal West Kent Regiment (the 10th) – a formation in which it would be possible 'for friends to serve together in sections, platoons and companies'. Apart from organised meetings, more impromptu appeals were also made wherever a ready audience could be addressed, as was the case in July 1915 when two officers of the 7th London Regiment made a number of impassioned appeals at the Penge Empire, whilst on leave from the Front.

By the autumn of 1915, the recruitment issue had become an important topic of debate. As a consequence, a conference attended by local councillors and recruiting agents was organised in Bromley. The conclusions drawn from the meeting were that those who wished to volunteer had now done so and that it remained for the Government to take steps to 'enlist men compulsorily'. The Government took its first steps towards compulsory enlistment with the introduction of the National Registration Act in August 1915, allowing the authorities to identify those still eligible for military service. As a result, local men between the ages of 18 and 41 were canvassed between October and December 1915, under the 'Derby Scheme' to see if they were willing to enlist if called upon. The disappointing response nationally forced the Government's hand and the Military Services Act was given royal assent on 27 January 1916. It required that all those aged between 18 and 41 on 15 August 1915 to be available for military service, with individuals graded and categorised into various classes of men, to determine when they would be attested. This resulted in some anxiety among local residents and, on 19 March 1916, a gathering of attested married men in Crystal Palace made a public protest. Their demand was that:

Mr Asquith and Lord Derby keep the promise made, in word and spirit, that every fit single man of military age receives the first call of their King and Country.

In reality the first classes of men to be called up for military service were single men and childless widowers between 18 and 41, although no 18-year-olds were to be sent abroad until the age of 19.

In connection with the Military Services Act, 1916, the first Penge Tribunal met on 14 March 1916 and dealt primarily with cases of single men appealing for exemption on the grounds that they were in reserved occupations, and from employers wishing to seek exemption for key staff. As the pressure of finding additional manpower for the Armed Forces increased, the Tribunal became much less willing to exempt individuals from military service. In addition, as more classes of attested men were called up, the Tribunal's caseload, which had originally required them to meet on average every 2–4 weeks, gradually diminished. However, by the end of hostilities on 11 November 1918, the Tribunal had dealt with 1,442 cases involving the rights of 701 persons.

Activity at the Crystal Palace during 1915 began with the closing of the house and grounds to the general public due to the need to expand the capacity of the Depot to 10,000 men, including new recruits. Officially named 'Victory VI', but known colloquially as 'HMS Crystal Palace', it continued as the Royal Naval Division's Training Depot until the end of hostilities in November 1918, after which part of the site was used to house the Imperial War Trophies exhibition. However, development of the site by the Admiralty also had pitfalls. Due to the number of recruits received, during 1915 it was found that drill instruction could no longer be accommodated within the Park alone. Although the Admiralty was unsuccessful in getting permission to use the Sydenham Public Recreation Ground in Mayow Road, Lewisham Council were agreeable to them appropriating Home Park, Bell Lane, since it was already being used for training the local home defence volunteers.

There is also a suggestion that the huge concentration of troops in the area helped to accelerate the number of cases of drunk-and-disorderly behaviour brought before Penge Police Court. However, the most serious reported incidents concerned public health. Early in 1915 rumours spread regarding a serious epidemic of cerebrospinal meningitis at the Palace. Claims and subsequent denials by the authorities persisted until the Commodore in command of the Depot placed a public statement in the local press to calm fears and confirm that only 18 cases had been detected, of which 15 had proved fatal. A much more serious epidemic occurred during the summer of 1918, when cases of influenza were reported at the establishment. By November 1918 there were reported to have been over 1,000 men taken ill, of whom 117 had died, and at the height of the crisis the Admiralty felt duty bound to close the Naval Depot for a period of two weeks. However, unlike the meningitis epidemic, the influenza outbreak was not confined solely to the Depot, but was part of a much deadlier 'flu' pandemic which gripped Europe during the latter part of 1918, and led to the untimely deaths of many local residents.

By 1915, a plethora of local Home Defence organisations, the result of patriotic appeals and the

Rifleman W.W. Webb, 13th Royal Irish Rifles, with his Sydenham wife. (AR)

whims of individual councillors or local residents, had created a rather confusing network of quasi-military formations with affiliations to a number of existing volunteer organisations. Whilst the Penge and Anerley Company was organised and trained under the rules of the National Volunteer Reserve, the South Norwood Home Defence Movement opted to affiliate to the Volunteer Training Corps. By May 1915 both units were able to regularly drill and offer military instruction. The Penge and Anerley Company carried out its first combined training exercise at Hayes Common with the Blackheath VTC on 2 May 1915. But there was a certain amount of frustration felt by both the local 'volunteer' companies due to a lack of purpose and direction in their role as a creditable defence force. For whilst they had been able to develop a scheme of training, including musketry and drill, they had been given no formal role to play in matters of Home Defence, and they failed to be recognised by the Army Council as part of the Armed Forces. Gradually, the situation became more favourable, with a further reorganisation of the Volunteer Force which brought about the amalgamation of the Penge and Anerley Company with the Sydenham and Forest Hill Company in June 1915 to form D Company, 4th Battalion, West Kent Volunteer Force. The new unit, whilst still administered and uniformed by the civil authorities, benefited from their employment from August 1915 on trench digging as part of a scheme of works for the defence of London, under the direction of the War Office. They continued to be employed on this task until well into 1917.

1916: Consolidation

By February 1916, membership of the Penge and Anerley Company had increased dramatically from 200 volunteers in November 1914 to a total of 680, of whom 141 had joined under the Derby Scheme. However, due to large numbers of trained volunteers being called up for military service only to be replaced by recently attested men, the Volunteer Company lost many of their experienced members. The rapid expansion of the Penge and Anerley Company also forced it to move from its original headquarters at Anerley Town Hall to a detached house at 31 Silverdale Road. In line with a further reorganisation of the Volunteer Force in October 1916, D Company (Penge and Anerley) of the 4th West Kent Volunteer Force became E Company, 10th Kent Volunteer Battalion. Early in 1917 Penge Council relinquished all remaining responsibility for maintaining the Volunteer Company and handed over administration of the unit to the War Office. This finally completed the process of consolidation which allowed the War Office to equip and train the volunteers for Home Defence and release further territorial and regular Army battalions for active service abroad.

1917: Women Show their Metal

As Britain approached the second year of the war, the Government faced a severe manpower shortage due to the large numbers of volunteers who had responded in Britain's hour of need. In order to replace these men, the President of the Board of Trade issued a directive in April 1915 calling upon women to apply for war work, primarily in textile manufacture, munitions, farming and clerical work. After the introduction of the Military Services Act (1916), women began to make significant inroads into the existing labour market, replacing men in the workplace. They found employment as postal workers, telegraph messengers, railway porters, ticket collectors and tram conductors to name but a few. By March 1917, women were employed in almost every sphere of work, including banking, finance and the Civil Service. Their employment in certain sectors, such as the railways, brought initial hostility due to a fear that their employment would lower wages, and, in other areas of work, scepticism about how women would cope. However, employers soon acknowledged that women were both reliable and trustworthy in the workplace and recognised their contribution towards the war effort.

Hardship at Home

As the Government prioritised the nation's resources in the prosecution of the war, local residents increasingly felt the effects of economic hardship and shortages. By August 1915, the need to restrict public spending forced the Local Government Board to refuse all but the most necessary expenditure proposed by Penge Council, which resulted in a deterioration of public services. The most visible effect was the state of the roads, which were not watered down during the summer months and were left in a continual state of disrepair due to a lack of materials and manpower. Residents also suffered from a downgrading of the local transport network due to a continuing drain on available manpower between 1915 and 1917, and increasing demands placed upon rail operators' rolling stock and track by the military authorities. In December 1916 local train operators reduced passenger traffic by making travel expensive and inconvenient. Fares increased by 50 per cent, and for some routes by 150 per cent! Off-peak services were reduced by closure of Anerley Station on Sundays and the Crystal Palace high-level station altogether. Tram and bus companies also suffered greatly from spiralling costs, due mainly to a shortage of fuel and growing wage demands. The most damaging single incident to hit them was a long and bitter industrial dispute over pay and conditions between Croydon Council and its tramway employers between 11 April and 9 June 1916. A settlement of this led ultimately to the costs being absorbed by the customer in the form of further fare increases.

In addition, with the growing scarcity of certain foodstuffs and raw materials, the price of manufactured goods and basic household items began to fluctuate. In such circumstances, local residents were encouraged to restrict their buying to British-made goods, to make economies in the use of domestic coal and water and to cultivate their gardens in order to grow their own food.

In December 1916, following growing public demand for allotments and a Board of Agriculture order encouraging local district councils to cultivate vacant land, Penge Council appointed an Allotment Committee under the direction of Councillor E.J. Hopper. The Committee's first task was to measure and register all vacant land in the district. The initial survey identified one-and-a-half acres on the Royston Estate; three-eighths of an acre in Elmers End Road at the corner of Oak Grove (now called Ash Grove); three-quarters of an acre in Samos Road at the corner of Bourdon Road; three-eighths of an acre in Stembridge Road; three-and-a-half acres in Oak Grove Road; and one acre in Milestone Road (Upper Norwood – Cintra Park). By February 1917 there were 116 plots under cultivation: 41 in Chesham Park, 43 on the Royston Estate, 13 in Milestone Road, 7 in Oak Grove Road, 7 in Bourdon Road and 5 in Stembridge Road. Some of these are doing very well to this day (see Chapter Ten).

To avoid a breakdown in public health and to protect the population against spiralling food prices, the Government directed the Food Controller to issue an increasing number of orders during 1917, fixing the prices of certain products such as wheat, barley, milk and sugar. However, by the summer of 1917 it was recognised that to alleviate the continuing shortages some form of rationing would have to be adopted. Penge Council set up a Local Food Control Committee on 14 August 1917, with an office at Anerley Town Hall. Initially, this administered the future rationing and distribution of domestic coal as ordered by the Coal Controller in July 1917. This was followed by the rationing of sugar in September 1917 and the fixing of the retail price for meat in October, all under the direction of the Food Controller.

For local traders there were additional hardships and difficulties to confront. Restricted opening hours resulted from the numerous lighting orders announced by the Home Secretary during 1915, compounded further by the Daylight Savings Act in May 1916. In addition, the introduction of the Military Services Act (1916) resulted in employers losing experienced and skilled staff at a time when the supply and distribution of raw materials, foodstuffs and manufactured goods were becoming more erratic and shortages more severe. It was little wonder that many local businesses, particularly retailers, failed under such trading difficulties.

By 1915, anxiety over the threat of aerial bombing increased, following earlier Zeppelin Raids on the East Coast – the most publicised being the bombing of Scarborough. The number of scares and alerts increased. For example, on the night of 19 January 1915 all special constables from South Norwood,

Women war workers making gas masks, c.1917/18. (AR)

Upper Norwood and Penge were mustered and held in readiness by the Metropolitan Police on telegraphic instructions from the Admiralty following a raid in the Yarmouth area. A further alert took place on 5 February 1915, due to rumours that five Zeppelins had been sighted over Hornchurch, Essex. The fear of aerial bombing was keenly felt by local residents. Advice from the authorities suggested that in the event of an air raid all basement and ground-floor accommodation should be utilised. In the case of Oakfield Road and Melvin Road Schools, they recommended that the children should congregate on the ground and first-floor levels during a raid. But, if requested in advance, parents could ask for custody of their children and remove them! However, advice from the authorities soon came under scrutiny. A letter in the local press dated 3 June 1915 from T.G. Dyson, (vice-president of the National Fire Brigade Union) suggested, in contradiction of Government advice, that cellars should be avoided and that householders should remain in their rooms, with two buckets filled with sand, earth or ashes situated on every landing. The first raid on London occurred in May, although the closest the district came to being on the receiving end of a direct aerial attack happened on 13 October 1915 when several stray bombs fell in the Croydon area during the most ambitious German attack on the capital thus far.

Throughout 1916 the Zeppelin threat remained, although the demoralising effect of the subsequent raids on London and the East Coast far outweighed any actual threat to the residents of Penge and Anerley. Yet the perceived threat still managed to generate fear and resulted in some unexpected trends. Estate agents claimed in the local press that demand for properties with basement accommodation had risen sharply since the war, and retailers noticed a further demand for dressing gowns and princess robes. From this one can only assume that residents didn't wish to be caught short during a raid or to lose their modesty if made homeless by bombing! Although the district was not under direct threat, several residents claimed to see a Zeppelin crash in flames over London on the night of 2 September 1916. It turned out to be the destruction of a Zeppelin 2–3 miles from Enfield in North West London.

By the summer of 1917, the Zeppelin had been overtaken by a new menace, the twin-engined bomber. In order to minimise the risk of casualties from this new threat, and in order to reassure the public, Penge Council, acting on advice from the Government and New Scotland Yard, evolved a number of new measures. In conjunction with the police, a system of advance warning and all-clear procedures was adopted to notify residents that a raid was in progress or that the threat had passed. The Council also reassured its residents that adequate medical arrangements were now in place to deal with casualties and that temporary shelter and accommodation would be made available for those made homeless by enemy action. By the end of 1917, the Council had also arranged for a number of public shelters to be used outside normal working hours, placing Melvin Road and Oakfield Road Schools at the disposal of local residents between 5p.m. and 8.30a.m.

1918: Year of Victory

As Britain entered the final year of the war, everyday life in Penge and Anerley reflected the strict war conditions imposed by the Government, with the issues uppermost in residents' minds being rationing and continued shortages. Even the success of Penge Council's allotment scheme could not stem the tide, for with all the vacant land requisitioned by January 1918, the Penge Allotments Committee found it increasingly difficult to find additional plots for cultivation to meet the continuing demand from local residents.

Growing shortages forced the authorities to introduce further rationing by 1918, to follow the rationing of coal and sugar at the end of 1917. As the crisis continued, the Food Controller announced further measures, which culminated with the rationing of meat, butter, tea, margarine, bacon and ham by the summer of 1918.

At a local level, responsibility for food distribution was placed with Penge Council's Local Food Control Committee, whose first real test occurred on 19 January 1918. A crowd gathered in Maple Road in anticipation of a delivery of margarine being made to local shopkeepers became restless when there were delays up the line at the Clapham Road sidings. The situation was eventually resolved when Councillor Hopper pacified the crowd by prevailing on the goods manager at Clapham to requisition another engine and bring the offending truck back to Penge Station, where its contents were eventually distributed to registered retailers.

In order to alleviate the suffering caused by the continuing shortages and to encourage households to economise on their domestic coal, gas and water supplies, moves were made by Penge Council to open a communal food kitchen. The Council's efforts resulted in such a kitchen being opened on 14 May by Lady Rhondda at the Manual Training Centre in Oakfield Road School. During its first week of operation, the kitchen supplied a staggering 1,000 portions a day, far in excess of expectations and requiring additional staff to maintain.

The final year of the war also brought with it political change, with the Representation of the People Act, 1918, which made significant changes to the electoral system. For Penge and Anerley it meant becoming part of the new parliamentary Borough of Bromley. All men over the age of 21 were entitled to vote in local and national elections, whilst women over the age of 30, for the first time in electoral history, were also eligible to vote.

By the end of September 1918, the tide had turned for the Allies on the Western Front with the start of a major offensive which culminated with the breaking of the Hindenburg Line. The prospects of a victory appeared tangible, and when news of the Armistice was received on 11 November 1918 in Penge and Anerley, 'the whole district entered whole-heartedly yet quietly into the nation's rejoicing', no doubt reflecting upon the cost of victory. There were few families or streets that had not been touched on a personal level by the loss of loved ones or friends.

Machine Gun Corps officer and men in Belgium on Armistice Day, 11 November 1918. (AR)

EPILOGUE

Though Penge and Anerley had answered the call, and as a district had been equal to the task, the cost was high. There does not seem to be an absolute figure for the number of men who served from Penge and Anerley during the First World War, but the Penge Roll of Honour, set up as a voluntary register of names, recorded 2,217 individuals as having served as at 28 November 1918. Of these, over 400 gave their lives, including the district's two Victoria Cross winners: Lieutenant Richard Basil Brandram Jones from Anerley, who was killed in action on 21 May 1916 whilst serving with the 8th Battalion, Loyal North Lancs. Regiment, and 50720 Private Herbert George Columbine from Penge, who was killed in action on 22 March 1918, serving with the 9th Squadron, Machine Gun Corps (cavalry).

1939–45: SECOND WORLD WAR

Another war had been long predicted, with the realisation that air raids would this time be a major threat to the civilian population. Thus, on Home Office instructions, Civil Defence, including Air Raid Precautions (ARP), was established as early as April 1937. By May 1939, Penge had recruited 902 of the 1,198 men and women volunteers it needed. Beckenham conducted full-scale blackout trials on 8–10 August 1939, a month before the declaration of war.

The platform still on top of Penge Police Station *(see p.100)* once held the district's air-raid siren which remained in place, with occasional tests, throughout the Cold War until the 1990s.

Upon the declaration of war on 3 September 1939, newspapers carried detailed instructions for every contingency: evacuation of children, provision of free Anderson shelters for the less well-off, first-aid posts (at Oakfield Road clinic and St Paul's Church Hall in Hadlow Place), closure of schools and cinemas, and, yet again, rationing.

On Government instructions, Penge Council set up a £10,000 programme to build public air-raid shelters throughout the district, but this took some months to complete; children in Arpley Road built their own in a day by sandbagging the cellars of a shop. Schools were closed for a few weeks until shelters could be built. They re-opened, initially taking a maximum of 60 children in relays, once there was enough provision. The shelters built for the then Boys' Grammar School remain to this day beneath the lawn raised for them at the front of the Royston School building. The question of whether school shelters could be used overnight by the general populace was long debated but finally conceded in 1941. With no underground railway in the South East, this was barely the option it was elsewhere, but considerable numbers sheltered in Chislehurst Caves. The cinemas and Penge Empire theatre were also allowed to reopen once they had air-raid precautions. Cinemas were allowed to provide limited entertainment on Sundays to keep up morale.

AUTUMN 1940: THE BATTLE OF BRITAIN

It was not until 15 August 1940 that an actual air raid hit South East London in the form of an attack on Croydon aerodrome which many watched from Anerley Hill. The main victims prior to that were accidents in the blackout, among the first being a Mrs Heasman of Evelina Road, Penge, who was hit by a No.75 bus in Parish Lane at the beginning of September 1939 and died of her injuries later that day in Beckenham Hospital. Later, Penge Council's Clerk and its ARP Controller, Mr Arthur Elson, died from head injuries received on 19 March 1941 while crossing Anerley Road, and paying more attention to the conflagration at Anerley Congregational Church

Remembering the damage caused by a VI flying bomb, which put The Paxton Arms out of use for 11 years. (PA)

than the oncoming bicycle of an ARP warden.

The first fatalities in Penge took place on 12 September 1940 when six people died and five were injured at 102 Oakfield Road. Three days later on 15 September, since designated Battle of Britain Day, there were 23 fatalities in the Penge district, the worst being nine people at 45 Crystal Palace Park Road. Some 20 casualties were treated at the Oakfield Road first-aid post. The worst single incident that year was on 9 October, when ten people were killed by a direct hit on the shelter in Anerley Road. On 31 October the popular headmaster of Beckenham and Penge Grammar School was killed at his house in Beckenham, along with his wife and teenage son – he could be heard calling from the wreckage, but was not reached in time. On 6 November Penge High Street was blocked by debris from a bomb that killed three people and demolished the Co-op store (at that time opposite where Sainsbury's is now). The year ended with the death on 29 December of 11-year-old Hazel Burgess at St Christopher's Kindergarten School on the corner of Lennard and Cator Roads – by a cruel twist of irony, her parents had left her there for safety over the Christmas holidays. The blast, caused by a gigantic 'parachute mine', containing a tonne or more of explosive, destroyed six buildings and damaged 420, including the neighbouring Holy Trinity Church and the ARP post.

Somewhat belatedly, one might think, after a total of 69 fatalities, though only four of them children, Penge was then included in the list of areas for evacuation of children to the country, and 600 – one third of the school population – left for Devon on 2 January 1941. But the worst of the bombing was over for Penge, at least for the moment. Apart from some serious incidents on the outskirts of the district on 16 April and 17 May 1941 when a total of 22 people were killed, there were to be relatively few fatalities for the next $3^1/_2$ years, and the population knuckled down to living with the hardships.

Bomb devastation at 8–14 Marlow Road, Penge on 7 October 1940. (LHC)

THE HOME FRONT

The extent of recycling during the war would make a modern-day environmentalist's eyes water. In a single week in 1940, Penge collected $4\frac{1}{2}$ tonnes of paper, $7\frac{3}{4}$ tonnes of iron, $\frac{1}{2}$ tonne each of brass and aluminium, and 25kg of bones. As was the case everywhere, iron railings were taken, and even the disused tram rails were dug out of the roads, although it is now known that much of this iron was never used. Later, it was to be made an offence to burn paper, hot-water bottles might be recycled for their rubber, and even bones buried by dogs were sought out. To reduce travelling, a 'Holidays-at-Home' programme took place in July 1942, with daily events including concerts, competitions and donkey rides for children in Betts Park, Penge Recreation Ground, Royston Field, and various halls.

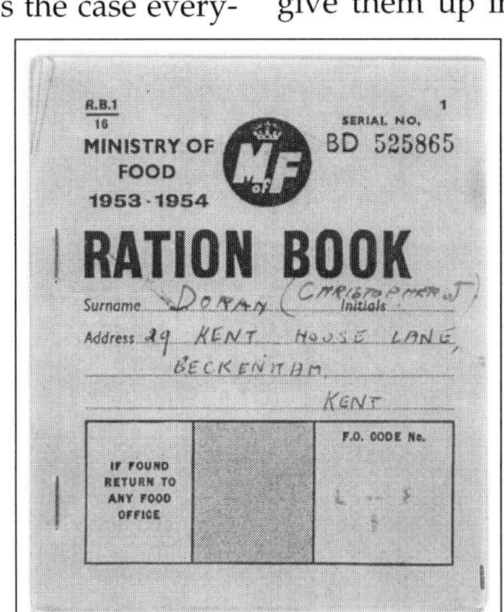

Ration books continued to be used in Britain into 1954. (CD)

As in the First World War, food rationing made it attractive to grow your own, but it took a while for Penge Council to organise allotments. The first 32 were taken up in May 1940, with 36 other applicants turning down offers on the grounds of locality. Parts of several parks were dug up, together with some waste land and large gardens; a number of bomb sites were requisitioned later. Warnings by the Crystal Palace Company of the poor soil quality in the Park went unheeded, and plots started there were soon abandoned. Most, though, were successful, with tenants reluctant to give them up in 1948 when the Council wanted to return them to public parks.

For those left without cooking facilities in damaged houses, feeding centres were set up in Churchfields and Melvin Road schools. On 31 December 1941, the one at Melvin School was opened as one of a nationwide network of 'British Restaurants' aimed to provide nutritious, low-cost meals to maintain the health of the population. They were staffed by the Women's Voluntary Service and proved popular with the general public, factory workers and schoolchildren. No less than 81,000 meals were served each year at Melvin Road in 1942 and 1943, with the service even making a profit of £460 in the latter. Women again served in many other occupations that had formerly been the province of men, even being found as BBC engineers.

FOR THE WOMEN ON THE HOME-FRONT!

WELDON'S
LADIES' JOURNAL
You will find this Splendid Magazine indispensable and invaluable.
Filled with Exciting Fiction, Exclusive Features, Helpful and Interesting Articles, Home Dress-making, and lots of new Knitwear designs.
Free Patterns are included with each issue.
PUBLISHED MONTHLY - SEVENPENCE

MOTHER AND HOME
The Ideal Up-to-date Family Magazine.
Packed with Splendid Short Stories —A host of Practical and Helpful Articles on Mothercraft, Cookery, Health and Beauty, Homecrafts and Gardening. Fashion and Knitting Pages.
A Free Pattern is given with every issue.
PUBLISHED MONTHLY - SEVENPENCE

GOOD TASTE
The Magazine for the Younger Woman.
Grand Complete Stories, a First-class Serial by a "best-seller" Novelist, Topical Articles, the Latest Beauty News, Smart Fashions, and the Newest Knitting Designs.
Every Issue contains a Free Pattern.
PUBLISHED MONTHLY - SEVENPENCE

PATTERN SERVICE. Any PATTERN ordered by 1 p.m. Tuesday or Friday can be obtained the SAME DAY at 7 p.m. NO ADDITIONAL CHARGES.

Newspapers, Periodicals and Magazines promptly delivered.
A GOOD RELIABLE EARLY MORNING SERVICE.
Private and Commercial Stationery and Account Books at London Store Prices.
FOSDICK'S Stationery & Bookshop, Ltd.,
131, THE HIGH STREET, PENGE. 'Phone: SYD. 8265.

Changing times during the Second World War at Fosdick's, still in the High Street today. (PCC)

In yet another repeat of the First World War, Belgian refugees flooded to the area. The Crystal Palace Park and buildings were requisitioned in the spring of 1940 and used as a reception centre through which thousands passed; the Penge Salvation Army Citadel served in the same capacity. The building of the former North Surrey District School (see Chapter Six) provided some of the accommodation.

Penge Court had a whole new set of crimes to contend with, such as blackout violations, ration fiddling, failure to leave vehicles immobilised, and dereliction of fire-watching duties. There was even a 'secrets case' where a lorry driver was fined £50 for communicating in the Goldsmith's Arms 'information which might be useful to an enemy'. His mistake was that in the pub were a number of RAF servicemen, some of whom were called to testify in Penge Court sitting in camera. Much was made of secrecy – even the newspaper reports of bomb locations gave but cryptic clues as to the location to avoid helping the enemy improve his aim. References like 'a large mission hall was badly damaged' plus the secretary's name, helped locals of the time to identify it, but do not make life easy for the historian 60 years later! Nevertheless, Nazi propaganda broadcaster 'Lord Haw-Haw' (William Joyce) frequently referred to the plight of Penge. (His unceremonious ejection from a pre-war meeting of the 'Penge Parliament' debating society must have left him with some antagonism towards the district.)

Various fund-raising schemes for the war effort were devised, beginning in October 1940 when Penge residents were asked to give to Kent's 'Buy a Spitfire' fund. In later years, the National Savings Movement promoted annual nationwide investment campaigns. Penge War Weapons Week, 19–26 April 1941, began with a target of £50,000, but this was greatly exceeded by the final figure of £90,182. In the following year, Penge Warship Week, 7–14 March 1941, raised £59,826 and resulted in its 'adoption' of the frigate HMS *Parrett* – which involved providing comforts such as dart boards, table-tennis equipment and rugs. Beckenham, being a larger and richer area, raised ten times as much and was allocated a destroyer, HMS *Sikh*, sunk off Tobruk on 14 September 1942, with the loss of 37 out of her 250 men. HMS *Parrett* survived the war. Plaques given to mark the association of these ships with the locality are now kept by its sea cadets. A major feature of each of these campaigns was a grand parade through the district. Other war-related entertainment included a boxing tournament at Royston Field on 15 August 1942, with protagonists from Canadian and British Army bases and the Penge Home Guard. Not to be outdone, the ladies followed on 5 September with a display by the Women's League of Health and Beauty, also at Royston Field, to raise money for the

Below: *Penge adopted the frigate HMS* Parrett *(similar to the one below). The commemorative plaque (right) carried on the ship was later given to Penge and Beckenham Sea Scouts and kept at their HQ in Kent House Road.* (CD)

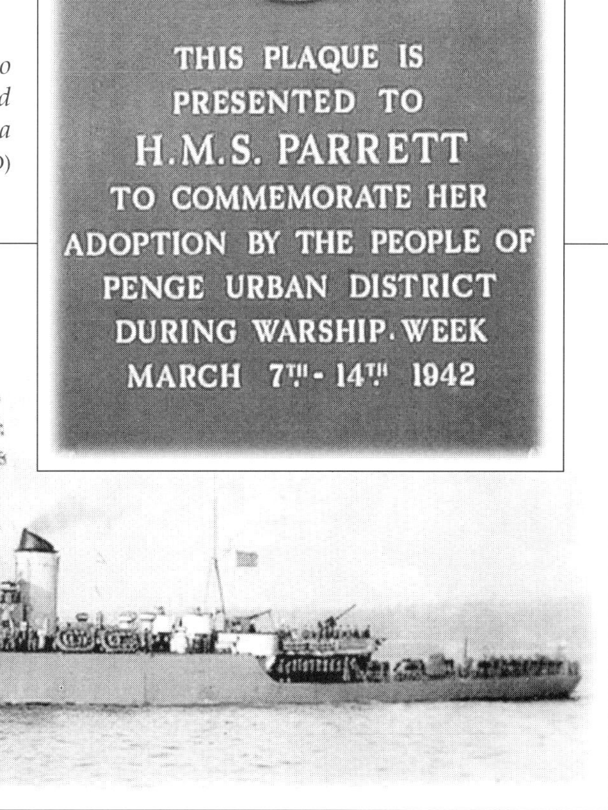

Procession for Penge War Weapons Week, Penge High Street, August 1941. (LBB)

Penge and Anerley District Nursing Association. The year 1943 saw 'Wings for Victory' week which raised £129,776, and 'Salute the Soldier' week, 22–29 July 1944, almost equalled this with £122,000, compared with a target of £110,000.

The Auxiliary Fire Service decided to mount a practice gas attack in Penge High Street on 12 April 1941 using a cylinder of tear gas. People who had come out without the gas masks which they were supposed to carry at all times, seeing the large number of police and AFS about, dashed home for their masks. In fact, the enemy never made gas attacks.

1944: Flying Bomb Summer

By the end of 1943 many were reckoning that the war was all but over, and the Home Guard was stood down on 3 December. However, the conclusion took longer than that, for 'Flying Bomb Summer', June/July 1944, was yet to come. Penge's first V1, Vergeltung eins ('retaliation one'), fly bomb, buzz bomb or doodlebug – call it what you will – hit the Crystal Palace end of the High Street on Sunday 18 June. It killed 11 people and caused widespread damage to houses and shops as well as to Penge Methodist Church (wartime damage to other churches is listed in Chapter Six). A second V1 on the same afternoon was shot down by anti-aircraft fire (presumably from the battery behind Anerley Town Hall) and fell at the Anerley Road end of Anerley Park. It was soon realised that shooting them down over residential areas gained nothing, and AA batteries and barrage balloons were removed. The worst incident occurred on 11 July when 11 people, mainly women and children, were killed and 48 injured outside the Crystal Palace low-level station. They had heard the doodlebug approaching but failed to get into the nearby shelter in time. Emergency steps were taken to resume evacuation of schoolchildren, which had stopped at the end of 1940, and a party was sent to Huddersfield in mid-July, but by this time the attacks were tailing off. Penge High Street received another serious hit on 21 July when 300 shops and houses were destroyed or damaged, but only one person was killed. Some 115 properties were destroyed or damaged and three people killed in Wordsworth Road on 3 August. The last V1 in Penge killed 7 and injured 18 at the gun site behind the Town Hall on 24 August 1944. The nearest V2s to the district landed in Lennard Road in January 1945 (without fatalities) and in Crystal Palace Park Road on 15 March (8 fatalities). In total, Penge was hit by 20 flying bombs, with more close to its borders. The official estimate was that half the houses in the district had been rendered uninhabitable. Penge gained the doubtful honour of receiving more hits per unit area than anywhere else in the country. One explanation is that the Germans were deliberately misled by a double agent into believing they had the correct range for Central London. On 8 May 2002, the 57th anniversary of VE Day, a plaque *(right)* was unveiled in Empire Square inscribed:

> *'To the people of Penge who suffered war and change showing courage, dignity and humour.'*

Bombs dropped during the Second World War which caused fatalities in Penge, Anerley and Crystal Palace. (CD)

Aftermath

The effects of the war continued well into the fifties, with pig-swill bins to collect food waste lingering on street corners, compulsory carrying of identity cards remaining until 1952, rationing not completely ending until June 1954 and conscription ending in 1963. Perhaps more significant is how much changed. Businesses that closed 'temporarily' for the duration never reopened – either the proprietors failed to return to the district (if they survived at all) or they had found other outlets for their energies meanwhile.

Many a search carried out for this book has simply met a dead end in 1939. Continuing shortages led to drastic cuts in public expenditure, with education the most publicised victim long into the years when the post-war baby boom was hitting the classrooms. An early casualty was nursery schooling started during the war to enable mothers to go to work – this was now deemed unnecessary.

The rebuilding of bombsites took many years, the block of shops at the end of Penge High Street where the Post Office now stands, for example, remaining derelict into the mid 1950s, as housing was given higher priority.

All's Fair in Love and War

After every major war, enormous resolutions are made to ensure that it will prove to be the last. Yet history tells us that every generation of homo sapiens seems to succumb to one or more. More homo than sapiens, the pundits might say. It is a case of short memories, others say; too much pent-up anger, suggest yet others.

While many still carry the scars of major wars, others can only imagine what life might have been like in such times. The surviving photographs of war-damaged buildings give some idea of what it must have been like to come home to find one's home and all its contents in chaos.

The Cold War certainly cost a great deal in financial and anxiety terms, but somehow was wound up largely non-violently. No doubt Penginians have served in more if small-scale conflicts in Cyprus, Kenya, the Gulf, the Falklands, Ulster, the Balkans and elsewhere. Whether closer union with the European Union, and enlarging this to take in more countries, helps reduce the chances of further wars remains to be seen.

Six

EDIFICATION & EDUCATION

In the fifteenth century Penge was a mere 'detached hamlet' of Battersea, as we saw in Chapter One. Its 12 families were therefore supposed to travel 11km to its Parish Church, St Mary's, to which they also had to pay taxes. In 1658 the inhabitants demanded a public inquiry into this situation, pointing out that their nearest place of worship was in Beckenham, where a church has been traced back to before 1100. Battersea's rector was paying a 'trifling consideration' to the Beckenham parish priest to look after his Penge parishioners. The inquiry, held in Kingston, suggested that Penge should be attached to a closer parish, but nothing was actually done.

It was not until 8 October 1837, when the population had risen to 270, that the first Anglican chapel was opened in Penge, diagonally opposite Penge Police Station. Its congregation soon outgrew its size and in October 1849 the present full Parish Church, St John's, was erected further up the High Street, beyond the Watermen's Asylum. As the population grew, other Anglican Churches were added, together with a Roman Catholic one, taking over portions of their predecessors' parishes. The Nonconformist, or Free, Churches have no parish system and were opened wherever there were enough people of a particular denomination. Since 1837, some 15 to 20 churches have appeared and a few have gone.

St John's Church, 2002. (PA)

PRIVATE ROOMS & TIN CHAPELS

For decades an almost universal pattern of church development was followed: people began to meet for worship in one another's homes, and when membership grew, they looked for space in a school, a public hall, or in one case a hayloft. Next they would buy some land, perhaps to erect a prefabricated corrugated iron church, eventually building a permanent one and maybe selling on the 'tin church'. Not all churches got that far. Among those of which no trace exists today are the United Gospel Mission in Woodbine Grove, Gilgal Mission and Tower Hall Mission on Anerley Hill, and a Unitarian Church using the Penge Public Halls in Station Road Anerley. Members of a Brethren group meeting in 'Green Lane Room' included Mr A. Olby, founder of Penge's one-time large hardware store, which was next door. The pattern of new Church formation did not end in the early 1900s, for as late as 1979 a number of people left existing Churches to form Penge Christian Fellowship. They first met in homes and halls, finally purchasing the former Co-op building at the corner of Green Lane and Parish Lane, where they thrive as Penge Family Church.

The Church of England followed St John's in 1859 with St Paul's, which started with an iron church in Anerley Vale, and moved to a permanent building in Hamlet Road in 1866. In 1883 it opened a mission church, St James', in Castledine Road. Down the hill, at the junction of Anerley Road and Croydon Road, Holy Trinity Church was built in 1872, with a hall in Melvin Road. A second Holy Trinity followed in Lennard Road in 1878. It is one of several churches bestowed by Francis Peek, a tea merchant and nephew of the founder of the biscuit and tea manufacturer Peek, Frean & Co. Christ Church was built in Franklin Road in 1884, with a hall in Green Lane.

St Anthony's Roman Catholic Church, in Genoa Road, started in 1878 in an iron chapel, moving to the upper floor of a combined church and school

The Congregational Church's 'tin hall', 1908–11. (PCC)

The Maple Road Salvation Army Citadel and (inset) *plaque to Mrs Commissioner Carleton* (top) *and First World War memorial* (bottom). (PA)

building in 1898. The present church was not erected until 1927.

Several Churches have used Mosslea Road Hall (now the Good Shepherd Mission), at the junction of Station Road Penge and Mosslea Road (of Staunton murder infamy, see Chapter Three). It was opened in 1885 as a mission hall for Holy Trinity Lennard Road, Station Road being called Trinity Road at one time. The London City Mission moved there from Arpley Road in 1948 and remained until 1966 when the missioner left and its members joined St John's. In early 1971 it became home for the Old Catholic Church, doing considerable work with handicapped youngsters. The tiny Old Catholic chapel of St Bonaventure, now located opposite Crystal Palace Station, was at one time housed in a room on the platform.

The first Free Church, Anerley Congregational, was started in 1856 by people meeting in a lecture hall in Jasmine Grove which it retained for its Sunday School until 1920. In 1876 it progressed to an impressive church building situated almost opposite the canal in Betts Park. In 1907, some members of Anerley Congregational Church left and built Penge Congregational Church in a part of Beckenham Road later renamed Penge High Street. Two ministers of the Penge Church, the Revd Ernest Barson (from 1909 to 1947) and the Revd Dr John Travell (1969 to 1989) achieved considerable local reputations through their community involvement.

Anerley Wesleyan Methodist Church first met in a house in Maple Road in 1862, built a combined church and Sunday School hall on the corner of Jasmine Grove and Oakfield Road in 1865, and added a larger church to it in 1879. Penge Primitive Methodist Church began at the High Street end of Mosslea Road with an iron building in 1871, replaced by a brick one in 1882. Baptists who met in two rooms in Hawthorn Grove in 1865 laid the foundations of the 'Penge Tabernacle' (Penge Baptist Church) in Maple Road in 1867, with several extensions in following years. In 1900 its members built Avenue Road Mission, which became independent as Avenue Road Evangelical Church in 1980 and was renamed to Avenue Baptist Church in 1993.

An unusual venture in 1875 was a combined mission, lecture hall, library, public baths, and coffee house in Parish Lane. Only the mission was financially viable, and after several changes of management it finally became the non-denominational Alexandra Hall Mission. It was noted for its soup kitchen for the poor, flower shows, and musical evenings by its Band of Hope singers. The New Jerusalem Church in Waldegrave Road was opened in 1883 by followers of Emmanuel Swedenborg, who had a series of visions that led him to some rather unconventional new doctrines. The building is unusual for its time, being made entirely of concrete using clay dug from its own foundations. It closed in

The Penge Churches' Good Friday March of Witness, 2002. (RM)

Beckenham Coffee House
AND
INSTITUTE,
Alexandra Terrace,
PENGE.

1—*Large Reading Room.*
2—*Public Smoking Room.*
3—*Coffee Bar.*
4—*Commercial Room for Tradesmen.*
5—*Reception & Dining Room.*
6—*Bed Rooms for respectable Clerks, with private Sitting Room.*
7—*Library, &c.*
8—*Recreation Room.*
9—*Class or Committee Rooms on hire.*
10—*Large Lecture Hall, for Concerts, Lectures, &c. &c., &c., &c.*

Lectures on Science, Literature and the Fine Arts occasionally delivered, and educational classes formed.

TERMS.
Honorary Members 10/6 per year,
Entitling members to free admission to all Institute Lectures and Concerts.
Ordinary Members 5/- per year,
Free admission to Lectures, Concerts (back seats), half price to reserved seats.
Half-yearly 2/6.
Quarterly 1/6.
Monthly 6d.
Single Admission to Reading Room 1d.

Beckenham Mission House, Institute, Coffee House, and Public Baths.
OPENED DECEMBER 13th, 1877.
Prospectuses, giving every information respecting the varied branches of educational work in connection with the Institute and Mission, can be had on application to the Manager on the premises. **Ladies admitted as members of the Institute.**

Beckenham
PUBLIC BATHS
Alexandra Terrace,
PENGE.

These baths are now open to the public; they are fitted up in a neat and commodious style, and have attached to them a comfortable waiting room, in which tea, coffee, cocoa, and other refreshmentsmay be had at moderate charges.

TERMS FOR BATHS.
Hot Bath 6d.
Cold do. 3d.
Two children *under 8 years of age can have a bath for* 6d.

LADIES' BATHS
Every week day excepting Saturday, from 2 till 4.30.

Open to Gentlemen
Any hour in the day, except those specified for Ladies, and on Saturday all the day from 8 a.m. till 9.30 p.m.

Every bather provided with two clean towels, and supplied with a bath of clear fresh water.

The Alexandra Mission Hall, 1888–1940. (CD)

Anerley Methodist Church, 1879–1940. (AMC)

Above: *Christ Church in 2002.* (CD)

Left: *Penge Congregational Church in 1912 – it is unusually ornate for a Nonconformist church.* (PCC)

Below: *Avenue Baptist Church.* (CD)

St Snthony's RC Church in Genow Road (left) *and original school* (right). (CD)

Penge Primitive Methodist Church building, converted into flats in 2002. (CD)

Above: *The New Church, Waldegrave Road.* (PA)
Right: *The original Holy Trinity Church.* (EP)
Below: *The original St Paul's, Anerley.* (EP)
Below right: *The magnificent Anerley Congregational Church, 1876–1941.* (EP)

1985, when it was converted into over 30 luxury flats.

Penge Salvation Army Citadel (as its meeting-places are called) opened in 1894 in Maple Road, but there are records of an earlier Salvationist 'Christian Mission Station' in Penge, and of meetings in a hayloft. Perhaps chief among its early 'worthies' were John A. Carleton and his wife, Major Carleton, who received the Order of the Founder – the Army's highest award. She was the Special Commissioner for the Army's periodicals; *The War Cry* alone enjoyed a circulation of 300,000 copies in the UK. John Carleton formed the Army's first 'songster brigade' in 1898 and also originated its international annual self-denial fund-raising. Kathleen Lavinia Bristow who began as a 'junior' in the Penge Corps was later to marry Wilfred Kitching who became the Army's seventh General (or international leader) in 1953. The London City Mission, formed under the patronage of Earl Shaftesbury, to serve the 'poorer classes', established mission halls in Arpley Road (around 1895) and Arthur Road (renamed Churchfields Road in 1907).

Faith & Fellowship

In the days of limited home entertainment, the churches provided many of the outlets for leisure-time activity through a variety of clubs. Penge Tabernacle even owned its own sports ground – 'Tablonians', opposite Cator Park in Lennard Road. Even today those who forsake the television and venture out to a meeting will most likely find it in a church hall. For children, something to look forward to was the annual Sunday school day trip to the country or seaside. Large crowds gathered at Penge West Station for the special train packed with groups from all around and destined for a coastal resort. Each church was allotted a section of the beach, where games were played and giant sandcastles dug until it was time for tea at a local church hall, and then home.

Who can tell how many young lives were, and still are, moulded through the Scouts, Guides, Sunday schools, and other organisations run by tireless leaders from the churches?

Inter-Church Co-operation

The churches recognised their need to work together and a Penge United Churches Committee acted as a meeting-point for the clergy. In May 1949 it was re-formed with lay participation as Penge Council of Churches. Its public activities included united services, 'June Study Evenings' on a different topic each year, a Good Friday 'March of Witness' around the district, and the Christian Aid collection which now raises over £3,000 annually. One of its achievements was the formation of Penge Churches' Housing Association in 1969. By 2002, this managed some 200 housing units and, together with its Friends' Association of volunteers, provides sympathetic, caring and efficient property services for its tenants. Penge Forum was formed under its auspices in 1971 to focus on secular concerns arising from the apparent neglect and misunderstanding of the district by the remote London Borough of Bromley. Forum in its turn established a Penge Festival Week each May, that includes entertainments by local organisations and a fête. The Council of Churches closed in 1991 when it was felt that a formal structure was no longer required, and joint activities are now organised by the clergy or others as need arises. Such a need was seen in the number of rough sleepers in central London which burgeoned in the 1990s. A group comprising members of several churches in the district is now part of a London-wide network supplying clothing and food to the homeless.

Preachers at the Palace

The Crystal Palace auditorium of former times, and its sports stadium today, have been filled by many large church events. The great Baptist preacher, the Revd Charles Haddon Spurgeon, preached there, as did The Salvation Army's founder, General William Booth. It was the venue for the Army's 25th anniversary celebrations in 1890, and from 1894 onwards it held mass meetings every three years. It was therefore appropriate that its centenary should be celebrated in the sports stadium on 26 June 1965. Pope John-Paul II (Karol Wojtyla) preached to Roman Catholics (mainly of Polish extraction) at the stadium in 1982, and Billy Graham held rallies there in 1989.

Wartime Destruction

Alexandra Hall Mission was badly damaged in one of the first bombing raids of the Battle of Britain on 20 September 1940, and not rebuilt. As in other cases, its members simply joined other fellowships. Anerley Methodist Church was destroyed on 8 December 1940, though the halls were repairable, with one converted for worship, as it remains today. Anerley Congregational Church was gutted by incendiary bombs on 19 March 1941 and not rebuilt.

Holy Trinity Anerley was totally destroyed on 24 March 1944 by the last piloted bomber to hit the district. Its worshippers moved to Christ Church in Franklin Road, whose own members joined with St John's. The Holy Trinity and Christ Church parishes were eventually combined, and in 1961 a hall was built on the Holy Trinity site. Penge Methodist Church was badly damaged in a V1 attack on 18 June 1944 and did not reopen; the building was used as a warehouse until it was converted into luxury flats in 2002. The LCM's Shaftesbury Hall in Arpley Road was destroyed on 21 July1944. Its First World War memorial was kept in the garden of No. 53 until the road disappeared in the Groves area redevelopment of the early 1970s. In addition, Holy Trinity Lennard Road, Penge Baptist Church, and St James' were seriously damaged but repaired

Peacetime Vandalism

St James' was never used as fully as before the war, and was closed after vandalism in the 1970s. Several churches suffered under a series of arson attacks on public buildings in the 1970s to '90s. Anerley Methodist Church was hit four times between 1975 and 1980, the worst on 9 July 1979, but it was repaired. An attempt on Penge Congregational Church was discovered in time. Another deliberate fire left Christ Church unusable. The site was sold, along with that of Holy Trinity Hall, Anerley, and a new church was built at the top of Maple Road in 1990. Its large basement area, known as 'The Hive', is used as a community centre. Holy Trinity Lennard Road was gutted on 11 September 1993. When it was rebuilt and reopened in 1997, the former chancel space was made into a garden that featured in the BBC's 'Songs of Praise' programme on 9 September 2001.

Several other Churches decided in the 1970s and beyond that it was time to redevelop their outdated and uneconomic buildings. Some just made internal improvements; others more extensive changes. In April 1971, St Paul's moved all its activities to the church hall (formerly St Paul's School) in nearby Hadlow Place. The Hamlet Road church was demolished in the winter of 1973/4 and replaced by a new dual-purpose church and hall which was dedicated on 16 December 1978. Penge Baptist Church closed the vast Tabernacle, selling the site for social housing which opened in 1990. The former hall alongside was adapted as a church.

Education Followed Close Behind

The major mass education reforms of the nineteenth and early-twentieth centuries all took place during Penge's formative years. The 1870 Elementary Education Act set up local School Boards and permitted them to make school attendance compulsory for children from five to ten, although education was not universally free until 1891. An Act of 1902 replaced the School Boards by Education Committees of local and county councils, and authorised them to control both elementary and secondary education. This Act also clarified the position of schools 'provided' by the council and those publicly financed but 'non-provided' (e.g. Church schools). The council controls education in both, except for religious education in Church schools.

The First Penge Schools

The deeds of St John's Chapel specified that when replaced by a church the building could be converted into a school for 'the religious instruction of the children of the Poor of Penge and its vicinity.' Thus its trustees' meeting on 11 July 1850 agreed that the chapel should become St John's Church of England School. A site in Maple Road was purchased for additional premises in 1859. St Paul's Church of England School was built in Hadlow Place, Anerley, around 1870, and St Anthony's Roman Catholic School in Genoa Road in 1898.

In addition to these three Church schools, Melvin Road School was built by the London School Board in 1880, with Oakfield Road School around the same time. Penge children could also attend Alexandra School in Parish Lane, started in 1875 by local landowner Mr Albermarle Cator who sold it in 1877 to the Beckenham School Board which considerably enlarged it. In 1890, Beckenham built another school in nearby Arthur (now Churchfields) Road, which also took some Penge children. St Paul's and St Anthony's were all-age mixed schools; the others were several schools in one building usually divided into mixed infants (five–ten years), senior boys, and senior girls. Mr Colin Hood lived for many years above his father's shoe shop at 143 Anerley Road, opposite the Town Hall. He recalls:

The original Penge Tabernacle. (VRP)

A pillow-making lesson at the Alexandra School, 1917. (LHC)

Boys at the Alexandra Boys' School, c.1915. Among them is contributor Chris Doran's father as a boy. (CD)

Woodwork class at oakfield Road School, 1906.

> *My father, Archie, born in 1895, went to Oakfield Road School until he was 14, he's the one in the middle row, by the 'X' in the 1906 photo* [above]. *He later became an apprentice in the shoe shop. Soon after WW1 he was first able to buy into it as a partner and later took it over, modernising the shop front and working there for a total of 54 years. We lived above; that's how things were in those days. Now I've moved out to Birkbeck Road and the shop is a solicitor's office.* [That's] *how it goes, these days.*

In fact, his father was lucky not to have been one of those taken out of school before 14 to augment the family's income. Parents were regularly prosecuted for this, although it was possible to get permission for children over 13 to leave early. For continuing education, Penge Local Higher Education Subcommittee started a Domestic Subjects Centre in 1911 at Melvin Road School, providing evening classes in cookery, laundry, and housewifery.

Classes were huge by modern standards – 50 or 60 pupils being common. Teachers were assisted by 'monitors' or 'pupil teachers' aged 14 upwards and themselves still under part-time tuition, either at the schools where they worked or at colleges in Beckenham. The pupil teacher system, seen as a way to support trainee teachers, continued until 1923, by which time scholarships for full-time training were available. School life was never easy – early records mention epidemics of measles, mumps, chicken pox, scarlet fever, etc., sometimes necessitating closure of whole schools. Their buildings were poorly lit, the need to improve classroom lighting being mentioned frequently. Another problem was that of some pupils starting the autumn term late, having been hop-picking in Kent, and returning 'unclean and verminous' as a report of 1920 complained.

Special Schools

The early Penge schools had no provision for disabled pupils – the 'physically and mentally defective' as pre-PC records termed them. A special unit at the Churchfields School in Beckenham took some such pupils, as did Anerley Residential School for Deaf Boys in Versailles Road, and the Royal Normal College for the Blind in Upper Norwood – none of these under Penge Education Committee's control. Many were sent far afield around the country. Likewise, delinquent pupils such as persistent truants were sent to euphemistically-named 'Industrial' boarding schools. The building in Versailles Road now serves Lewisham in this capacity as Anerley Boys' School. Next to it, running behind Madeline Road off Anerley Road, was the North Surrey District School, opened in November 1850 and run by the Boards of Guardians of six boroughs as a boarding school for children of paupers. It added training for employment to basic literacy and numeracy skills, making full use of its vast building and three- hectare (seven-acre) site. The *Illustrated London News* of 23 November 1850 describes its various rooms, including 14 dormitories, classrooms, apartments for teachers and other staff, work- and storerooms, plus two reception wards where children could be quarantined for 24 hours until examined by a medical officer. The multiple-room pattern, adopted partly to avoid the spread of disease, seems to have been common for this type of school; it is described in 'Lowood' school in the novel *Jane Eyre*, where an epidemic fis described.

Private Schools

Albermarle College, opposite Holy Trinity Church in Lennard Road, was an exclusive Church of England High School for Boys, whose managers included the Church's first vicar, the Revd Samuel Whitfield Daukes, and the Mr Francis Peek we met above. It also hosted evening classes run by the Penge and Beckenham School of Science and Art. St Christopher's School, on the Cator Road side of Holy Trinity Church, offered elementary education for boys and girls from 5 to 11. Anerley College in Selby Road boasted in a 1913 advertisement that its four resident masters were all 'university men', and of a pupil getting 100 per cent in Cambridge Locals Arithmetic. The South London School, originally at 8/10 Anerley Hill, later at 57 Croydon Road (where

This house was built as a school as part of a local residential development in 1866–8 on the site of Porcupine Farm. Later it was managed by the nearby Alexandra School, built in 1875, and then converted into flats. (CD)

Yeoman House now stands) provided a 'sound English education in modern times' for children aged 5 to 14, guaranteeing its older students (14-17) 'when proficient, assisted with introductions, etc., until settled in a satisfactory appointment.' Also in Croydon Road were The Crispin School at No. 65 and Kent House College. Others included Anerley Park College at 22 Anerley Park, Belvedere House School at 30 Belvedere Road, Miss Fox's Private School at 4 Castledine Road, and Thornsett Road School at No. 11. Doris Pullen tells of other small schools in Chapter Nine. All of these are long gone, but since around 1990, private secondary education has been available at Harris City Technology College in Maberley Road, Anerley, where children of 11 upwards can enter one of its four faculties: Arts, Communications, Science, and Technology.

The Crystal Palace Lends a Hand

The Crystal Palace Company established several schools beginning in 1859 with the School of Art, Science and Literature to teach subjects that included literature, history, geography, modern languages, elocution, Classics and mathematics. Some of its students, numbering 400 in some years, went on to gain distinctions at Royal Academy schools. There was a large ladies' division, a junior section for girls under 16, and a centre preparing students for Oxford and Cambridge local examinations. When a previously unknown 19-year-old Arthur Sullivan rocketed to fame overnight after the presentation of his first work, 'The Tempest', at the Palace on 5 and 12 April 1862, he was appointed professor of pianoforte and ballad singing. Teachers at the School of Music set up in 1861 included Henry Leslie, Manuel Garcia, Julius Benedict and Ebenezer Prout, all of whom achieved fame in the musical world, as did August Manns, the Crystal Palace concert conductor. Mr J.W. Wilson and his son, also named J.W. Wilson, formed the School of Practical Engineering in 1872. The father had worked on the 1851 Exhibition as well as the re-erection of the Palace in 1854. The school's drawing office, foundry, pattern shop, smiths' shop and electrical section were housed on several floors of the South Water Tower, an adjacent building (see pp118/119), and No. 14 across the road. The .two-year course covered mechanical and civil engineering. Among its students were Capt. Sir Geoffrey de Havilland (1882–1965) who formed the De Havilland aircraft company, a forerunner of British Aerospace, and Mr Morgan of Morgan's Cars. Less academic than the above was the Crystal Palace Great Riding School which had stabling for 400 horses.

Expansion after First World War

The 1918 'Fisher' Act raised the school leaving age to 14, creating secondary education for all children from 11 upwards. This, along with the growing population of the district, resulted in severe overcrowding, a problem exacerbated by the age and design of the buildings. A 1921 report on Oakfield Road School complained of classes exceeding 60, and in 1924 St Paul's School, with over 200 children of all ages in four rooms, was condemned as 'unsuitable for continued recognition'. A major reorganisation therefore began in 1926, when some land behind the Town Hall belonging to the North Surrey District School was compulsorily purchased to build Anerley Junior School, which opened in the autumn of 1930. This took children from St Paul's School, which then closed, and Oakfield Road Infants. St Anthony's School gained some space in 1927 when the church was built next door, releasing the upper floor of the shared building. A shortage of playing-field space led to the purchase in 1925 of Royston Field at the corner of Franklin Road and Croydon Road. Beckenham Education Committee established the Beckenham County School for Girls in Lennard Road in 1919, and in 1929 opened Alexandra Infants School in Kent House Road to take the youngest pupils from the main Alexandra School in Parish Lane. In 1939 it added Stewart Fleming Primary School in Witham Road, named after its first chairman, the Revd R S Fleming of Beckenham Baptist Church.

Penge's reorganisation also consolidated senior boys at Oakfield Road School and senior girls at Melvin Road. Oakfield Road retained a junior mixed school, and Melvin Road still had infants. The senior schools were renamed to The Penge Central Schools for Boys/Girls in 1937. The St John's Schools ended split working between the Croydon Road and Maple Road sites in 1937 when all operations moved to Maple Road, where a new classroom was built with the proceeds of the sale of the Croydon Road site. A most significant contribution to secondary education took place in 1930 with the move to Penge of the Beckenham Technical Day School, one of four institutions in a building adjacent to Beckenham Baths now occupied by The Studio. The chosen site, at the junction of Kent House Road and Penge High Street, was previously filled by four large houses and a farm. Through a series of name changes, it became Beckenham and Penge Grammar School for Boys, which set a high standard of academic achievement,

Formerly the boys' grammar school, this site now houses Royston Primary School downstairs and Kentwood Educational Centre upstairs. (CD)

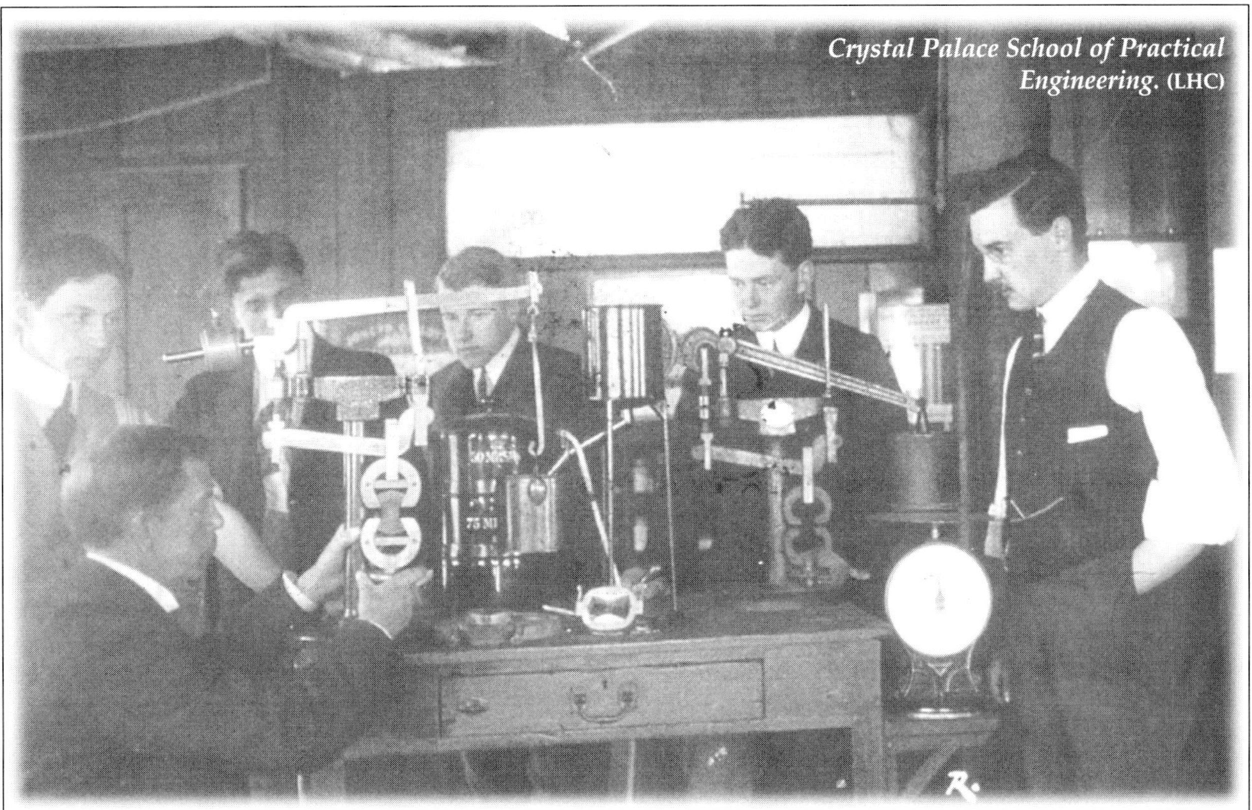
Crystal Palace School of Practical Engineering. (LHC)

not least under the headmastership of Mr L.W. White who ruled the school with a rod of iron from 1941 to 1962.

Continued Growth after Second World War

The 1944 'Butler' Act established a three-tier secondary system of secondary modern, technical, and grammar schools in ascending order of ability, and raised the leaving age to 15 or 16. This, together with the post-war bulge, put further strain on school accommodation. The Ministry of Education's solution was 'HORSA' – 'Huts On Raising School leaving Age'. Under a further provision of the act, Kent Education Committee took control of education in Beckenham and Penge in 1945/6, and added these huts to several existing school sites. A popular Penge Evening Institute was started at the Melvin Road site, the only institute of its kind in Kent. Reports of its annual prize-givings show that subjects included upholstery, millinery, basketwork, dressmaking, cookery, leatherwork, woodwork, boot- and shoe-making, shorthand, and typing. As early as 1960 the school had an evening class to teach fifth-formers use of electro-mechanical calculators.

HORSA provided only a short respite and more new schools were soon needed. Oakfield Juniors moved to Malcolm Road in 1951 as Malcolm Primary School. Around the same time, Melvin Road Infants moved into huts on the Croydon Road side of Royston playing-field becoming Royston Primary School. Alexandra Junior School was opened on a former sports ground in Cator Road in 1954 to take younger pupils from the Parish Lane school, which then became solely Alexandra Secondary Modern School for boys. Back in 1948 it had won some acclaim when its swimming team became South of England champions. James Dixon Primary School in Anerley Park was opened in 1955, named after a Penge Councillor in recognition of his life-long service to Penge and in particular to education. A new block was added to St Anthony's School in the same year. A replacement for the Girls' Secondary School was started in 1958 on more of the land of the long-closed North Surrey District School, in William Booth Road off Anerley Road. But the Melvin Road building lingered on in use, completion of the new school being little more than a promise for another 20 years.

Bromley Takes Over

Responsibility for local education was transferred to Bromley Borough on its creation in 1965. Replacement of buildings over 80 years old was a priority. Alexandra School closed in 1968 when the boys moved to a new Kelsey Park Boys' School in Beckenham. In the same year the Penge Secondary Schools were renamed Kentwood Boys' School and Rock Hills Girls' School (recalling the one-time Rockhills Common and Paxton's house, see p121). These name changes heralded introduction of comprehensive secondary education throughout the borough which did not take place for another five years due to wrangling over various schemes – at one

The original St John's School, diagonally opposite Penge Police Station, early 1900s. (LHC)

Melvin School, now demolished. (EAH)

Old Penge Library at Baroda House, 98 Oakfield Road, 1899–1928. (LHC)

Penge Library, Maple Road, 1959–present. (PA)

TELEGRAMS:—"BRAILLIST, LONDON."
TELEPHONE:—330 SYDENHAM.
ENCLOSURES..............

NEAREST RAILWAY STATIONS:—
"Gipsy Hill," or "Crystal Palace," from Victoria or London Bridge (L.B. & S.C.Ry.)
"Crystal Palace," from Victoria, Moorgate Street, Holborn Viaduct or Ludgate Hill (S.E. & C.Ry.)

Royal Normal College & Academy of Music for the Blind,
UPPER NORWOOD, LONDON, S.E.

PATRONS: THEIR MOST GRACIOUS MAJESTIES THE KING AND QUEEN

PRESIDENT: THE RT. HON. LORD HOWARD DE WALDEN AND SEAFORD.
CHAIRMAN: THE RT. HON. LORD LAMINGTON, G.C.M.G.
PRINCIPAL: SIR FRANCIS CAMPBELL, LL.D. F.R.G.S.
HON. TREASURER: THE RT. HON. LORD STALBRIDGE.

28th June, 1910.

Dear Lord Stalbridge,

On behalf of Lord Lamington and the Executive Committee I am writing to enquire if you could favour us by presiding at our Prize Festival. Any afternoon between the 18th and 25th July, both dates inclusive, except Tuesday the 19th, is available. Would you also mind asking if the ... It is a
Dowager Duchess of Westminst...
very long time since any ...
been to the College, and we ...
family represented at the ...
ing, will you please teleph...
Duchess will be able to fa...
You will be glad to ...
papers are already printi...
kind enough to sign.

Believe me,
Yours ...

The Rt. Hon.
Lord Stalbridge.

OBJECT: In each department the instruction is directed to the practical end of preparing the Blind for self-maintenance.

INSTRUCTION. The course of instruction includes the following departments:—Physical Training, General Education, Science and Practice of Music, Training of Teachers, Typewriting and Shorthand, Pianoforte Tuning.

PIANOFORTE TUNING. Certificated Pianoforte Tuners sent to any part of the London Postal District. Agencies in many provincial towns. Terms on application to The Manager, Tuning Department.

TYPEWRITING. The Typewriting Department is prepared to execute rapidly and accurately all descriptions of typewriting and duplicating.

RESULTS. The success in life of many Teachers, Organists, Pianoforte Tuners, Typists and Business Men testifies to the efficiency of the training given in the College.

APPEAL. Those who live in the shadow of a "great darkness" are surely entitled not only to our sympathy, but to our practical assistance. This National Institution is without endowment. Donations and Subscriptions earnestly requested.

VISITING DAY. The first Thursday of each month except January, August and September, 3.15 to 5.0. Tickets forwarded on application.

Royal Normal College and Academy of Music for the Blind,
UPPER NORWOOD, S.E.

Annual Prize Festival,

4.15 P.M. THURSDAY, 13TH JULY, 1905.

H.R.H. THE DUKE OF CONNAUGHT WILL PRESIDE.
H.R.H. THE DUCHESS OF CONNAUGHT
has graciously consented to present the Prizes.

THE PRESIDENT, LORD HOWARD DE WALDEN,
Requests the honour of the Company of Yourself and Friend.

The holder of this Ticket is requested to enter the College Premises at "Walmer," Church Road.

ADMIT TWO.

R.S.V.P. TO DR. CAMPBELL AT THE COLLEGE. P.T.O.

Above and left: *The emphasis on 'normal' in the title of this nineteenth-century establishment reflects the relatively new phenomenon of educating the blind.* (EP)

Right: *Royal patronage was always highly valued.* (EP)

Alexandra Infants' School. (PA)

point the then Minister of Education, Mrs Margaret Thatcher, had to intevene.

A heavy blow was dealt in 1969 when Beckenham and Penge Grammar School for Boys was moved to Langley Park, where the Girls' Grammar School had relocated from Lennard Road ten years earlier. Kentwood Boys' School took over the boys' grammar school building, enabling the Oakfield Road school to be demolished. Arsonists destroyed part of St John's School buildings in April 1977, but they were about to be replaced anyway when the school was completely rebuilt on the same site, reopening in September 1978.

Among these were gains, but another bitter blow was about to strike. In 1985 Bromley Council, having reviewed its secondary school provision in the light of falling numbers, decided to close the two poorest-equipped schools in the borough – Rock Hills and Kentwood – despite the obvious geographical hole this would create. Penge protested, but to no avail, and both schools closed in 1987, forcing many secondary school girls, and all secondary boys, to commute elsewhere. Ironically, a shortage of secondary school places in Bromley was created a few years later when the 1989 Greenwich Judgement ruled that Local Education Authorities cannot give priority to their own children over applicants from neighbouring boroughs. The closure of Rock Hills allowed the Melvin Road building to be demolished, and Anerley Junior School, behind Anerley Town Hall, shifted a few hundred metres into the newer Rock Hills building where it was renamed Anerley Primary School. Royston Primary School went to the ground floor of the one-time grammar school building now vacated by Kentwood. Finally, Churchfields Primary School moved to a new site on the opposite side of Churchfields Road in 1989.

More Changes in the 1990s

The Education Reform Act of 1988 imposed a National Curriculum that came into force in 1990. Primary schools must teach the 'Core Subjects': maths, English and science, and 'foundation subjects': history, geography, music, technology, art, religious education and physical education. All Penge schools supplement their teaching with educational visits and school trips, often overseas. They have clubs for sports, music, computing, classroom subjects, and other activities. Most schools have returned to serving cooked midday meals after the nationwide unsatisfactory experiment with cost-saving 'convenience foods' which began in the 1970s and '80s, the first local schools to suffer this having been Kentwood and Alexandra Infants' in 1971.

School life is still not easy – significant challenges faced in an area of socio-economic disadvantage are children with learning difficulties and those with English as a second language. All its schools cater for these needs with special units and help as needed from Bromley's Education service.

Continuing Education

When Kentwood School moved out of the former grammar school building, Kentwood Adult Education Centre was opened on its upper floor, providing a wide range of courses ranging from art history to yoga. Hawthorn Centre, at the Maple Road end of Hawthorn Grove, is run by Bromley College of Higher and Further Education. It was set up in 1999 as a joint initiative partially funded by the Crystal Palace Partnership under the Single Regeneration Budget Scheme (see Chapter Fifteen). It offers courses in computing, office administration, childcare, English as a second language, parenting skills, and assisting in the classroom.

Libraries

The Public Libraries Act of 1850 authorised use of local taxes to maintain buildings (though not to purchase books!), but the Penge library service did not begin until 1892 when a temporary reading room was opened in Station Road Anerley. A permanent library was opened at Baroda House, 98 Oakfield Road, on 1 July 1899. In 1928 it moved to Oak Lawn at 194 Anerley Road. Under the librarianship of Mr H.G.T. Christopher after the Second World War, it developed a high reputation with books up to university level, and in 1946 was the first municipal library in the country to lend out gramophone records. Subsidence cracks appeared in the Oak Lawn building in 1950, and by the mid-'60s it was in a dangerous condition. In November 1968 the library was therefore moved to a purpose-built single-storey building just along Anerley Road at No. 206D. Regrettably, the more academic books were removed in the process. In April 1987 it was re-sited in the former magistrates' court at Anerley Town Hall – more impressive surroundings, but half the size. Following an experiment in 1940 with a reading room in the London City Mission Hall in Arpley Road for those living down the hill in Penge, a small branch library was opened in 1950 at 101 Penge High Street, now a side-room of the Crooked Billet public house. It moved to 186 Maple Road in December 1959.

A train emerging from Crystal Palace Tunnel shows the overhead lines that were used before third-rail powering became standard throughout the Southern Region of former British Railways. (LHC)

A typical tram undergoing its official inspection before operating on the High Street, Croydon Road, Anerley Road and Hill. Its depot in Oak Grove Road survived until early 2002. (LHC)

Seven

Economic Activity

We have already seen that significant trade came to Penge from 1809 via the canal and its Penge wharf. Very little is known of this wharf today, although one hand-sketched map of unknown provenance suggests where it was located. Even less is known as to how the important Beckenham Road, now Penge High Street, crossed the canal. It could have gone under or over the canal, and if over then by a fixed or a moving bridge; and if a moving one then either by a sliding, rotating or lifting structure. The fact that this uncertain map shows the road somehow passing over the canal cannot be much relied upon; it also shows the Crystal Palace branch of the London to South Coast railway as passing under the mainline, instead of over it.

The Railway Age

The canal's replacement by the railway in 1839 made commuting a practicality and the district soon proved popular with city merchants. Such an affluent populace immediately attracted traders of every hue and colour. With the arrival of the Crystal Palace in 1852–4, came firstly 6,000 construction workers and later operators of the 1,001 entertainments which it embraced.

The district's second railway, the London Chatham and Dover (LCDR), arrived in 1849 and, following some accidents and derailments, soon earned the nickname of 'Land 'Em, Smash 'Em and Run-Over Railway'. It served the district by Penge East Station. Muriel Searle makes a couple of interesting points regarding the lengthy Penge Tunnel under Sydenham Hill. She notes that it:

... was lined with bricks made from its own clay as the bore was being excavated. Almost from the start, pessimists believed it would collapse onto a train, due to the hill's instability... In the event a wartime bomb bored through the hill, through the roof, and into the

Penge was never afraid to experiment, but two ideas that never really took off were the 'Sydenham Hill' tunnelled pneumatic train, which appears to have only run within Crystal Palace Park; and the nearby Croydon to London Henry Pinkus overground alternative.

A South Metropolitan tram advertises Hudson's soap and Robertson's marmalade, Anerley Hill. (JD)

A junk trader in Anerley Road in the early 1950s. Whatever one's feelings about today's state of the place, this view demonstrates a clear improvement on former times. (LHC)

tunnel, and still failed to satisfy the old predictions.

The railways were originally steam-hauled of course, making it absolutely necessary to close all the train windows when approaching Penge Tunnel. This tended to lead to schoolboy jokes like the one in which a passenger opens the heavy leather-strap-operated windows after the tunnel, while another immediately closes it. Says the first, 'Hi, mate, what's yer game?' Whereupon the other replies, 'Draughts. Your move.'

But around 1928 electrification became practical and more economic; a train was ready to move off immediately the staff arrived, instead of requiring hours of stoking up. Initially 6,000V overhead lines had a slight economic advantage; later the third-rail 750V system had the edge and was adopted throughout the Southern Region.

Last to arrive, and first to go, was the Crystal Palace high-level station, served by a tunnelled branch from the LCDR. Since its prime purpose was to cater for the Palace trade, it did well to survive until September 1954. Its once splendid station area is today an entire housing estate, though its foot tunnel to the Palace site, an amazing and listed work of Italian architecture, remains today, awaiting new uses (see Chapter Fourteen).

Trams & Trolleys

The industrialisation of Penge and Anerley mimicked that across much of Britain throughout the Industrial Age. Improvements in transport enabled those with a slightly better product to more readily oust slightly poorer products and more skilled and/or better motivated employees were able to market themselves across larger areas to secure higher incomes. Both these features stoked the melting pot of competition and drove others to raise their standards or retreat.

Driving these transportation improvements were the canals, followed closely by the railways. Overlaying this broad network came a closer mesh of trams and trolleybuses which filled in the gaps between the Crystal Palace and Penge Stations with those of South Norwood and West Croydon.

And upon these networks the humble bicycle made full use of improving street surfaces everywhere; not just bicycles for commuting and pleasure, but also for delivering food to many a fine mansion.

Popular Shopping Area

From the 1920s the population rose again and the High Street was soon filled with several department stores like Rogers, Olby's, Bryce Grant and indeed entire parades of major shops like the Grand Parade, still most architecturally decorative high above the clutter and clamour of ground-floor marketeering (see overleaf). As Searle notes, the area's reputation for good-value women's clothes and linens attracted customers to travel from Bromley for a bargain coat or dress. In the 1950s and '60s a lady would more likely bus into Penge than buy at Bromley's middle-class emporia.

Trade, manufacture and commerce follow the vicissitudes of technology, fashion, custom, whim and standards of living. They always survive on the edge, sometimes most visibly as a junk dealer's premises from the early-twentieth century in Anerley Road clearly shows. A few trades endure. The Maple Road Street Market is thought to have its origins more than 100 years ago. Pitches Nos 1 and 2 have been held by at least four generations of the Brown family in the last 50 years.

Yet even this sector has seen phenomenal change. Half a century ago four shops in ten sold food. The first 100 yards of Maple Road alone sported five grocers, three butchers and four other food shops, recalls Tommy Goff, keeper of the shop two doors up from the Salvation Army Citadel – a shop nameless today and trading mainly in fresh eggs, packets of sweets and greetings cards. It was known as Anne's Shop when his mother ran it, and as the Maple Road

Table 1: Population Overview

Statistic	Anerley	Penge	Both	Bromley	% of borough as a whole
Population, 1991	11,082	10,092	21,174	290,609	7.3
ditto, estim, 2001	12,123	11,587	23,710	300,071	7.9
Area in acres	217	125	342	15,143	2.3
Pop. per hectare, 2001	23.9	35.9	30	13.4	224
% pensioner hslds	22.7	23.2	23	34.2	67
% ethnic minorities	13.9	14.5	14.2	4.7	300
% ditto, ages 0-19	21.7	20.2	21.0	6.2	340
% pop. married	16.5	17.4	17.0	23.8	71
Unemployed, 2001	5.7	6.4	6.0	3.0	300
% youth unemployment	12.1	14.3	13.2	5.1	260

The Central Parade shops in the High Street.

Bazaar before the war when the Dalrymples had it.

Today, with the maturity of the supermarket world, only one shop in ten sells food, while four in ten now offer ready-to-eat meals. Their range, embracing cuisine from at least half a dozen Asian countries, reflects an ever-growing sophistication in tastes, not to mention depths of customer pockets.

Today's Employment Scene

No one knows how many businesses or employers there are in the district, nor how many they employ, let alone how many are self-employed. Indeed, many of our searches for such data hit the buffers when we were advised:

> *Employers often don't want to declare how many they employ; and the self-employed don't want to tell the income tax nor the benefits office what they're doing on the side.*

But we do have quite a bit of information from the decennial census returns and local quangos (quasi-nongovernmental organisations). One such quango, the Bromley Business Centre, proved most useful, as was the Bromley website, 'www.bromley.gov.uk'. The census ward data revealed the information shown in *Table 1*, previous page.

Here the first two lines show that the district's recorded population rose 12 per cent in a decade, compared with just 3 per cent for the whole borough in the same decade. The second and third lines show that while the district had nearly 8 per cent of the borough's population, these people occupy just 2.3 per cent of the land, so its housing density was 224 per cent of that of the whole of Bromley. And if the third of the district comprising parks like Crystal Palace Park were equally densely populated, the crowding

Table 2: Social Deprivation

Statistic	Anerley	Penge	Both	Bromley	% of borough as a whole
Lone parents, % of pop.	3.23	3.76	3.5	1.15	304
Schoolchildren on free meals, %	52	31	42	16	250
Households with no car, %	43	45	44	25	171
Households without central heating, %	21	20	21	12	160

Table 3: Education

Statistic	Anerley	Penge	Both	Bromley	% of borough as a whole
Key Stage 2 Science Results, %	45	56	50	74	67
Key Stage 2 Maths Results %	40	43	41	66	62
Key Stage 2 English Results %	49	59	44	73	60
Pupils in primary schools	518	1,279	1,797	24,704	7.3
Children 'looked after' by Social Services	25	29	53	78	68

would be consistently higher still.

Ethnic minorities in the district were 14 per cent of the population in 1991, compared with under 5 per cent for the borough as a whole. Ethnic youngsters formed a quite high percentage of the population across the borough, especially in Penge and Anerley. But then the district's entire history has seen considerable migration, both inward and outward (see Chapter Three).

Unemployment at 6 per cent was triple the borough's 2 per cent in June 2001. By gender, in the district the male unemployment rate of 8.6 per cent was nearly three times the female rate of 3.0 per cent while in Bromley altogether the male rate of 2.6 per cent was just twice the female rate of 1.2 per cent.

For social deprivation we have figures for 1991, shown in *Table 2*, above. From these we see that Penge and Anerley had three times the percentage of lone parents than the whole of Bromley; two-and-a-half times the rate of children on free school milk and getting on for twice the rate of car-less households.

If significant indicators of social deprivation had been published a generation ago, these might have focused on TVs, fridges and washing machines to show such large divergencies. And had the comparison been undertaken two generations ago, they might have focused on the differences in availability of indoor WCs, baths and running hot water. Around the district one was twice as likely to find a household without central heating than in the whole borough, but that only means the district's a little behind and catching up.

It is as if Penge and Anerley follow Bromley by a generation or so, as indeed do other deprived parts of the United Kingdom. Compared with other areas in the UK, Penge and Anerley has Bromley close by to give it a helping hand. But on the other hand, being 'condemned' to live cheek-by-jowl with such relative affluence can be quite dispiriting. The question has always been a delicate one to cope with. Today we also have further and more advanced measures of progress; social and educational data as follows from 1998. Who was it who said, 'Only what gets measured, gets improved'?

Key Stage 2 are the nationally-set, locally-organised tests given to every school child between seven and eleven. They focus on what are considered the three most basic subjects today: science, maths and English. The figures in Table 3 show that in 1998 children in Penge and Anerley primary schools were only doing two-thirds as well as those from right across the borough. Bromley of course does rather better than the rest of the country, and so our district isn't that far behind the rest of nation; but these figures do show, as they say, that there's considerable room for improvement. At the margin, where those are in most desperate need of care – and a few of these, nationally, do tend to make the headlines – Penge and Anerley have 53 people in care out of a total of 78 in the entire borough. We may have come a long way since the days when Harriet Staunton (of Brixton, Cudham and only eventually of this area) was so terribly treated (see Chapter Three) but still, to use another educational cliché, we could

Table 4: Crime, 1998

Statistic	Anerley	Penge	Both	Bromley	% of borough as a whole
Reported crimes per 1,000 pop.	138	136	137	85	161
Reported burglaries per 1,000 pop.	48	29	38	18	211
Reported robberies per 1,000 pop.	3.4	3.0	3.2	1.2	267
Offenders arrested per 1,000 pop.	28	29	29	12	240

Table 5: Health

Statistic	Anerley	Penge	Both	Bromley	% of borough as a whole
Jarman scores (Scores > 0 deprived)	22	29	25	-19	-
Long-term illness as a % of the pop.	10	11	10	10	100
Hospital discharges as a % of the pop.	21	22	22	23	93
Infant mortality rate	10	-	10	5.2	200

Table 6: Home owners

Statistic	Anerley	Penge	Both	Bromley	% of borough as a whole
Owned by occupier (fully owned) %	8	9	9	27	161
Owned by occupier (mortgaged) %	43	42	42	51	211
Privately rented % plus miscellaneous, %	16	13	14	8	267
Housing Association rented %	33	36	35	14	240

do better – and no doubt are moving in the right direction.

Education, or lack of it, leads on to crime, or perhaps more of it, as *Table 4* for the year of 1998 indicates. Crime figures have been notoriously unreliable, so over the years more and more effort has been put into improving their accuracy and reliability. For instance, it's often said that less-educated people are more likely to commit crime. This could mask several more fundamental points: firstly, that less-educated people are more likely to get caught; secondly, that if those doing the search spend more time looking amongst the less-educated folk, then the figures will be pushed up and a bias perpetuated.

However, many ordinary folk have a great fear of crime, and the data does show that however you look at it the district's crime figures are between 161 per cent and 267 per cent of those of the borough as a whole. The simplest conclusion, again long since cliché, is that something needs to be done.

As far as health goes, the figures in *Table 5* relate mainly to 1991. The Jarman scores of social deprivation are positive numbers if there's serious deprivation, and negative numbers for areas substantially better off than an average area for Great Britain. Intriguingly for the area, the next two lines of data in *Table 5*, 'Long-term illness' and 'Hospital discharges', show that Penge and Anerley fared very much the same as the rest of Bromley; that is, we were no more often ill nor did we stay in hospital any longer than was the case elsewhere. With all that deprivation, we must be as tough as any, even though the table shows that twice as many Anerleyans died in infancy.

As can be seen in *Table 6*, in 1991 nearly three times as many residents in Bromley owned their homes outright when compared with Penge and Anerley; not only that but their homes may have had twice the market value or more. Penge and Anerley on the other hand had 60 per cent more residents in private rental and over twice as many in 'publicly funded' rental.

Wide as these discrepancies appear, there is one mitigating factor. Remember the migration from inner London to outer London? Quite a significant proportion of those 'snapshotted' in 1991 for the data would have been those recently leaving their parents' homes and still on their way to moving into mortgaged property later in life, and in a further-out part of town. The Bromley website contains much more similar data, but here we'll sign off with just the last item shown therein. In the 1998 local elections, those turning out to vote in Anerley totalled 34 per cent, in Penge 35 per cent, but in the whole of Bromley, 41 per cent.

The Voluntary Sector

A great deal of the world of work, essentially, is the ability to get on with other people; suppliers, colleagues and customers. Some find this easier than others. With constantly increasing focus in schools these days on individual performance, sometimes these key socialising skills get relegated. There is no doubt that some individuals recognise this, and recognise it early. They don't necessarily join a club just to share, say, their passion for stamp collecting or aerobics. They also join to practise getting on with others in preparation for getting on well at work, and for what today is being labelled as networking.

It has often been said that British citizens are far more likely to be a member of a voluntary club or interest group than are those from most other developed countries. The Bromley website shows that there are over 36 broad categories of clubs. Clicking on just one of these leads to a list of a further 45 in just the 'General Hobbies and Interest Clubs' category. And even this misses out several like soccer, bridge playing, Masons (both male and female versions) and others not yet registered. Further investigation of any of those 45 groups reveals how to get in touch with them; yet another marvel of the Internet. We estimated in a recent High-Street survey that there are over 1,000 clubs to choose from – all typically requiring a committee to run it, including a chairman, secretary and treasurer at the very least.

And then there are the informal groups, the neighbourhood groups, the churchgoers and the regular pub meeters. So why is it that so many feel so lonely? For time after time, as one bumps into friends, neighbours and strangers in the park, one comes across the disaffected, the shy, the timid, the street corner hangers-out, the singles, the fearful, the sick and the infirm.

With so many clubs and groups, it almost seems as if there are more members than there are people living here. The contradiction lies in the fact that people are often members of more than one group, perhaps several. When it comes to social participation, it almost looks like there are two camps; the haves and the have-nots, and this has nothing to do with money or poverty.

There is one very clear glimmer of hope for improvement on the horizon; more and more are taking to the internet where it is no exaggeration to say that an entire new world of opportunities is opening up, never mind that in these early days much of it seems very much like a rather bewildering jungle of frustration. The canal, the railways, the Palace, even Crystal Palace Football Club, and much more besides, took a considerable time to blossom. But what they all have in common is that they show that perseverance pays. The small embryonic firms of today include the seeds of tomorrow's multi-nationals.

Employers & Employees

Penge's own Business Coordinator for the Crystal Palace area, Mike Ellis, has the most comprehensive list of major employers in the district – he carries it in his head. He aims to visit 200 to 230 of them a year and estimates that there may be as many as 900 in Penge, Anerley and the adjacent Lawrie Park wards which he covers, although he admits some 90 per cent of them are of below ten employees.

Work here may best be divided into three groups; commuting out of the district, working locally and the self-employed. Commuting has, from the start as we've seen, been the largest source of work. Whilst this was mainly to central London, there has in recent years been a major switch towards borough centres such as Bromley, Croydon and Lewisham. Although London is where the highest incomes are found, it is also where the highest proportion use public transport. This is now over 80 per cent. Street congestion, with 'rush hours' now extending to three hours each end of the working day, encourage this high use of public transport. Generally, such congestion doubles a journey's length but can often quadruple it.

The largest local employer as in many areas is the Government, mainly local government. Their employees fall mainly into three groups: education, social services and environmental services. Once there was a clear distinction between public and private, but today we have a range of quangos spanning this divide. Close to one end of this amorphous group are the Hexagon and the Broomleigh Housing Associations, with about 190 and 50 staff in the district respectively. And at the other end, Mike Ellis' own organisation with about 20.

Muirhead employed 1,800 in the 1960s, and grew to some 2,400 through acquisitions in the 1970s. But by 2002 they were down to around 300, although this still leaves the company ahead of other large ones like the Hanover Park Group (190), Safeway (140), European Springs (120), Homebase (110) and the ubiquitous Clarke's Coaches. The last of these, Ellis estimates, had around 100 employees through the winter and more than twice as many each summer.

Other significant local employers on Ellis' list included Aluvens (32), Ancaster Garages (60), Burnham Signs (40), Carlton Offset (50), Columbia Industries (60), Dylon International (40), Market Place Publishing (40), Marketing Database Services (30), Maybray Precision Casting (90), McDonald's (55 in Penge, 42 in Upper Norwood), Peacock Stores (20), SG Smith (50) and STS Flooring (50).

Deducting all of these figures from the number estimated to be in work, some 13,000, still leaves a goodly number of self-employed. Although we have not been able to quantify this, anecdotal evidence suggests that this figure has been growing significantly for at least a couple of decades now. Nationally the Government puts this at ten per cent of all workers.

Investment

Often it is investment that makes us rich – investment in education, in housing, in commerce, in infrastructure, in defence and so on. Yet throughout history too, many Penginians have found that robbery is an easier way to make money; over the centuries they suffered at the hands of Scandinavian, Roman and Norman invaders, and conversely, they later marvelled at the trophies of Empire, won by the British and exhibited in Crystal Palace. Yet it was investment in the canal, the railways, the Victorian houses and the Palace which brought much wealth to the area. In addition, the settlement of 'incomers' within the area has meant that Penge is constantly growing and evolving. All these occurrences have made Penge what it is today.

Downhill all the Way

Chapters One and Two outlined the phenomenal rise of Penge, Anerley and Crystal Palace; Chapter Three, the first of its big troubles. The next four chapters considered this in some further detail and depth, over the following hundred years or so.

Such ups and downs are part and parcel of life; many civilisations have risen, fallen and even been lost. Yet others rise like the Phoenix, as the Roman Empire has largely led to the Western world as we know it today. The question for us today is how and when do trends reverse and matters improve? Investment is clearly a key issue; the more we invest today, the greater the jam tomorrow. And investment in Penge is clearly on the rise, as we shall see in the forthcoming chapters. One can invest in all kinds of areas; buildings, transport, industry, commerce and administration. Yet, never mind that a balance between all of these is needed, it's generally reckoned that education provides one of the largest returns on investment.

Now the last chapter showed how, in recent decades secondary education moved inexorably out of the district and into adjacent areas. Good news or bad? In a sense, it's a blessing in disguise; if adjacent areas at this moment are providing better education – although there's often been too little solid evidence for this – then it can be argued that the best thing to do for Penge and Anerley is to educate its youngsters there.

Investment is expenditure now in anticipation of greater benefits later. Some call it postponed gratification. And in education that postponement can be quite some time. But already signs of green shoots are becoming visible.

Eight

People & Politics

From the early days of the establishment of Penge and Anerley as a centre of human activity few of its key architects were born here. Those playing significant roles in the area include:

Thomas Hood, 1799–1845, writer of humanist poems like 'The Song of the Shirt'. Widely translated into German, Russian, etc. Sub-editor of *London Magazine* during its heyday. While his earlier poems were full of comedy, often black, his later outstanding ones, including *The Last Man* and *The Bridge of Sighs*, were moving protests against the evils of the day – sweated labour, unemployment and double standards of morality.

In her book *Penge*, Mrs D. Pullen tells us that he lived at 12 Queen Adelaide Road, from 1867–72, although these dates do not tally with the information gleaned from the encyclopaedia in Anerley Library. The mystery was only resolved when we found she was describing Thomas' son, Tom (1835–74). Elsewhere Hood is credited as being editor of *Fun and Living* until 1874.

Sir Joseph Paxton, 1801–65. (PA)

Sir Joseph Paxton, 1801–65, gardener and architect to the Duke of Devonshire; superintendent of his estate at Chatsworth; late entrant and winner from a field of 20 for the design of a temporary and controversial glass and steel-framed exhibition hall in Hyde Park in 1851; and launcher and manager of the company which bought the land and had this building, now called the Crystal Palace, brought by hundreds of cart-loads to be re-erected at Sydenham Hill, while doubling its glazed surface area. Later he became MP for Coventry and wrote a treatise on the cultivation of dahlias.

Admiral Robert Fitzroy, 1805–65, Captain of *The Beagle* in which he took Darwin on his journeys of discovery around South America and the Galapagos Islands. While Darwin lived on one side of Penge, in Downe, he often visited his friend Fitzroy who lived on the other side, at 140 Church Road, Upper Norwood. Indeed Darwin's *The Voyage of the Beagle* was the third of a three-volume work of which Fitzroy wrote the first two. He was the first Head of the Meteorological Office, devised a barometer and a system of weather forecasting upon which today's methods are still based and was Governor General of New Zealand.

None of this, sadly, is referred to on his tombstone which stands in the churchyard of All Saints Church in Upper Norwood. Terry W. Jenkins wonders whether this has anything to do with the fact that he was a manic-depressive and eventually took his own life.

Isambard Kingdom Brunel, 1806–59, was the builder of the Great Western Railway, GWR, long known as God's Wonderful Railway. He was also a keen director of the Crystal Palace Company. As mentioned in Chapter Two, it was he who made Paxton's huge fountains meet their aspirations by designing suitable water towers which even survived the great fire of 1936.

Charles Darwin, 1809–82, certainly needs no introduction, and has been mentioned several times in this review. He lived at Downe House, at the other end of the Borough to Penge, but often passed through it on his visits to Owen's dinosaur statues and his friend Admiral Fitzroy in Upper Norwood. He is buried at Westminster Abbey.

Above main: *Charles Darwin.* (ME)

Inset, left: *Brunel, designer and builder of the Great Western Railway, the Great Eastern and Western Ships and the water towers, contributed to the splendour of the park at Crystal Palace.*

Inset, right: *Camile Pissarro, self portrait.*

Edward Lear, 1822–88, painter, nonsense writer, art master to Queen Victoria and great-great-uncle-in-law to Brian Vernon. Lear has a lasting connection with the district in the form of a limerick, which recalls some of Penge's ancient roots:

There was an old person from Anerley,
Whose conduct was strange and unmannerly.
He rushed down the Strand
With a pig in each hand
But returned in the evening to Anerley.

Joseph William Wilson, 1829–89, became the founder of the illustrious Crystal Palace School of Practical Engineering in 1872. He remained Principal until his death, when his son succeeded him to the position (see Chapter Six).

Camile Pissarro, 1830–1903, French Impressionist painter, who made a name for himself by adopting the pointillist technique. In 1870 he came to Britain with Monet and lived at 2 Chatham Terrace, Palace Road, Anerley. Thus many of his paintings, both of Penge and Paris alike, are to be found in the homes of Penginians. His works feature prominently in the Tate.

Reverend Charles Haddon Spurgeon, 1834–92, buried in Norwood Cemetery. He was a Baptist and Primitive Methodist preacher extraordinaire, launcher of many good works and founder of the Spurgeon's College for theological students in Upper Norwood. In 1857, after the Indian Mutiny, the directors of Crystal Palace invited him, aged a mere 23, to conduct a service in the Palace. Over 23,000 people attended and nearly £500 was collected, to which the directors added another £200, plus a further £50 towards a Metropolitan Tabernacle Fund.

Joseph Gywer, c.1835–1901, a potato salesman and poet 'by Royal Appointment', he lived for a while in Woodbine Grove. His autobiography was first published in 1875 and again, substantially enlarged, in 1900 and is quite an ego trip. This second volume recalls that the first one sold 6,000 copies and spread across the world, but just at the zenith of its sales a disaster occurred which for a time banished all hopes for it. A fire at his publishers destroyed all the plates for it which were uninsured. One poem alone 'Sketches of Margate etc.' ran to 1,040 lines. He recalls how another of his poems on the 'Illness and Recovery of the Prince of Wales' was sent, without his knowledge, to Queen Victoria, resulting in his receiving five letters of appreciation from members of the royal household.

Thomas Crapper, 1837–1910, was one of several eminent sanitary engineers of his era to develop and market the water closet, or WC. He lived at 12 Thornsett Road from c.1897–1910, where a blue plaque displays his name. He was well thought of in his field and even drew the attention of the Royal Family, installing sanitary equipment at Sandringham when it became a royal residence. The colloquialism, 'I'm going for a Tom Tit' stems from his name.

Sir Hiram Stevens Maxim, 1840–1916, was an American civil, mechanical and electrical engineer whose Captive Flying Machine was erected on the site of The Rosary in Crystal Palace Park in 1904. This must have delighted thousands as a fairground centrepiece. He invented many things, from automatic gas engines to incandescent light bulbs, but is most famous for the first machine gun, which was used in the Boer War of 1899–1902 and improved by Vickers, with whom he collaborated, for use in the First World War.

Harriet Staunton, née Richardson, 1841–77, a most unfortunate woman who, after coming into an inheritance, was lured to a terrible death by starvation over several months, during which her first child was born and died, by the conspiracy of several close relatives and friends (see Chapter Three).

Dr W.G. Grace, 1848–1915, one of England's greatest cricketers, who lived for many years in Lawrie Park Road and is buried in the Elmers End Cemetery. The nearby pub in Elmers End Road is named after him. He captained the Marylebone Cricket Club and England, recording a batting average of 40 and a bowling average of 18 in 35 years of first-class cricket. A modest doctor, he began playing first-class matches aged 16. In one such match, Kent v Notts., at Crystal Palace Park, he scored 50. Aged 24 he toured Canada for England and a year on captained England in Australia. Even by 1899, aged 50, he was still representing England there.

Émile Zola, 1840–1902, journalist, painter, morose novelist and spokesman for the Impressionist Movement, stayed at Crystal Palace in 1890 and 1893, while fleeing from the French Government in 1899 after writing *J'Accuse,* following an anti-semitic persecution of Dreyfus in 1898. After Dreyfus' vindication Zola returned to France to become a popular hero.

Dr Alexander Muirhead, 1848–1920, founded Muirhead Ltd, originally at Elmers End, now in Oakfield Road, Penge, and brought electricity generation to the area at the turn of the century. His company has a rich panoply of notable inventions to its name, including a 1930s electromechanical form of real-time computing for submarine torpedo guidance, ships' stabilisers and the ubiquitous facsimile, or fax, machine. The fascinating way in which the fax machine came to the world's notice is told in Chapter Eleven. Contributor Paul Vernon recalls working alongside his highly reclusive son, Dr

Heron Muirhead, for some years before the family firm was floated on the Stock Exchange in the 1960s.

Frank Bourne, OBE, 1855–1945, lived at 16 Kingshall Road, where a blue plaque commemorates his role as the most senior NCO in the Battle of Rorke's Drift, 1879. He retired at the end of the First World War, when he was given the honorary rank of lieutenant colonel, and he died on VE Day, 8 May 1945.

Andrew Bonar Law, MP, 1858–1923, Chancellor of the Exchequer, Lord Privy Seal and Tory Prime Minister from 1922–23, lived in Oakfield Road. He introduced conscription, as well as paving the way for peace after the First World War.

Sir Arthur Conan Doyle, 1859–1930, lived at 12 Tennison Road, South Norwood between 1891 and 1894. Terry Jenkins tells us that during this time he wrote his best Sherlock Holmes stories, including the *Adventure* and the *Memoirs* series, from a first-floor study room. As with so many others, it was the removal of the Palace to Sydenham Hill which attracted him and his wife Louise here, finding this property after touring the area on a tandem tricycle. Not surprisingly, No. 12 is a blue-plaque site.

Walter de la Mere, 1873–1956, poet and writer, lived in three local houses: 195 Mackenzie Road (1899–1908), 5 Worbeck Road (1908–12) and, two years after Thomas Crapper lived there, he died in the house next door, at 14 Thornsett Road (1912–25). A blue plaque commemorates his life here, where he wrote his memorable epitaph 'Fare Well', and the oft-recited 'The Listeners' which begins, 'Is there anybody there? said the Traveller/Knocking on the moonlit door.'

Enid Blyton, 1897–1968, the famous children's writer, lived in nearby Westfield Road and Chaffinch Road.

John Logie Baird, 1888–1946, pioneer and inventor of television, demonstrated his invention by filming for transmission, horses and carts passing outside the South Tower of the Crystal Palace.

The Hon. Roden Noel, a minor poet, lived in Anerley, as did **Miss H. D'Anvers, later Mrs Bell,** author of *Parted*. **Tony Bradman,** writer of *Peril at the Pirate School, Adventure on Skull Island* and others was also a Penginian. And **John Freeman,** eminent critic and nature poet, lived in Weighton Road. **William Walker,** a notable diver who secured Winchester Cathedral by devising novel ways of working on its foundations while under water, **Frederick Wolsley,** a car designer and inventor of sheep-shearing equipment, for which he was honoured by the Australian Government, and **Samuel Rowbotham,** founder of the Flat Earth Society, are all buried in the local Elmers End Cemetery.

Frank, now deceased, and his sister-in-law Peggy Spencer, TV ballroom-dance teachers extraordinaire, for many years were based at Royston Road, more recently at the Spencer Dance Centre, Woodbine Grove, now demolished.

Brian Vernon, 1912–95, civil servant, humanist, captain in the Second World War, school governor and father of five, is one of the subjects of Chapter Nine.

Ewan McColl, 1915–89, founded the influential Theatre Workshop with Joan Littlewood, his second wife. In 1945 he changed his name from James Miller when his theatrical and scriptwriting career flourished in London. His partnership with Bert Lloyd, Alan Lomax and Peggy Seeger, his third wife, started The Great Folk Revival. At the time of writing, his wife Peggy Seeger still lives in their local family home in Stanley Avenue, Beckenham, where they'd been since around 1960.

Doris Pullen, 1920–, now of Venner Road, was born in Newlands Park, and went to Sydenham for her education and to Penge for her shopping – where she always obtained better value for money. She wrote comprehensive recollections of each, from 1975 to 1978. After raising a family of six she turned to write books on Forest Hill, Dulwich and Beckenham. A founder member of the North-West Kent Family History Society and Crystal Palace Foundation, she became a Fellow of the Society of Genealogists.

The Spencers: international ballroom-dance teachers. (PCC)

Doris Pullen with her husband, John. (DP)

Annie Fernando, 1925–2002, of Croydon Road since 1980, widely known as about the most friendly person you could hope to meet. Almost single-handedly she tends the richly stocked one-fifth of an acre Victorian gardens about her large Croydon Road mansion.

Bill Wyman, 1936–, was born and bred in Penge High Street, educated in Beckenham and Pange Grammar School, and went on to become the lead guitarist in the world-famous pop group, the Rolling Stones. Steve Collins, a classmate, remembers many a pub crawl with him during those long dark winter nights of the 1960s. Bill was invariably in the centre of things, even then.

Brian Wright, 1947–, freelance writer, actor and BBC script editor, lived in Penge, where as a 'fulfilled if feckless unemployed teacher' he wrote the hilariously entertaining *Penge Papers* in 1985 – the volume which may well have triggered a ripost in the form of this one.

Kazuo Ishiguro, 1951–, novelist and winner of the Whitbread Book of the Year, 1986, lived in Penge and was one of the students of the first MA course in the UK on creative writing at the University of East Anglia.

Hanif Kureishi, born in Nagasaki in 1954, son of an English mother and a Pakistani father. His father was a journalist who wrote two books on Pakistan and longed to be recognised as 'a proper writer'. Hanif on the other hand has enjoyed success with his highly acclaimed work, *My Beautiful Launderette*. It was screened on Channel 4 in 1986 and named 'Best Film' by the *Evening Standard*. Then came *The Buddha of Suburbia*. Set locally, this book portrays Penge, Anerley and Norwood in a positive light.

Paddy, a well-recognised Penginian since the 1980s. (PA)

New immigrants to the UK like Mr Ahmed Patel have been known to work 80-hour weeks. (PA)

Ordinary Folk in the Limelight

The shift in interest from an emphasis on mighty heroes to ordinary folk is mimicked by the entire country's culture; name any famous British engineer, for instance, and he – or she – is likely to have reached their fame many years ago. Look at those celebrated on our bank notes; George Stevenson on the £5 banknote, Charles Dickens on the £10 and Michael Faraday on the £20. That two of these three were engineers makes one think; are there any engineers enjoying fame who herald from the post-war period? Maybe not. Today, discoveries like the computer, jetliner and gene code are all made by teams; including some in Penge and Anerley; for instance facsimile transmission.

Spontaneously, Table 39 at the Moon and Stars is adopted by painters Ron Whellan, Dai Davies, poet H.P. Carpenter of Thicket Road, 'Sergeant' Nick Walker, John 'The Comedian' and writer Huw Jones. Here is where the world's wrongs are righted, ideas are melted and new orders wrung. It is situations like this which meld mere 'societies' into something umpteen times richer, like 'communities.'

It would indeed be strange if that last great bastion of individuality, politics, should follow the trend from the individual to the team. Yet already we are used to that being so – in local politics, at least, for generations. A recent High-Street survey found only 7 per cent could name our MP, Jacqui Lait, despite her having polled every householder recently. Furthermore, less than 1 per cent could name our member of the European Parliament, making one wonder just whom he represents. Many feel most strongly that we are far from ready to have anything more to do with Europe and all it stands for. And yet compare a newspaper or TV newsreel with one of a year or two ago and one can see that noticeably more coverage is given to European matters. Some 25 million Britons go there each year, and similar numbers of Continentals are welcomed here, in Penge and Anerley as elsewhere.

Especially over the last 50 years Penge and Anerley have welcomed newcomers. But not for the first time. With the arrival of the railways, as we have seen, came the navvies, many of them Irish. With the building of the Palace, came the cockneys, as we've also seen. With the coming of wealth, and major inequalities thereof, emerged the South Londoners. And with the rebuilding of Penge and Anerley after the Second World War came immigrants from all over the new Commonwealth, the Caribbean, the Indian subcontinent and SE Asia. They rebuilt the roads, they manned the buses and trains, they ran the shops and a few even set up much larger businesses. Slowly, some say too slowly, they permeated up the social, cultural, religious, business and political hierarchies.

Caroline Stokes, now living out in Bromley, recalls that her grandfather, Mr F.A. Smith, was Chairman of Penge Council in 1953 and again in 1964 as it prepared for absorption, along with Beckenham and Orpington, into Bromley, one of the 33 newly-created London boroughs. Her grandmother, Mrs E. Smith, was a founder-member of Penge's Meals on Wheels. Caroline Stokes says:

As members of the local Inner Wheel they were shocked at the appalling numbers of old people dying from cold and starvation at a time when rationing was still very strict. They felt that something should be done to ensure the elderly and housebound received at least one hot, nourishing meal a day. One of the ladies, Dolly Styles, opened up her own kitchen where huge tureens of soup were prepared, using bones from the butcher and vegetables from the market. This was poured into 2lb jam jars; a veritable fleet of volunteers took these round to any person they thought was in need. The number soon rose to 90 a day! The only transport in the early days was a motorbike-cum-sidecar, lent to them by the London City Missioner of Wheathill Road.

After my grandmother became too old to continue deliveries her place was taken by my aunt, Mrs Jay Cooke, who also became a long-serving Chairman of the Melvin Hall Day Centre. My mother as Secretary delivered meals from 1977 to her death in 1999 and my sister and I have carried on the family tradition since the 1980s.

Cllr F.A. Smith, last Chairman of Penge Council, at the Civic Reception marking Penge's absorption into Bromley, with Mr Bunting, Clerk, and their wives. (CS)

Down Among the Dead Men

The local place of rest, Elmers End Cemetery, originally called Crystal Palace District Cemetery, now Beckenham Crematorium, is not just an extremely well-kept, privately-owned but publicly-available park, sporting a waterway richly stocked with rainbow carp and cascading falls by its decorative crematorium. Nor is it limited by being next door to the peaceful South Norwood Country Park, to which Canada geese return for a good night's rest on its lake's island (safe from prying foxes) after their daily visits to Crystal Palace Park, where they are fed by the large number of visitors. The cemetery is also a place of rest for many distinguished souls.

It was one of the first to be privately owned in London when formed in 1874 and first brought into service in 1876. The impetus came about from the filling up of graveyards surrounding local churches like St George's in Beckenham. The move towards such secularism was quite avant garde in those days and the company had to spend quite considerably on landscape gardening, architectural chapels and posters. There were two chapels to handle the demand, until one took a direct hit during the Second World War and was finally demolished in the early 1960s. Both the care taken over the landscaping and the publicity may be gauged by the poster *(see overleaf)* which proudly announces, 'Adjacent to Penge, Sydenham, Forest Hill, Thornton Heath, Bromley, Gypsy Hill, Croydon, Addiscombe, Norwood and South of London generally.' Anerley was not considered worthy of a mention; and the now adjacent Birkbeck Station was not yet worth building.

The prices for interments have rather risen since this very early announcement; the lowest price of £1.50 has risen nearly a thousandfold in just a century; the highest, for either of a pair of mausoleums, still available in pride of place just inside the main entrance, by nearly ten thousandfold, to £30,000. The 1883 bill of charges, fees and regulations for 'divers services' provided by the cemetery shows a vast difference and is surprising. Even though people's average height has increased by at least two inches over time, the size of graves has come down considerably from 9ft by 4ft to today's 7ft by 2ft 6ins. However, it should be noted that the brickwork included in both the above prices and spaces did at least prevent the considerable settlement and tilting of tombstones which one sees these days – which some local authorities have decided to remove as they pose a health-and-safety risk!

Among the more memorable bodies laid to rest here are Frank Bourne, Thomas Crapper, W.G. Grace, Samuel Rowbotham, William Walker and Frederick Wolsley.

For many years across the road from the main gates were the monumental stonemasons, Cullens. One had to have a bit of a personality when working in a place of this nature and one such stonemason was Skipper Dicky Marshall. There was nothing he didn't like more than friends calling in on him to ask how the business was doing. 'Oh, it's a dying business, you know, a dying business,' he'd reply, which he'd follow up with the heartiest of guffaws. Sadly, however, by the 1970s, with the pressure on land and rising costs generally, there was a major move towards cremations. The cemetery company changed its name to 'Beckenham Crematorium and Cemetery', Cullens went out of business and Skipper Marshall emigrated with his family to Australia.

The Blue Plaque Scheme

It goes without saying that the Blue Plaque Scheme, whereby notable local heroes are honoured, well after their death, is, like most things in life, too little too late. And one could go on to argue that this state of affairs is worse here than elsewhere in Bromley or the rest of London. But that sort of argument misses a more important point. This scheme is a good thing which has been supported and promoted by Penginians. In the immortal words of JFK, 'Ask not what the state should do for you, but rather what you can do for the state.' Who would you commend for recognition, blue plaque or otherwise, for services rendered in our community?

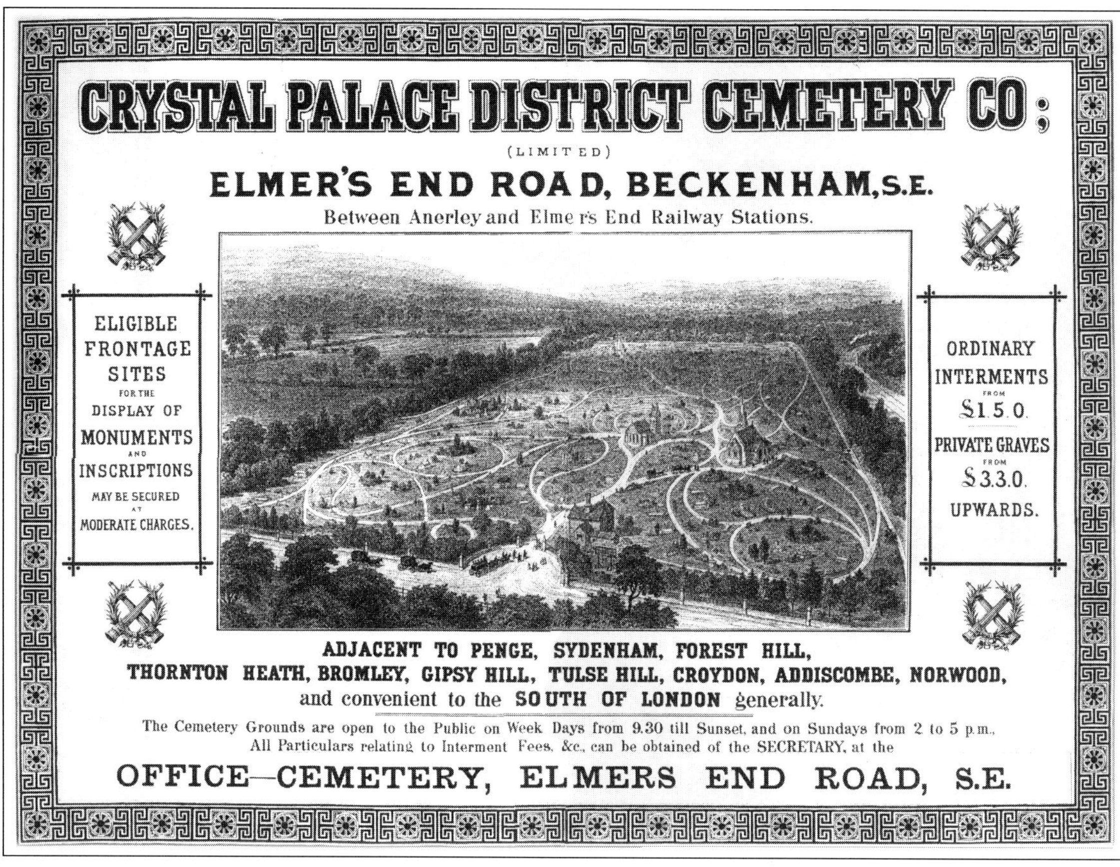

CRYSTAL PALACE DISTRICT CEMETERY,

ELMERS END ROAD, BECKENHAM, S.E.

BETWEEN ANERLEY AND ELMERS END RAILWAY STATIONS.

Adjacent to PENGE, SYDENHAM, FOREST HILL, SELHURST, THORNTON HEATH, BROMLEY, GIPSY HILL, TULSE HILL, CROYDON, ADDINGTON, NORWOOD, AND CONVENIENT TO THE SOUTH OF LONDON GENERALLY.

OFFICES:—No. 107a, FENCHURCH STREET, LONDON.

CHARGES AND FEES.

	Area of Ground.	Purchase of Ground.	Brickwork in Cement, with York Landing.	Fees on each Interment: Adult.	Fees on each Interment: Child under 10 Years.
	feet. feet.	£ s.	£ s.	£ s.	£ s.
BRICK GRAVE—10 feet deep	9 by 4	14 14	19 19	4 4	3 3
Extra per foot in depth	...	...	1 8		
BRICK GRAVE—10 feet deep	9 by 6½	19 19	25 0	4 4	3 3
Extra per foot in depth	...	...	1 15		
Ditto in select situations, 15s. and 21s. per sq. foot.				Including digging to 6 ft.	
PRIVATE GRAVE in front rows, with privilege of placing a Monument	9 by 4	14 14	...	4 4	3 3
PRIVATE GRAVE in Reserved Ground, with privilege of placing a Monument	6½ by 2½	{ 6 6 / 5 5 }	...	2 10	1 15
PRIVATE GRAVE in other parts, with privilege of placing a Monument or Grave Stones	6½ by 2½	4 4	...	1 18	1 5
PRIVATE GRAVE, with privilege of placing Grave Stones	6½ by 2½	3 3	...	1 18	1 5
PRIVATE GRAVE in Special Ground, with privilege of placing Grave Stones	6½ by 2½	2 2	...	1 11/6	1 1

Digging beyond Six Feet to

	£ s. d.		£ s. d.
7 feet	0 2 0	14 feet	0 18 6
8 „	0 4 0	15 „	1 1 6
9 „	0 6 0	16 „	1 5 0
10 „	0 8 0	17 „	1 8 6
11 „	0 10 6	18 „	1 12 0
12 „	0 13 0	19 „	1 16 0
13 „	0 15 6	20 „	2 0 0

Excavating for Brick Graves 3/6 per cubic yard.

INTERMENT IN UNPURCHASED GRAVES, INCLUDING SERVICE IN CHAPEL.	1st Division.	2nd Division.	3rd Division.
	£ s. d.	£ s. d.	£ s. d.
Adult	1 18 0	1 12 6	1 5 0
Child under 10 years	1 5 0	1 1 0	0 15 0
„ „ 7 days (without service)	...	...	0 5 0

FEES ON REMOVALS FROM OTHER PLACES OF INTERMENT.

			£ s. d.
In a BRICK GRAVE	in addition to the price of purchase	per Coffin	£2 2 0
PRIVATE GRAVE		do.	1 1 0

EXTRA CHARGES AND FEES.

	£ s. d.
For interring a Still-born Child	0 3 6
For privilege of placing a small memorial stone on unpurchased Grave	0 3 0
For opening and re-closing Brick Grave, 9 by 4	1 1 0
Ditto ditto 9 by 6½	1 15 0
And for removing and replacing Monuments, Tombs, Head Stones, Curbing and Railing, as per special charge.	
For extra ground beyond the size of Grave, in the Front Rows of centre Road, per square foot	1 1 0
Ditto in select situations, per square foot	0 15 0
Ditto in other parts, do. do. 7s. and	0 10 0
Step entrance (if required) according to special agreement.	
Turfing Private Grave, 6 ft. 6 in. by 2 ft. 6 in.	0 2 6
Certificates of Burial	0 2 7
Searching Register	0 1 0
Grant of Grave (exclusive of stamp)	0 2 6

REGULATIONS.

All Fees and Charges are to be paid, and notice given at the Offices, 107a, Fenchurch Street, E.C., at least 36 hours preceding the proposed interment.

For the construction of a Brick Grave, four clear days' previous notice must be given, or an extra fee will be charged.

To re-open a Grave, the consent in writing of the owner must be obtained, and deposited at the said Offices.

The size of the Coffin must be given when bespeaking the ground, &c.

Chaplains are provided by the Company. Should the friends of the deceased wish their own clergyman to officiate, he may perform the ceremony, provided that notice thereof be given at the Offices at the time of ordering the Interment.

The Hours for Interment are at 11 a.m. and 4 p.m. from 1st March to 31st October, and at 11 a.m. and 3 p.m. from 1st November to 28th February. Interment at other hours on payment of 7/6.

No Coffin, unless in lead, can be removed after six months from date of burial.

No Interments permitted on Sundays, Good Friday, or Christmas Day.

Monuments or Grave Stones are subject to the approval of the Company, and must be erected within Six Months after purchase of the exclusive Right of Interment in any Grave, or the same will not be considered private, unless License for further time has been obtained.

A Drawing of every Monument, and Copies of Inscriptions, &c., must be submitted for approval, and Orders for the admission of Monuments, Grave Stones, &c., obtained at the Offices.

All Brickwork to be executed by the Company's workmen.

All Monuments, Grave Stones, and places of Burial to be kept in repair by the Owners, or the grant of the Grave will become forfeited; but such repair will be undertaken by the Company, if required.

The Registrar's Certificate of the Registry of Death, or the Coroner's Warrant (when an Inquest has been held), must be delivered to the Officiating Minister, or the Superintendent, previous to the interment of the body.

No fees whatever are payable by the Parties to any Parish, *from* or *through* which Bodies are removed for interment in this Cemetery.

The public are admitted on week days at 9.30 a.m. till sunset, and on Sundays at 2 till 5 p.m., during the pleasure of the Board.

Certificates of Burial can only be obtained at the Offices.

Office Hours 9 till 5, on Saturdays 9 till 2, Sundays, Christmas Day, Good Friday and Bank holidays excepted.

Officers and Servants of the Company are strictly forbidden to receive any gratuity.

For the CRYSTAL PALACE DISTRICT CEMETERY COMPANY (Limited).

Feb. 1st, 1883. JAS. WM. FORBES, *Secretary.*

Eligible Frontage Sites may be secured for the erection of Monuments, &c.

The Company undertakes the planting and maintaining of Graves with Flowers, Shrubs, &c., at moderate charges.

Nine

Points of View

A greater contrast of personalities like Doris Pullen, Brian Vernon and Elena Gelpke would be hard to find. Being older than most, Doris Pullen worries that she should set down a little more of the history of Penge and Anerley, 'Before I forget it completely', she says. 'It could happen.' These are some of her memories:

Crossing the footbridge [see p.100] *at Penge East Station to buy a paper, I realised this bridge had hardly changed over the 80 years I've known it. Only the lighting has changed; no longer does a gaslighter ride up on his bicycle to reach up with his long pole to light the fragile mantle. They wouldn't last long these days. And the lamplighter's successor can be better employed on other more important matters.*

If I turned right, past the station and into Mosslea Road where that dastardly murder of Harriet Staunton took place, I'd reach the Primitive Methodist Chapel where my uncle was organist, my aunt was in the choir and my brother was married in 1936. [For its later history see Chapter Six.]

If I turned left, along St John's Road, I'd pass St John's Church on my left, opposite King William IV Almshouses (below). *This was a set of homes specially built in the 1840s for the widows and daughters of naval officers. But before reaching St John's I'd walk by the large houses, one being a private school where I was a pupil from 1926 to 1928, aged six to eight, and the surgery of Dr Penny and Dr Dawson. They both treated me when I was ill.*

The Watermen's and Lightermen's Almshouses, as the asylum is now known, was built on land given by John Dudin-Brown and using money raised from subscriptions. Its architecture was unique and it was erected to house watermen and lightermen who had worked on the barges on the River Thames. This attractive building still stands today although the individual homes are now privately owned. I think that Penge owes a great deal to our seagoing forefathers.

From the end of St John's Road I would cross the High Street and find, in Maple Road, that the street market is still there today, if not as active as it once was before the big stores opened. I think Sainsbury's must have made a big difference to the shopping habits of so many people. Nevertheless, the first two stalls are still run by the Brown family after over 50 years.

Nearby, the Crooked Billet, on the High Street's corner with Penge Lane, has changed its appearance several times during my lifetime. When I walked by the pub as a child, women were often sitting on the steps with their children while the men were inside. It always reeked of beer on that corner. The public toilets were in the middle of the Triangle in front and there was a water trough for the horses to drink from as they were then being used for pulling heavy loads piled onto carts.

King William Naval Asylum Penge

Old and modern: Eurostar passing the listed footbridge at Penge East. (RM)

The imposing Penge Police Station, complete with a platform dating from the Second World War which was built for an air-raid siren. It is the oldest working station within the Metropolitan Police Force, built c.1872. (PA & RM)

I have certainly seen many changes in my lifetime. When I started life we had coal fires, gas lighting, no running water, mangles to wring out the washing, no telephones, no typewriters, no refrigerators, no electricity; so many things have changed to make life easier now for women.

Some façades along Penge High Street do still look the same but the shops have all altered. However, the imposing Police Station is still there in the very heart of Penge, although I doubt if the cells are as full of drunks now as they used to be! In my young days it was quite a common sight to see a trolley being wheeled along the street with a drunken body slumped on the top.

The Penge Empire Theatre was the centre of entertainment and the cinemas ran a good second film with the programme changing twice a week. Before the days of television people would go out for their amusement which was comparatively cheap. You could go to the theatre and sit 'in the gods' for 6d. This was not comfortable, because you sat on hard forms and high up in the building, but it was fun.

The churches were far more active then than nowadays. The Salvation Army Citadel and the Baptist Tabernacle were in Maple Road where they 'gathered up the poor'. It was good to hear the SA singing and marching behind the brass bands in the street.

In some ways I would say that despite the hardship life was more cheerful and less stressful before the war than it is today, although perhaps that is because I was luckier than some.

Everyone now has so much to do and time goes by so quickly. Perhaps it seems that way because I am so much slower now. Where have the years gone? I feel my life has slowed down but I hope to write a bit more before I go! This article I hope will show how much change can come about in a lifetime – what will be recorded about Penge in the new century and millennium? How much of Penge as we know it today will still be there in 2080? I hope that the Watermen's and Lightermen's Almshouses might be preserved as a museum because the architecture is unique. But I doubt if any of the other buildings stand much chance, except perhaps the Police Station. Yes, Penge is still different to other places – still 'on the edge of the wood' – but an active lively place, earthy and full of bustling life.

Left: *The bustling High Street.* (RM)

Below: *William, the fifth generation of the Brown family to be running the first two stalls in the market. He was preceded by Thomas (senr and junr) and Jim (senr and junr).* (PA)

The Changing Role of Women

There's no doubt in my mind that the lifestyle for women has changed considerably during my 80-plus years. My mother, born in 1885, had a quieter life, with less strain than I have experienced. I'd say, as her family were 'in trade', it was a middle-class atmosphere. The men worked for the money, helped by their wives making 'a bit on the side', dressmaking, cooking and hairdressing. When I was young one did not have a tax man watching you as you earned a little extra to assist the family. We were encouraged to be independent and to look after our own.

The rule was 'find a home of your own.' My grandmother made wigs in the kitchen, helped her children to buy their property and started her sons off in small printing businesses.

My mother had a musical talent and had some private pupils in her younger days – she had been educated enough to teach a little. I know she was sent to school at the age of three, as even in those early days of compulsory schooling there were women who would take a few children into their homes and teach them to read and write for a small fee each week. I was sent to a 'dame' school when I started and in Sydenham there were quite a few of these little unregistered schools in private houses.

I lived in Newlands Park and there were several such 'schools' around; Miss Lee-Smith's, Miss Rackstraw in Wiverton Road, Miss Pickering in Venner Road, Miss Hoare in St John's Road, Miss Twentyman in Townsfeld Road – all within half a mile of our house. These maiden ladies did a good job and the children behaved and were not problems like they so often are today. We would be told off and had to be quiet and there was no playing about. If we misbehaved we were smacked. I was ridiculed until I learned to do as I was told. I was not aware that it was doing me any great harm, but by today's standards my treatment would be considered inhumane. I was made to stand in the corner and was given the cane, but it didn't worry me too much. So I grew up not expecting to have it all my own way and through this discipline I learned to accept my lot and obey orders more or less!

St John's Church, Penge.

201, Sydenham Road, and other cottages, Sydenham, once in Kent.

My mother had married at the age of 23 and only had two children. My brother was born in 1911 and I came along in 1920. My father was serving in the Royal Flying Corps and the RAF and Mother kept the house going alone. Sometimes she would let off rooms to paying guests for extra money. My father came home on leave from time to time, so I did not actually live with a man in the house until I married at the age of 18.

I don't remember ever seeing my father in bed with my mother – when he came out of the Forces at the age of 64 they shared a bedroom but slept in single beds. He died aged 67. At times, Mother used to stay in lodgings near the camp where he was stationed and when I was 14 she moved into married quarters with him for a while.

I stayed at home with an aunt who lived with us. I would say that my mother was completely faithful to my father. Strange men never came to our house, only relations. I presume that my father was faithful to her too. I hope so! At least in those days any hanky-panky was kept very quiet. No one talked about it if anything did happen. Scandal was not allowed – nor would illegitimate babies have been born in our family. You married or were ostracised and an outcast if you had a baby unmarried. Women had their households to run. We had a largish house and Mother had domestic help. Auntie did quite a lot of the cooking, a woman came in to do the cleaning and washing and Mother did the flowers, needlework and played the piano, beautifully, for hours on end. But I am pleased to be able to remember her doing this. She had been ill after my brother's birth and her face was paralysed on one side, but I thought that she was lovely and very ladylike in appearance.

Women of my mother's generation looked after their homes and children while the men went off to work. The man usually controlled the money and doled out whatever he felt like giving to his wife to spend on the family. If he was mean she did not get very much but some men were generous – though most of them expected to be looked after, waited on and have their marital rights. Things have improved for women now. They can, and do, say 'No!' Because I had this rather strict upbringing I found that I was able to accept disappointments and did not expect too much. I did not always get my own way – though Mother did! My mother, being the wife of a regular airman, was sometimes expected to live on the camp. I grew up very quickly. I trained as a hairdresser and I had more freedom and time to enjoy it. My brother had moved into lodgings and married in 1936 and in 1939 I married a man 12 years older than myself.

The war started soon afterwards, my husband and my brother both joined the RAF and, like my mother, I too became a serviceman's wife. London was being bombed and I had to go away sometimes to get some sleep. I travelled around the country for a while staying near to where my husband was stationed, until he was sent overseas and I came back to Sydenham. The war and the bombing was still going on, life was never 'normal'. In 1944 our house was destroyed by a flying bomb. My husband had been posted overseas to South Africa. I had been evacuated and gone to stay in lodgings in South Wales with my mother, near my father's camp – but then I had a child of two and a baby of six weeks, so it was difficult to manage. I came back to stay with another relative near Hounslow, on the west side of London, and stayed there a while. Then, when the old home at 66 Newlands Park had gone, I came back to my brother's house in Newlands Park, which was empty.

After the war my mother came back to a house requisitioned by the Council and I moved in with her again. The men came back from the war – I had another baby and my mother found another house, and so did I and we were able to live separately again.

My father came home and out of the RAF, in which he served for 30 years. However, he soon died of cancer. I was not happy with my husband after he came back from South Africa, and had a divorce. I remarried in 1952 to a widower with two children. The damage done by the war years was rectified and we all settled down again, but our lives had changed considerably. My life was completely different and by 1952 with five children we had very little money to buy a house or feed and clothe them, but my husband and I both worked hard and pulled ourselves out of the trouble we were in. The war was responsible for the great changes in our lifestyles.

Women had to manage without men during the war and, when they returned, they were tougher, harder, not so patient, and certainly not so willing to submit or be subservient. They wanted their own money and they wanted more. They wanted their own way and they didn't see why they shouldn't have it. I suppose the change had really started at the beginning of the century when men were in control. Women then had to obey. Their job was to make the home comfortable, feed the family, clothe them by knitting and making garments sometimes out of old materials. Jumpers were often unpicked and the wool rewound, washed and re-knitted. Large coats and dresses would be cut down for the children. Everything was re-used and thrift was encouraged. Most women tried not to waste because in this way they saved money and thus men did not have to work so hard for it. Food was cooked at home. The meat was often killed locally. Animals were slaughtered in Penge behind Aitkens the butcher's shop next to the Crooked Billet. Rabbits were caught wild or kept in cages in the back garden, as were chickens. So a good many people had their own supply of eggs.

I remember in about 1925 there were fields in Newlands Park, opposite our house, with sheep grazing there. Milk was delivered to our door and ladled out by the milkman into our jug. The fishmonger walked around the streets with a basketful of fish on his head. A muffin man would ring a bell selling his wares and the 'cat's-meat' man was also a familiar sight.

Street singers and other entertainers sang in the streets. They'd walk along in the centre of the road holding a cap out hoping someone would give them some money. I remember a man singing 'Only a Rose' in the middle of Venner Road outside the house.

The baker drove his horse-drawn wagon along with bread in the back and the greengrocer would call, although then many people grew their own vegetables in their gardens or on their allotments. Food was fresh and tasted very different to the frozen food of today, and consequently was cheaper.

There is no doubt that between 1900 and 1950 there had been many alterations in lifestyle caused by new inventions, such as cars, electricity, wireless, telephones, television and all the other electrical and mechanical gadgets brought out during those years.

More followed, of course, during the next 50 years, and by 2002 there were as many brain teasers like computers, email, tape recorders and the Internet.

No one under 50 can remember life without information coming to you 'over the box' or just by car. They could not imagine living without electricity, having to rely on oil lamps or gas; heating only by fires after firewood had been gathered to light the coal dug first from the ground.

No doubt children brought up in this mechanised world of 2002 would not be able to visualise life without the help of refrigerators or computers. Now there are switches or buttons for everything. Everything must be quick and efficient and luckily it usually works. No wonder women's lives have changed.

I feel sorry for men nowadays because they are challenged so much and can't show their manhood in the same way. Before these inventions we needed them for the hard manual tasks – now these jobs are no longer there. Women can now be independent. They are more equally educated and have ideas and more skills. They no longer wear themselves out by having babies. They are stronger in many ways. [Editorial note: It is not widely known, as it was a state secret in those days, that after the Second World War when grammar schools were introduced with their 11-plus entry exams, the girls' papers were marked more severely as there weren't as many places and it was felt to be more important for the nation to have the men better educated.]

Babies made so much work for mothers in the past. Now there are no nappies to wash. There are medicines and vaccines galore. Once I had five of my children all ill together with chickenpox, but they all recovered.

I suppose that future generations will think that videos have been there forever. It is all clever stuff today and half of it I can't understand and am glad to live a simpler life, not having to cope with computers which crash. I would rather have an old typewriter and carbon paper, although I must admit I often use a photocopier; I like to see whatever I have written – especially if it goes into a book.

A Tribute to Brian Vernon (1912–95)

Brian Vernon of Kingshall Road, a continuation of Parish Lane, lost a lung through tuberculosis during the Second World War and had to limp along through the rest, the best, part of his life.

Typically the doers divide the world as they see it into two halves; the doers and the 'be-ers' – those who try to do things and those who try to be something. Or someone. They even had an epigram for them: 'those that can, do; those that can't, teach.' Now that's not a particularly nice, let alone fair, thing to say of anyone, so it's rapidly going out of fashion these days, especially as nowadays fewer than 18 in 100 of us are genuine makers, over 82 in 100 of us are pen-pushers, advisers or organisers. The redoubtable John Adair, director of training for the British Army – a doing organisation if ever there was one – once wrote a book on leadership, in which he biographied those whom he thought were the 12 greatest leaders of all time. Naturally these included celebrities like Churchill, Genghis Kahn and Socrates. But the greatest of all, he concluded, was not a soldier, politician or writer at all. He was about as meek and mild a chap you could ever dream of meeting: Jesus Christ.

Now Brian Vernon was not much of a Christian, despite being brought up by a Protestant mother (who had much to do with the founding of the WI) and an atheist father, and being educated in a Quaker school. Brian's father also lived here while serving as a councillor for the London County Council, an MP for West Dulwich and a governor for Dulwich College and for Alleyn's School for girls. Brian's Quaker school in the West Country led him to the London School of Economics. He then had a job as an egg-liaison officer in the Ministry of Farming, Fishing and Forestry, initially based in Cambridge. (He only settled in Penge after nearly being killed by

Brian Vernon of Kingshall Road. (PV)

a blast during the Second World War.) Today the Blair government has more recently subsumed even all that into the still-longer-titled Department of the Environment, Farming and Rural Affairs.

Brian Vernon had an interesting attitude towards religion. Perhaps he was not entirely alone in this. He felt that most religions consisted of two quite fundamentally separate and distinct aspects, even if most people kept them most inextricably entwined. These two basic aspects of religion were their moral code and their god-leader. In the Christian faith these are represented by the Bible and the Ten Commandments on the one hand, and the triumvirate of God the Father, the Son and the Holy Ghost on the other. He believed that while the moral code was essential to the formation, harmony and development or progress of any society, the God-leader might or might not be. This latter position probably placed him in the school of agnostics, rather than atheists, were it not for an additional stance he took. Although not a phrase he would have used, he would certainly have nodded approvingly towards the question, 'Did God make man, or did man make God?'

As Vernon sat in his Penginian sitting-room, struggling with his one remaining lung, he would have been aware that it was one of the most dangerous questions ever to pose, dangerous in the sense that it readily led to feuds within families, between families, uprisings, death sentences, wars and even crusades lasting for centuries. And it was certainly a question which would once have branded a person a heretic and condemned him or her to burning to death at the stake.

Brian Vernon was both a quite ordinary man as well as a quite exceptional one. Asked what he ever did, at first one might be quite hard-pressed to answer it. He didn't run a company, head a well-known government department or even write a book, although he came quite close to the latter, even to the extent of asking the Pope to commission it and have his Church publish it. But he did raise a family of five children in an exceptionally benign and non-fractious manner. Ask each of those children what were the greatest things about him, and they'd probably all reel off a quite different set of aspects, though they might just agree on that one hardly noticeable feature – the fact that he always found a way around an argument, rather than plunging straight into it.

His eldest, Adeline, recalls his diplomatic prowess soon after she began dating an acquaintance of her brother Paul. Naturally at the earliest moment in their relationship she was expected to bring him home for tea, which she obligingly did, and a pleasant meal was passed in the politest and most civilised manner. Not until the next day did her mother, Elisabeth, pronounce that this fellow was far too effeminate to ever make her a suitable partner and that this would be the end of the affair. Adeline, never mind she was over 18, was devastated, and appealed to her father. He noted that she wasn't too happy in her library job either. He had a very good and trustworthy friend who would make enquiries about a far more rewarding job, teaching English as a foreign language – to adults – in Spain. A short period away from the domestic hothouse would allow cooler heads to rule in due course, and he would stand by her then, if she stood by him about this.

With a most heavy heart it was a deal she felt she could go along with and thanked her father, almost with relief. The family friend found her a good post in a private school, run by a proprietor, a widower with two children, who taught Latin. Before you could say 'Jack Robinson' she married him and gave him two more children. Only later did it emerge that her first date was more than just effeminate. But then the word 'gay' hadn't been coined in those times.

Brian's second child, Paul, when coming up to his teenage years, was asked by his father what he might like to be. For daughters, 'to be' was literally the right word in those days. For sons 'to be' was merely a euphemism for 'to do'. What would you like to do, when becoming a grown-up? It was the same

Elisabeth, Brian's wife, Crystal Palace Park, c.1965. (BV)

The Vernon family, including in-laws. (PV)
Left to right: *Paul, Adeline, Joka, Brian, Peter, Joanna, Anne, Annette, Richard.*

Paul Vernon, 1959, with 'L' plates on his 1934 Austin 10. Over a ten-year period, Paul repaired or replaced most of the car's components. He is with his father, Brian, outside their home in Kingshall Road.

Above: *The Vernon family, 1967.* Left to right, back: *Richard, his father Brian, cousin Alfred and brother Paul;* front: *siblings Biff and Annette, their mother Elisabeth and sister Adeline, with her husband Miguel.* (BV)

Above: *Head girl at Holy Trinity School, Annette Vernon, with Wilfred, wearing his Bishop Challoner School uniform, 1965.* (PV)

Right: *Wilfred Vernon in his treehouse as a child, 1962.*

question his physics teacher had asked, though adding, with a wimpish smile, 'if you grow up'. An architect was what Paul wanted to be and he looked into it. He was fascinated by library magazines for architects, but reckoned that compared with his father's job in the civil service, it might be a rather risky one. He also said he didn't want a boring job. 'All jobs become routine within a couple years,' Brian replied. 'Even the knowledge you gain at university becomes obsolete within five years.' Fortunately Paul knew his father well, and knew he was being kind and supportive, even in this severely realistic manner. So, having enjoyed meccanoing and damming up the tiny stream, Penge Brook, all his childhood, he settled for engineering and made a tolerably good job of it, taking great care to avoid boredom at all costs.

Vernon's third, Richard, had been quite impressed with Brian's horticultural interests. Although Brian left most of their large garden to his wife Elisabeth to fill with a myriad of blossoming flowers, and for small sections to be fenced off for each child to do whatever they liked in, he stuck mainly to an allotment wherein he grew much of the family's vegetables. He was one of the few guys who knew that to feed an Englishman entirely on meat required 17 acres for sufficient animals to graze upon, but to feed someone entirely on vegetables took only one acre. One only ate meat to guzzle up more calories, vitamins and proteins in less time – and vegetables to add interest, through their greater variety. So Richard studied botany, became a tropical agriculturalist and later on an information technologist, ending up writing a couple of definitive textbooks on tropical agriculture.

Vernon's fourth, Annette, also followed some of her family's footsteps and, after becoming head girl in her convent grammar school, became a teacher, first in history then sociology and eventually worked as deputy head of a special school. She was encouraged to devote so much of herself to the job that it literally drove her into the ground and she died aged only 56 – but not before raising three wonderful children of her own.

Vernon's fifth, Wilfred, first took a deep interest in botany, then zoology, but soon realised this was a dying business. The nineteenth century had seen the country's farming community shrink from 80 per cent of the workforce to 20 per cent. The first half of the twentieth century had seen this shrink still further, to five per cent after the Second World War and to barely 1.5 per cent by its end. So Wilfred decided to become a teacher. When asked what he taught, he'd reply, quick as a flash, 'Children'. When pressed he would admit to specialising in geography and geology. But after three years of this, in the 1970s, he found the value of his house, just off Avenue Road, Penge, had stratosphered to more than the total of his teaching salary in the same three years. So he sold up, became a smallholder in Lincolnshire and began raising a family quite outside our capitalist society altogether, eventually doing a little peripatetic teaching to pay the electricity bills – he never mastered candle-making from animal blubber – and to replace his ageing car. There being a screaming shortage of maths teachers, he mugged up enough of this each evening to cover his lessons the next day and ended up on the national committee writing the new maths textbooks for the country in his spare time, slowly running down his livestock of five cows, two goats, one pig, a dozen geese, six hens and a cock.

But what was Brian's real legacy? Well, it was whatever could be passed on to Adeline's four children, Paul's two, Richard's one, Annette's three and Wilfred's four, before he died. And although he didn't leave much in the way of written work behind him, he did prepare a major work, his *opus magnum*, a treatise on contraception. All of those children and grandchildren of his very nearly didn't happen, for several reasons. Vernon first met their mother-to-be, Elisabeth, by accident, when she was working as an au pair in Camberwell in 1936, and then by design in Hamburg in 1937 and in Rome in 1938. Elisabeth was an ardent Roman Catholic, brought up in an age when mixed marriages were a taboo. Yet somehow she fell passionately in love with him and combined this passion for him with her incredible faith as a Catholic, so much so that she was quite blind to the possibility that, the more she tried converting him to Catholicism, the more she was turning him away from her as a possible husband.

Her countless sleepless nights, her impassioned beseechings on the few times they were able to meet, the fanatical if amorous letters she sent continuously, her pining for his replies, never mind their cool, down-to-earth logic, have to be studied at length before one can begin to appreciate the depths of her love and devotion to him.

A couple more like chalk and cheese it would be hard to find. To cap this, she was a German, he a through-and-through Anglo-Saxon. Come 1938, Elisabeth was getting desperate. Desperate times call for desperate measures. She actually wrote to the Pope for dispensation for a mixed marriage, and obtained this. But that was only the start. Then she found the Nazis dillydallied over granting her an exit visa to Britain. It was not an auspicious time.

Brian, warming to the idea of so determined a woman making a great mother for his dreamed-of children, also began pulling out the stops. Why were they delaying Elisabeth's exit visa, now in 1938? She couldn't say. Letters were being steamed open and read. They had to be extremely careful. Then Brian had a brainwave. He wrote to her, saying that unless the visa was forthcoming in three weeks, he would have words with his high-ranking colleagues in the Foreign Office. It did the trick, and she was on her way to Britain within a fortnight, and to the man who'd told the only white lie in his life to make this possible – not to mention a dynasty of new Vernons. Others have been canonised for less.

Sir Winston Churchill, whose main claim to Penge and Anerley was that he was chauffeured through here daily when working in Parliament and sleeping in Chartwell, famously defended the concept of democracy by claiming, 'It may be a terrible form of government, but it's the best form ever devised by mankind.'

Brian Vernon also claimed a footnote to the concept of democracy. Democracies, he noted, could be defined as the only form of government whereby one individual, or group of individuals, hands over the reins of power voluntarily to another. But just as importantly, he noted, almost in passing, only under democracies is there no widespread starvation.

Contraception for the Family

Brian Vernon's treatise on contraception was based upon one simple, almost trivial, discovery which might have done much to restore the Roman Catholic Church's loss of reputation this last century or so. He discovered that in its solid and sound teaching regarding faith and morals, a minor error had crept into some translation work in the early 1920s. This had led to the Church adopting an attitude against the contraceptive pill, in the 1950s. While the Church had been totally against all forms of deliberate killing, and had maintained that the sacrament of marriage was primarily for begetting children, the purpose of marriage was not exclusively for breeding the next generation. It was also for rearing them to be good and useful contributors to society. For that, in an increasingly complex world and in a world needing fewer children to be bred to maintain itself, the rearing aspect of begetting was to play an ever more important role. One had to keep disparately different people, like a mother and a father, more firmly together in the face of ever-growing forces pulling them apart.

As an economist, Vernon noted that one of the beneficial aspects of generally rising wealth throughout the nation was that women, en masse, were developing the economic clout to do something about their poor treatment and were going independent just as soon as they could. Men had always treated their women badly, he said, but only now had women been able to do something about it.

What the pill provided, for the first time in history, was for a woman, post emancipation, to take control over her sex life and as far as morals were concerned this could now be directed towards keeping the marriage together for the benefit of all concerned, not least of all for the children. But although Vernon wrote this up as best he could, in the form of a pamphlet which he sent to all the cardinals, it got no further in his lifetime. Quite a few replied expressing both their interest and their warmth towards his viewpoint, including, significantly, a pretty unheard-of Cardinal Karol Wojtyla from Poland – later chosen to be the next Pope.

Vernon was also one of the early spotters of a flaw in the 1965 Sex Equality Act. He maintained that it should have been called the Equivalence Act, due to the 'many physiological, sociological and psychological differences between the genders' that rendered the concept of equality meaningless. But he accepted that the simpler implication of equality of opportunity and pay. 'That can happen a couple of generations down the road,' he said.

A view of the Palace from the east, showing scenery that is still visible today. The house in the foreground was once Shortlands House, although it is now Bishop Challoner School. (JD)

Elena Gelpke

Brussels may be becoming best known for the source of legislation not emanating from Westminster. Once it was best known for being near Waterloo, where, in 1815, Wellington's defeat of Napoleon changed the shape of Europe completely, and the world significantly. But for Penginians it also has another significance. For some years now Anerley Writers Circle's most far-flung member, Elena Gelpke, lived in Brussels and has been paying several visits a year to Anerley.

She's an accomplished speech writer and has published a full-length memoir of her life spent touring the world's worst trouble spots for the UN published in 2002. She writes:

Elena Gelpke on one of her many visits to Penge. (PA)

When I first visited Anerley I had to travel from Waterloo Station by taxi, the planned pick-up by my host's car failing due to a breakdown. Who would have thought that it took the taxi driver more than an hour – it appeared that there were three Croydon Roads in the area? But once arrived, what a wonderful old Victorian house this appeared to be, with stairs to an enormous front door flanked by roses and other flowers up each side. Fortunately this concealed all the garbage and litter blowing in from a rather unlooked-after street.

I liked Anerley and Penge right from the start. It has the typical air of a big city; fast and energising in its variety, which is quickly noticeable when shopping or passing people in the streets. There are the long-native British, there are the Blacks and there are the Asians; in short, a wonderful mixture of people representative of our wide world. Having lived so long in midtown New York, I therefore felt immediately at home.

But Penge and Anerley had other things which struck my fancy. Such as its architecture. Take for instance right along the High Street one finds the mid-nineteenth-century quadrangle of cottages in which poor people once lived. The buildings were impressive with their lovely gardens. And if you wanted to read up on its history, you would find a library just around the corner, one of several in the neighbourhood. Here again one would find a wide mixture of people reading their daily newspaper or whatever. Then there were some wonderful parks – dog owners do keep your dog on a lead! I was once bitten rather badly by one. But setting this aside, what really struck my fancy was the Crystal Palace Park with its dinosaurs. Oh, how these animals looked real, gazing down on us from behind trees from afar. Unfortunately there were then considerable works going on in the park, and I haven't been able to look at my beloved animals for some time now.

Going uphill in the park, next was a wonderful small museum with all the remnants of bygone times – a truly romantic place to walk around in – what with lion heads still capping the plinths there where the ceremonial steps once led up to the Palace itself.

This part of London has it all – parks, nature reserves, the movies, pubs for my host to eat jacket potato dinners in, not to mention bacon, eggs and mushrooms for myself.

Ten

PUBS & PLACES

Penge had a pub before anything else. Few people know as much about Penge's pubs as Ron Whellan, longtime resident of Raleigh Road. Even where he hasn't made Penginian pubs the subject of a painting, or depicted their signs in a notice, he has a clear picture in his mind of their people, their brews and their atmosphere.

The Crooked Billet is clearly the oldest pub in Penge; some say the oldest building, but that would be to overlook that it has been rebuilt several times. By the eighteenth century its staff were refreshing travellers between London and Dover. Legend has it that Penge was so heavily wooded that to guide travellers the score of paces from the main road to where overnight shelter could be found, a sign had to be placed by the roadside. This took the form of a bent, or knotted, branch. The bent-over tip of this crooked billet led to the pub's name. According to Doris Pullen the pub was first built in 1827 and rebuilt in 1840, but local historian Alan Warwick, back in 1982, felt that it was over 200 years old by then. What can certainly be proved is that the building was damaged during the Second World War – so seriously that the top floor had to be removed.

Many a passer-by has wondered what a crooked billet was, since the removal of this illustration of a gnarled tree branch.

It seemed odd, back in 1996, that to attract more custom the then landlord felt obliged not only to modernise the pub but to re-name it La Salsa and give it a Mexican flavour. Of course, what the clientele wanted to know was that its ales were still as well-fermented as ever.

Since then, the name has reverted to its centuries-old Crooked Billet, the fading sign is still absent and the ageing public toilets in front have not only been removed but the public area beautifully paved, complete with a modern clock tower and shelter reflecting the wings of the pterodactyls in Crystal Palace Park. Some locals worry that no simple bench could be provided, but such benches would, it was said, only attract 'undesirable' characters or behaviour. Civilisation has a long way to go.

The Pawleyne Arms at the bottom of Croydon Road and the Robin Hood at the top vie as to which is the next oldest. The former is famed for having only a beer licence, not needing its own car-parking space nor having to supply meals; and the latter for having allegedly been the haven of highwaymen.

How many times have route directions been given using pub names like the Crooked Billet, the Pawleyne Arms or the Robin Hood? But Penge has lost more than its fair share of pubs. The Porcupine once stood somewhere near the Alexandra, though no one seems to know just where. It may well have been named after Porcupine Farm in Parish Lane across the road from the Alexandra. The Watermen's Arms stood where the High Street's Superdrug now is – one medication replacing another?

'BETRAYING THEIR OLD NAMES'

What next? Who knows! But the Railway in Oakfield Road and the Hop Exchange and O'Briens in Maple Road are 'dark', or closed. The charlatan Hollywood East still betrays its old name of the Park Tavern on

The Crooked Billet on Penge Common

"Ye Olde Crooked Billet" Hotel

HIGH STREET, PENGE

Built in 1827. Rebuilt in 1840
Extension in 1925

Now completely modernized with alterations embodying all up-to-date features of comfort and convenience.

Select Accommodation and Catering

Headquarters of all the chief Local Clubs and Societies

Luncheons, Teas, Suppers

Proprietor—W. A. FREEMAN

Telephone : SYDenham 0606

LUNCHEONS • DINNERS • TEAS

EVENING MEALS A SPECIALITY

Proprietor—
W. A. Freeman

Telephone—
SYDenham 0606

99 HIGH STREET, PENGE

THE OLDEST LICENSED HOUSE IN THE DISTRICT

Comfortable Lounge • Music and Dancing Licence

Date: 1936

The Alexandra. Its upper floors are protected against vibrations caused by passing trains. (PA)

Hollywood East, complete with a deceptive mural of itself. (PA)

Twenty-five to the Square Mile

PengePubs

and other watering holes

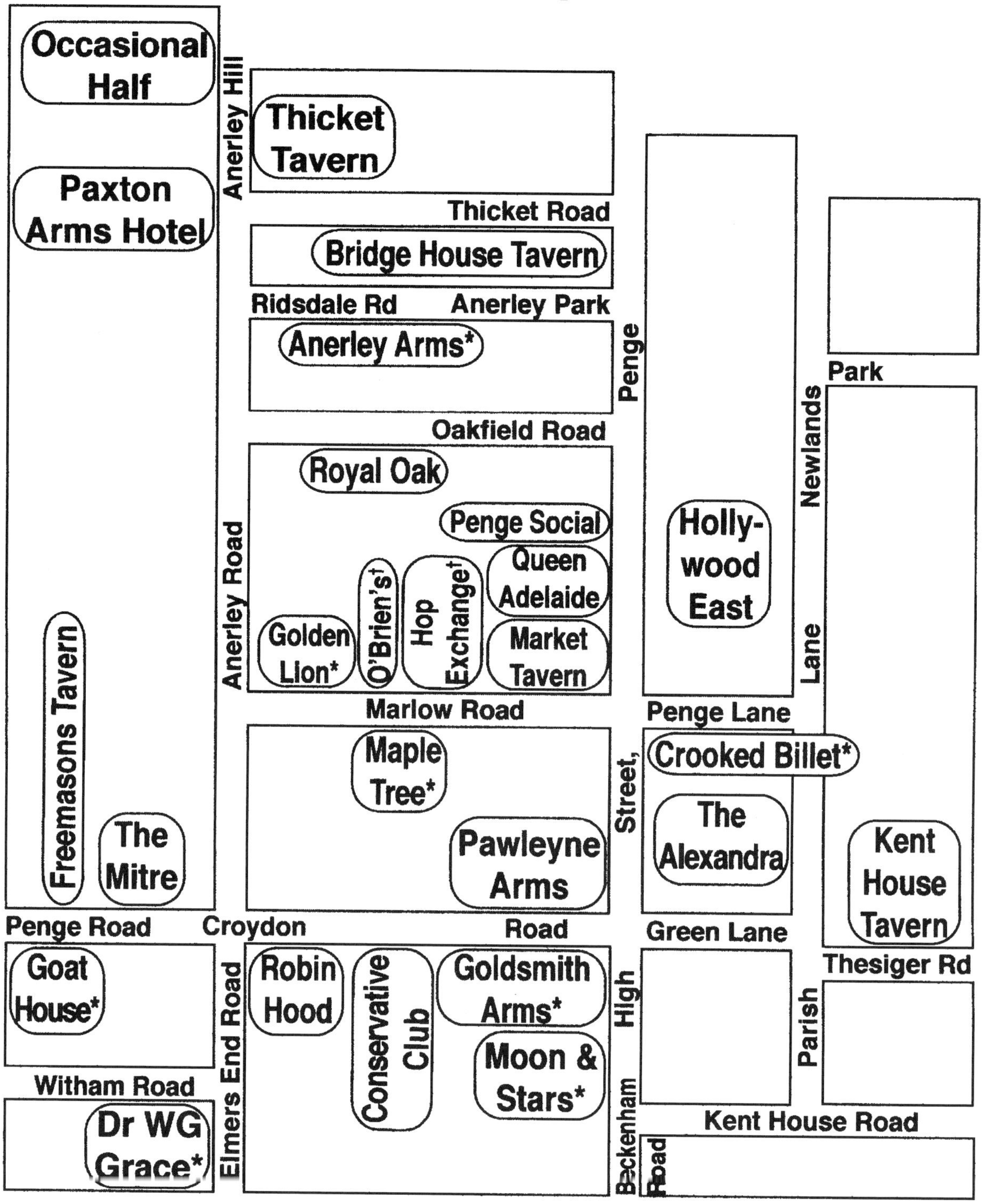

*Jacket potatoes served here

†Dark at time of going to press

Left: *The Anerley Arms.*

Above: *The Golden Lion.*

Left: *The Market Tavern, ever popular with Maple Road street traders.* (All PA)

The Moon and Stars. (PA)

Above: *Pawleyne Arms, with only an ales licence.* (PA)

Below: *The Robin Hood.* (PA)

the 40ft-square mural of itself on its rear wall. And the much-cherished Dew Drop in Maple Road is now the Market Tavern. Penge's latest pub, opened in 1995, is the Moon and Stars. It is a fitting monument to the Odeon cinemas and bingo hall that graced the site for many a year. While this refreshment place was modernly styled for the jet-setting yuppies market, it's just as often filled with 'woopies' (wonderfully older people), not to mention family parties in the district's one and only pub with a large non-smoking area.

Altogether, the considerable number of pubs in the district does result in Penginians having a quite exceptional range of beers and lagers available.

The Maple Tree.

The Mitre.

The Royal Oak. (All PA)

Not Just the Right Elbow

Pubs are fine for sedate entertainment; but what about when something more active is required? When passing by a local primary school during dark winter holidays, one might be surprised to see all its lights blazing. The gym would be full of athletic-looking ladies doing their aerobics. But what might really attract one's attention would be the car park, full of cars, to carry these people the few hundred yards home – a sad indicator of the need to protect oneself from harm on dark evenings.

There is plenty on offer for the active in Penge: swimming, badminton, squash, volleyball, table-tennis, roller-blading and much else besides, both at the National Sports Centre, Crystal Palace Park (NSC) and Beckenham Road Leisure Centre; tennis and indoor bowls can be enjoyed at Anerley Road and Kingshall Road; you can trim sails at Sylvan Road, play soccer at Betts Park, Crystal Palace Park and the High Street and Royston Field Recreation Grounds: take up dancing and drama at several halls throughout the district and take part in cricket, fishing, snooker and other activities at various locations. The NSC was erected in the 1960s. It and its high-rise tower blocks have won few architectural bouquets and their massive built-up 'footprint' in the very centre of what was originally a park to match the best in the world seems a far worse intrusion than any old or new Palace at the top site. At the time of writing its future still hangs under a darkening cloud.

Changes Everywhere

Penge began the nineteenth century with the largest greenhouse in the world, as the Palace was colloquially known, a top-division soccer club and then a grand theatre and music hall. In the early-twentieth century these were augmented or replaced with three cinemas. Then, as tastes changed and public transport improved, Penginians tended to look further afield for their entertainment; the West End, Croydon, Beckenham and Bromley. Doris Pullen wrote in her 1975 Penginian reminiscences of Bryce Grant, Rogers, Olby's, the Co-op and all; departmental stores which served Penge well for most of the twentieth century. She waxed lyrical about the Empire Theatre, later the Essoldo, and the King's Hall and Odeon cinemas.

Then, most ubiquitously, with the coming of more and more radio, music centres and TV, and most recently the home computer, nearly all local entertainment centres closed. All that was left was for stores and shops to provide the equipment and servicing for these home-entertainment facilities. However, these new facilities do little to cater for one's social needs; disco centres apart, they are all too often used in pretty lonely environments. Organisations like Scouts, Guides and youth clubs, forever struggle to keep up with current needs. Youngsters are still to be found everywhere on street corners, 'promenading' as Victorians called it, as ever before.

Above: *The pterodactyle-like shelter in front of the Crooked Billet is the area's latest example of 'change'.*

Left: *Youngsters at Crystal Palace Farm.* (PA)

Penge Square, where grass remains green and clean and off-street parking prevails. (PA)

Greening Sweeps In

Penge, once an outpost of Battersea, Surrey, then an appendage of Kent, later being part of the parliamentary constituency of Beckenham, finally – a word to be used with great caution – in 1965 became part of Bromley, a borough in the new Greater London. This marked a whole new era. Bromley was not proud of a largely working-class district in its new and 'Green' borough, and set about gentrifying Penge on a large scale. First came street greening, starting in the Station Road and the Kent House areas. All over the place pavement widths were doubled for a few yards and a tree or two planted on territory recaptured from the car. In the 1960s the entire Groves Estate was flattened and rebuilt, an area of some nine streets, but unfortunately with such minimal consultation that the levels of deep-seated anger were only stirred up further, taking decades to subdue. High-rise tower blocks just didn't work; people felt hemmed in. Lessons were learnt and in the eighties the Weighton Road development was handled rather more sensitively; nothing over four storeys, plenty of open grassed areas, private balconies or small gardens, and neighbourhood-watch schemes were essential. Levels of anger remained cooler, as the lower levels of litter and graffiti showed.

Rustic street furniture appeared up and down the High Street, from Kent House Road to Thicket Road, and elsewhere too. Sleeping policemen, as speed humps were called, slowed down rat-runs. Several roads were closed to through traffic. Hanging flower baskets became more widespread. Shopping-centre decorations were introduced for Christmas time. The year 1996 saw the sixth and last set of recycling bins installed in the district, and they were hailed as a much-needed facility, euphemistically called 'amenity centres'. If the Council had introduced them too early in the march towards civilisation, it was said, they'd only have been vandalised. It was another thing the Council seemed to get right.

In the same year the humps came to the Avenue Road area, complete with several other traffic-calming measures, with promises of the same for the Marlow Road area when funds became available. By 2002 such money still hadn't been found; or maybe it was felt that traffic had calmed sufficiently on its own account without such intrusive measures. Perhaps this too was something the Council really had got right. The problem of inadequate off-street parking, regretfully, remains a task for later chroniclers to chart. Double parking and traffic chaos is all too often the inevitable result.

Crystal Palace Museum

In July 1979 a dedicated team of volunteers formed themselves into a Crystal Palace Foundation, negotiated a long-term lease on the splendid 1872 building erected for the Crystal Palace School of Practical Engineering and set about collecting as much memorabilia as they could find. According to Mervyn Harrison, the Foundation's founder chairman, many of the statues, which had been removed for safe keeping during the Second World War had been lost, damaged or sold.

Nevertheless, the group soon commandeered more than enough pieces to fill the museum and

Crystal Palace Museum. (RM)

Below: *Actress Joan Ware as Queen Victoria and Eric Price as her equerry, at the fund-raising Crystal Ball, Stanley Halls, November 1981.*

Above: *The Palace fund-raising Subway Superday, May 1993. Sir Bernard Weatherall, then Speaker of the Commons, and his wife are introduced by actress Joan Ware to her daughter, Cathrin. Foundation member Eric Price is in attendance.* (Both EP)

provide excellent displays. The official opening, by the Duke of Devonshire, was held in June 1990.

An active member of the foundation has been Eric Price (who has also contributed significantly to this publication). He has played a prominent role in the museum's fundraising – which on more than one occasion has taken the form of fine dances in period costume.

Jellied Eels – A Speciality

Crystal Palace has become a gastronome's delight. There are eating places of all kinds: Mongolian, Thai, Chinese, Indian, French and Italian, to mention a few. There are even a few serving English food amongst the 40-odd eateries. Some of these serve traditional London eels – fresh or jellied – and pies.

As early as the Middle Ages, Terry Jenkins advises, Ely in the Fens enjoyed a flourishing trade in which eels were sent, live, in barrels to London. Such was London's appetite that eels were even shipped here from Gloucester and Holland.

Once there were over 500 piemen in London, hawking their wares on trays balanced on their heads, as did the muffin man whom Doris Pullen described in the previous chapter. But their days were numbered with the opening of the first pie shop in Southwark in 1844; shops which invariably adopted the new traditional style of a large open window each side of a central door *(right)*, staff wearing aprons and hats as they sat on wooden benches at marble-topped tables surrounded by tiled and mirrored walls. Who knows whether Churchill's new shop may herald a renaissance in this new trade?

Churchill's pie and jellied eel shop has revived an ancient local trade. (TWJ)

Caravan Parks, Paxton's Place & German Embassies

Tucked away almost out of sight in the most northerly corner of the Park, our district and the entire borough of Bromley, is an international caravan and campsite, the nearest one to central London. A site for 58 tents, 84 caravans and any number of the 40-foot recreational vehicles our American cousins are so fond of. Joint managers Steve and Jayne Stinton recall how there had been a camping and caravan site further south along the Parade but when the lease came up for renewal they were asked to move, so they insisted on a far longer lease the second time.

Compared with much of the rest of Crystal Palace Park, the site is an oasis of lawns, blossoms, shrubs and trees of all shapes and sizes. Their office is precisely where Sir Joseph Paxton's house, Rockhills, stood when he supervised the rebuilding of the Palace *(see overleaf)*; indeed the site now roughly mimics his private gardens and much of its ten-foot wall remains today, surely one of the few listed brick walls in the country!

After being there some years the Stintons stumbled upon a blue plaque commemorating this, and had it installed on this garden wall. Through a fanlight in their office one gets a mole's-eye view of a large red sandstone-carved eagle with outstretched wings, high on the top of a gabled roof.

Exploring outside, one finds this is on an imposing mansion, right opposite that blue plaque. Closer inspection still reveals that the mailbox in the porchway beside the front door bears the Alpine horn insignia of the German Bundespost *(below)*. Again the Stintons came to the rescue by advising this was built as an outpost of the German Embassy, perhaps the ambassador's residence, no doubt for impressing visitors whom they could then conduct around the Palace exhibitions, concerts, balls and other great events of the day.

The Alpine horn insignia of the German Bundespost

Allotments

Bromley is London's largest borough and claims to be its greenest. From the Middle Ages to the nineteenth century, enclosures of common land led to the poverty of the peasant, rural depopulation and riots against the rich. Allotments were just one attempt to better the lives of those worst affected.

Bromley has 52 allotment sites – several in Penge and Anerley – and encourages their development with annual prizes for the finest wine, honey, cottage garden, site maintenance and organic produce. It promotes sustainable waste reduction, mulching and soil conditioning – six sites have their own shredders – and the council's accredited with providing the 'Best Practice' examples in England. Jan Cousins, Maberley Road Allotment Association's secretary, explains to our contributor Terry Jenkins:

> *Once, allotment holders sported a cloth-cap image, or seemed a retreat for the elderly or lonely; today sites like our Maberley Road allotments, converted from a Victorian house's tennis courts, is a thriving community centre. Not only are young people growing their own produce but many bring their children, some of whom have small gardens of their own.*

Organic cultivation is of increasing interest; the association's Trading Hut stocks organic manure, compost and fertiliser, sage is grown next to cabbage to keep insects away, and chives help keep mildew and fungi from other crops, Jenkins reports. 'But more difficult pests have been local youths who break in, steal, cause damage and recently burned down the entire Trading Hut; fortunately our insurance replaced it with a better one.'

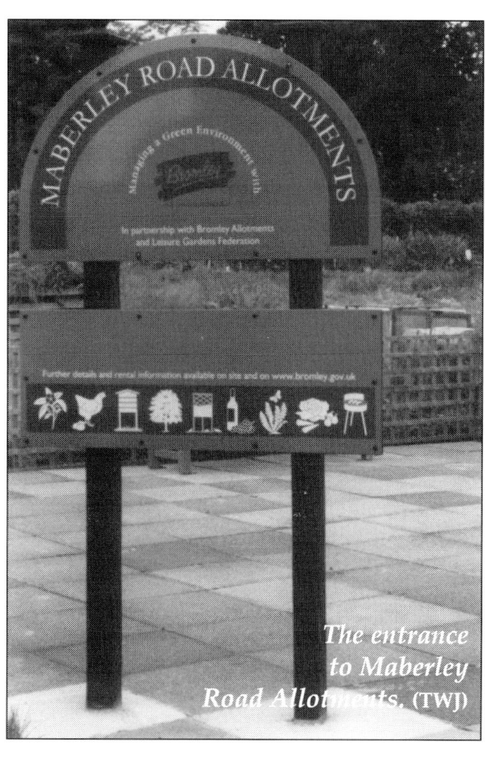

MABERLEY ROAD ALLOTMENTS
The entrance to Maberley Road Allotments. (TWJ)

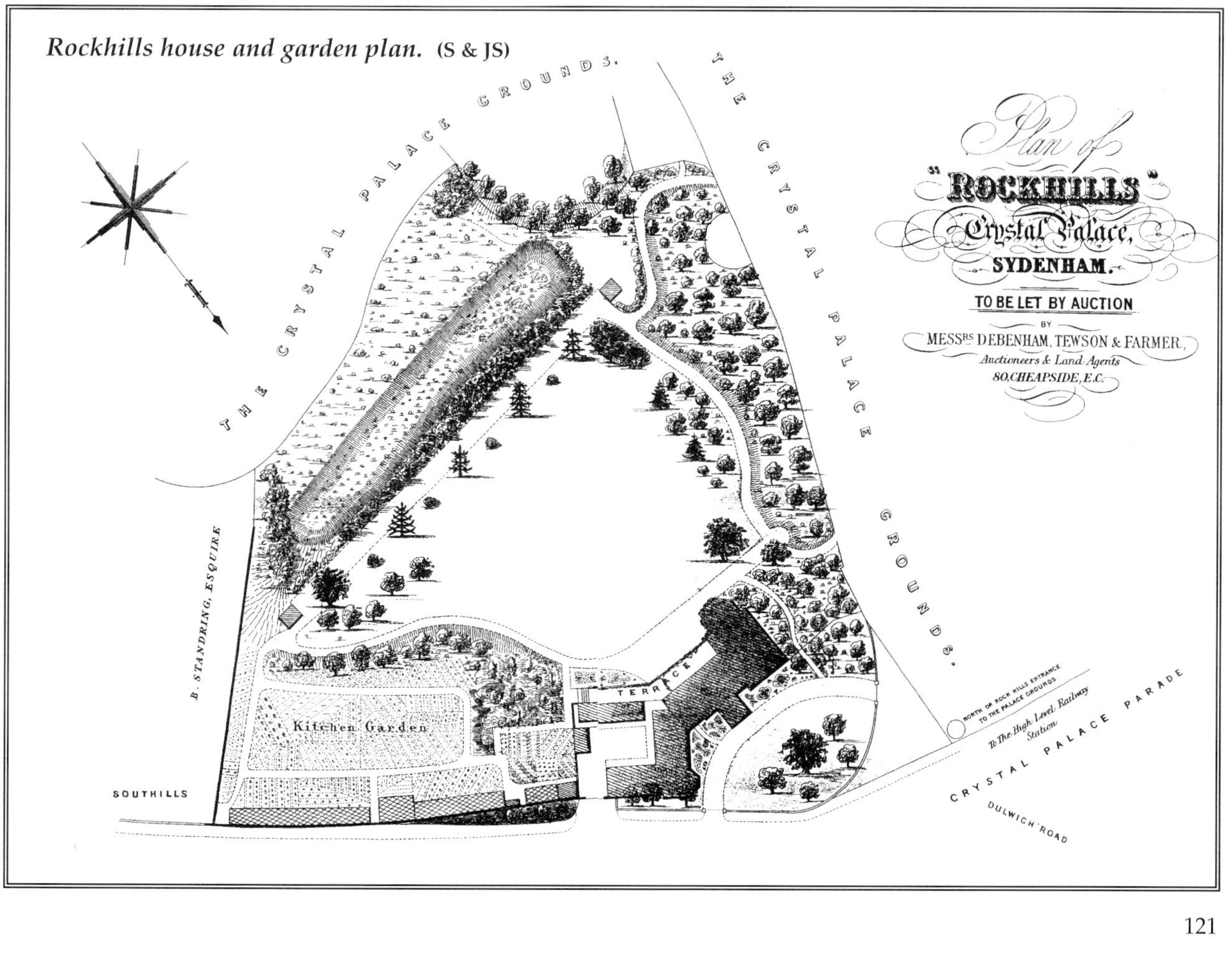
THE CRYSTAL PALACE GROUNDS.
THE CRYSTAL PALACE GROUNDS.
Plan of
"ROCKHILLS"
Crystal Palace,
SYDENHAM.
TO BE LET BY AUCTION
BY
MESSRS DEBENHAM, TEWSON & FARMER,
Auctioneers & Land Agents
80, CHEAPSIDE, E.C.
B. STANDRING, ESQUIRE
SOUTHILLS
Kitchen Garden
TERRACE
To The High Level Railway Station
CRYSTAL PALACE PARADE
DULWICH ROAD
Rockhills house and garden plan. (S & JS)

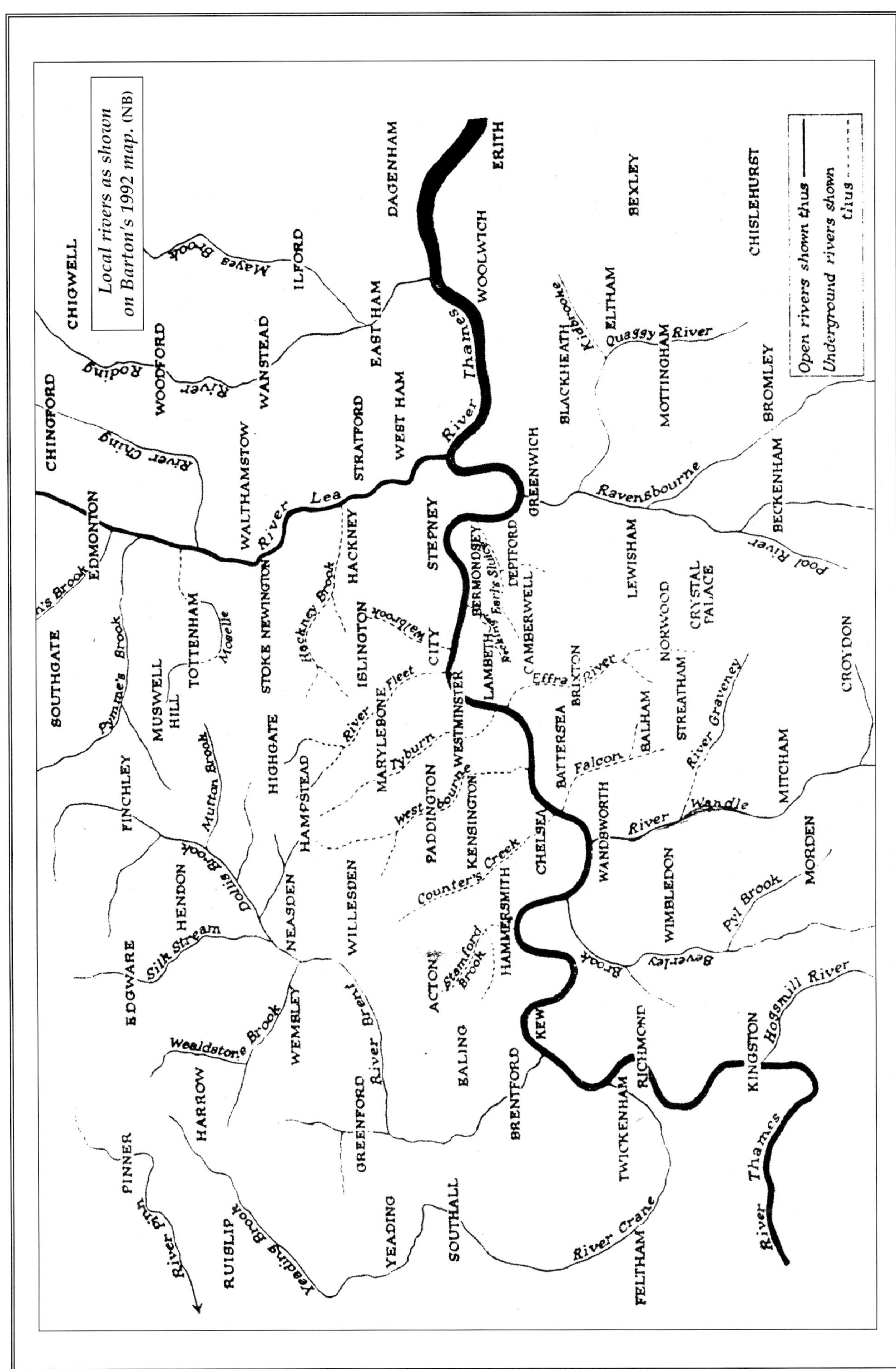

Local rivers as shown on Barton's 1992 map. (NB)

Eleven

WATER, WATER

Not many folk know this, but Penge and Anerley are riddled with streams and brooklets. Even Barton's celebrated book, *London's Lost Rivers,* includes no mention of Penge, let alone its several little streams. If one were among the 60 species of fish – now returning to a Thames cleaner than it has been since its nadir in the early 1950s – one would come upstream to Penge, where the air is at London's finest, in order to breed. Heading up the Ravensbourne you would leave the Quaggy on your left before turning right into the Pool River for Beckenham. At Cator Park you'd be spoilt for no less than three, later four, choices. First, there's Penge Drain, now entirely underground, yet having a most auspicious origin. Its final fling, its last hundred metres through Cator Park, where it drains into the Pool River, was open until the 1960s. Boys who grew up there in the 1950s might remember its twin concrete sides set at 45 degrees from a foot-wide flattish bottom. They'd run down one side and use their momentum to get themselves up the other, or they would dam it up using sods of earth from the surrounding grasslands. If several lads built a series of dams, what fun they could have at tea time when the top one was breached. This would release a tidal wave which would smash open the next and so on like some enormous cascade of dominoes.

Today, with everything so tidied up and imagination stifled at every turn, even this length of the stream has been encapsulated in concrete and lost underground. It is little wonder children get bored in double-quick time and turn to graffiti. Only aquatic aficionados can trace the waterway, often marking the boundary between Penge and Beckenham, for example at the start of Beckenham Road and Penge High Street. Its boundary course is marked by an obscure boundary post outside 85 Tremaine Road, Anerley, above which, as a fish, you'd still have a long, dark and mysterious way to swim before reaching the pleasant uplands of Norwood Reservoir.

But beware of dinghy sailors' keels cutting through your water as they race on Sunday mornings, or the fishermen stalking you throughout the open season with lines they can cast right out to the centre of a lake built at the high point of Croydon Canal to keep its locks filled with water gathered from much of Beulah Hill. Another arm of Penge Drain, going off to the right just upstream of Cator Park, takes you the full length of the High Street to drain from the upper, intermediate and lower, or once 'tidal', lakes of Crystal Palace Park.

Secondly, if you kept straight on through Cator Park (the waterway Barton shows as Pool River should rightly be called the Chaffinch Brook, see our author's amendments to his map, *p.124*) and you avoid the right-hand spurs to South Norwood Country Park, where if the fishermen don't get you the many species of wildfowl almost certainly will. It would be better to remain in the quiet and calm waters from Long Lane Wood.

There's little doubt that the waterway by Chaffinch Road and Clock House Station is called the Chaffinch Brook. For 50 years, Southern Region Railways and Beckenham Council argued as to who was liable for the Brook's constant flooding and tripping the circuit breakers of the railway's third-rail power supplies, invariably stopping the trains in the morning rush hours. Never mind Penge and Anerley commuters who suffered all this while.

Thirdly, continuing your upstream search for good breeding grounds for you and your fellow fish, you could well turn left at Cator Park and into the

Bridge on the Road to Beckenham.

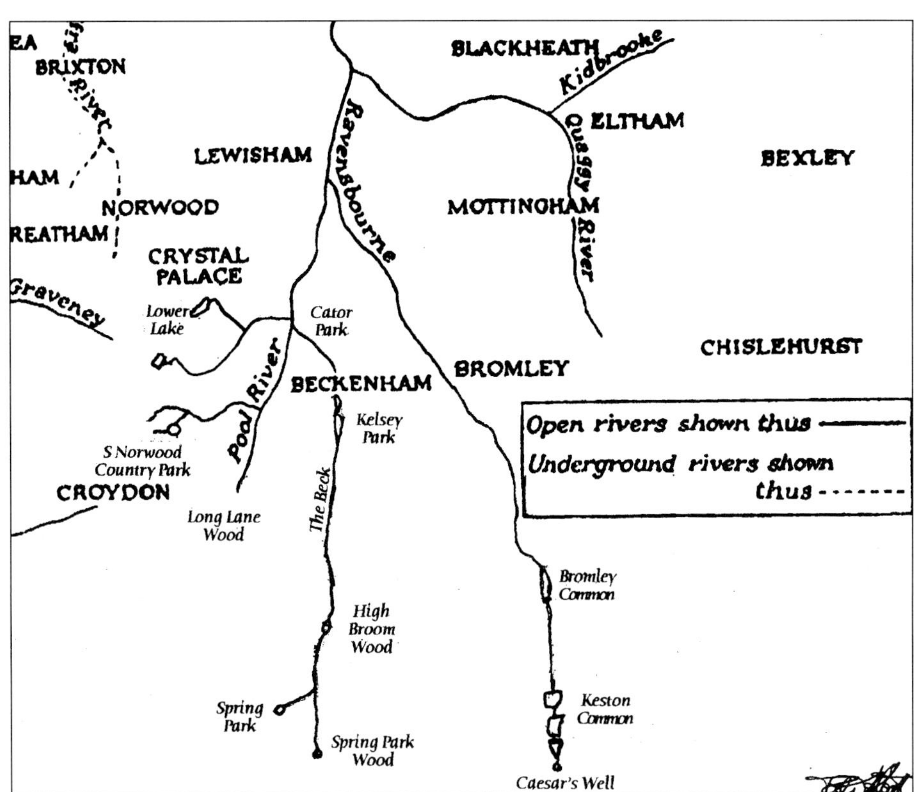

Barton's map enlarged for Penge's streams. (PA)

rich waters of The Beck. But take care not to be attracted by the beautiful lakes and exotic flora of Kelsey Park. Great danger lies here, not just in the form of the several waterfalls but also from several families of herons nesting in quite cramped conditions on a small island. However, if you can get an especially satiated heron to carry you on and drop you off above these lakes, you can trace The Beck to way above Beckenham, Eden Park, Monks Orchard, Shirley and right up to a muddy patch in the jungles of Threehalfpenny Wood above Addington Bottom.

The Penge Canal

For centuries large tracts of Penge and Anerley were quite impassable. The high ground was a densely overgrown wood, penetrable only to pigs which were kept there. The low ground was such a quagmire in winter that it was hardly worth constructing a passageway for the few dry months. Only the London–Dover road past the Crooked Billet and was an exception. One problem was that while turnpikes could only collect limited dues from passers-by to maintain the highway, canal owners could levy everyone using it to repay the monies invested therein – but not until economical labourers from Ireland, who'd been treated so badly there that they would do anything to escape, made canal building viable. They were called the navvies from the navigations they provided all over England (see also p.34).

Penge Canal, soon called the Croydon Canal, ran from West Croydon in the centre of Croydon to the Surrey Docks in Rotherhithe. Skirting Forest Hill and Crystal Palace it went up at least 28 locks and down about another four. It carried lime, chalk, clay, timber, Fuller's earth and vegetables from the hinterland behind and beyond Croydon to London via the Surrey Canal and the Thames, and it carried coal and manufactured goods from the docks to Croydon. There were wharfs at Penge, near where Penge West Station now stands, and stopping-off points to admire the scenery across Penge Common, near where Anerley Station now stands. That must have placed it under the circulating birds in John Pullen's picture of the place *(p.125)*, even though the contours of the ground there today make this hard to visualise.

Most maps and descriptions of the canal, which ran along the line of the (later) lower railway bridge here are unclear as to whether the canal was built under the road or over it at this point, or indeed as to whether there was a moving road bridge. However, we have tracked down a commentary by a Bernard Brown of Brixton, in a published article of unknown provenance and date, which reads:

> *To supply Beckenham and Bromley with goods brought by barge, a wharf – Scott's Wharf – was constructed north-west of the Beckenham Road* [now Penge High Street], *which... passed over the waterway but when the railway came the road was realigned to pass under it.*

One of a series of six maps, sketched locally during the 1820s does reinforce this notion. Although of course Brown just might have relied upon this map to make the above assertion.

A week after the canal's opening on 22 October 1809, *The Times* reported on the grand cavalcade assembled on one of the company's barges at Sydenham 'to celebrate so interesting an event'. The 'gay fleet of barges' passed Scott's Wharf at Penge, the newspaper told its readers, continuing:

> *... by means of which the towns of Beckenham, Bromley and a considerable part of Kent are accommodated with coals, manure and all other articles of merchandise at a greatly reduced rate of carriage. Here they entered Penge Forest; the canal passes though this forest in part so elevated that it affords the most extensive prospects,*

comprehending Beckenham and several villages and seats, Shooters Hill, Addington Hills, Banstead Downs and numerous other picturesque objects in the counties of Surrey and Kent.

Made of Conflict, Not of Peace

However, the canal had been made of conflict, not peace, harmony or beauty. During the 1790s England had been at war with France and needed to get a great deal of heavy material safely from London to Portsmouth. In 1799 no less than three rival schemes were being developed for the first leg to Croydon. These included an easterly canal through the Pool and Ravensbourne valleys, a lengthy canal up the Wandle River basin and the Surrey Iron Railway (SIR), horse drawn of course, up through Streatham. The first of these, called the Croydon Canal, was the first scheme to be promoted, albeit to a false start. Mill owners on the River Wandle feared it would divert the head waters of the Graveney, upon which they depended (see *The Book of Carshalton*). This also handicapped the second scheme. Its longer route through more expensive Surrey land also made it economically less viable. The third scheme, the SIR, as reported in the *Living History Publications Local Guide No 7*, was proposed by a group of Wandle Valley industrialists, also in 1799. By July 1800 they had 'resolved [this] to be carried into execution as soon as possible.' But by October of that year a variation of the first scheme was proposed by the already celebrated engineer, Rennie. He noted that a higher route, through Penge and Brockley, would be both shorter and, hanging on the side of Sydenham and Forest Hills, would be an embankment canal requiring earthworks only on one side. Considerable heights would need to be surmounted and he left the financial backers to choose between locks and inclined planes up which 25-ton boats would be heaved by steam engines. The scheme with the former would cost £64,000; the latter £47,000.

Separately, a Grand Surrey Canal was also being promoted in Parliament, running from Rotherhithe through Camberwell, Clapham, Mitcham, Croydon and on to Epsom on its way towards Portsmouth. By 21 May 1801 the first part of this, up to Mitcham, was authorised by Parliament. An initial portion of this would also be needed by the Croydon Canal. The *Guide No. 7* reported that:

Penge Wharf is thought to have been where the birds are circling. **(VRP)**

The house just visible in the middle distance among the trees of this 1815 'View of Penge Wood' by H. Browne could be Penge Place, the first local mansion of any significance. It was located on a site some 300m downhill from the BBC TV mast. **(CL)**

Also on the 21st May, Parliament authorised the SIR... and the Croydon Canal was approved on 27th June, so giving the go-ahead to all thee routes within five weeks.

The railway from London to Croydon was opened in May 1805 and extended on to Merstham by July; but it could only carry modest loads. And what with Britain winning the Battle of Trafalgar in October, defeating the French navy and capturing many of its ships, enthusiasm for continuing the links to Portsmouth very much waned.

However, the Grand Surrey Canal spent most of its money more profitably, creating what are now known as the Surrey Docks, which opened in April 1807. The Croydon Canal had been authorised by Parliament in 1801 to raise and spend up to £30,000, but arguments as to how much water would be needed where, and whether to use locks or inclined slopes, delayed construction and development until the Grand Surrey had completed its connection in July 1807.

This did have one advantage; it shortened the canal to just over 9½ miles. But by then, thanks largely to Wellington's Napoleonic Wars, costs had escalated and a further Act of Parliament was required to raise further funds. By the time that construction and financing costs were added up, in 1811, these initial costs exceeded £164,000 or three times the official estimate. Such hiccups are not just features of modern times, like the Channel Tunnel or the Dome. The Humber Bridge ended up costing 18 times its estimate and the Woolwich Barrage was so much over budget that no one has yet dared publish its overspend.

Now Nearly 1,000 Years Old

And yet the canal's origins are far older than most would imagine from the above. Its predecessor also was the product of wartime strategies, as the *Guide No 7* reminds us:

In 1016, the Dane, Canute, embarked his army at Southampton and sailed to Greenwich where he made a fortified camp. London, the one major stronghold of the new monarch Richard Ironside, was virtually invincible, especially with the [naval] obstruction of London Bridge. Canute therefore dug a canal for some four miles across and south of London, but Edmund gained further support and in due course Canute had to use the canal as a retreat.

Why, then, was the canal, built to serve Croydon, so important to Penge and Anerley? Well, as local writer George West put it so well:

If the canal had been constructed along an alternative route via Woodside and Lewisham, as advised as a preferred route by the promoter's engineer, John Rennie, it would have bypassed Penge by several miles. As it was, the canal was built through Penge; and when it failed it left the hamlet with a legacy of a railway provided before its time [indeed, one of the earliest in the whole of London].

The railway brought quick and easy transport [especially commuters from a grime-ridden London] *and, probably most important, it brought the Crystal Palace because, when the time came to move the Palace from its temporary site in Hyde Park, one of the main factors influencing the decision to rebuild it at Upper Norwood was the close proximity of the canal's successor, the railway line passing through Penge and Anerley.*

If it had not been for that the Crystal Palace might well have been rebuilt somewhere else. There was no shortage of applicants. The opening of the Palace at Upper Norwood on the Heights of Sydenham in 1854 was a most significant event for the whole surrounding area, bringing people and trade and public recognition to this part of South London.

It could be said that just those who were drawn to this area, notably those of Upper Norwood, were the most vociferous in their objections to the successor Crystal Palace, in the 1990s. If only they'd had the foresight which George West alludes to here. But more of that anon (see Chapter Fourteen).

Above: *Nelson's victory helped the Penge Canal cause.*

Below: *Most large projects overspend.* (RM)

Drinking-Water

It's a well-known fact that once we have conquered a problem, we put it aside and forget all about it – until such carelessness lets it resurface again. Around the time of the Harriet Staunton dastardly deed of 1877 (see Chapter Three) the same invention occurred twice coincidentally – in Highgate and in Hamburg – before coming to Penge. Throughout the nineteenth century some of the greatest concerns surrounded the prevalence of all kinds of disease. Early on Louis Pasteur had shown that these were spread by microbes, bacteria and viruses, but no one knew how – until it was spotted by a doctor that all those in his area who caught cholera were drawing their drinking-water from a certain public pump. When he had it padlocked, the outbreak ceased.

Shortlands pumphouse and well. **(RM)**

Now although everyone knows that water can be made safe by boiling, it was left to engineers to devise a method 20 times cheaper, and therefore affordable – by passing the water through at least 20 inches of sand. In no time at all filtration plants were being constructed at the upstream end of town; sewage filtration plants downstream – everywhere except at Penge and Anerley that is.

By the time this discovery was being acted upon, the 'toffs' were already leaving the area. Penge and Anerley were left to gather rainwater as best they might from wells and from the hillside of Crystal Palace; and only later on connected to the ever-spreading London network and the smaller if nearer Beckenham network supplied from deep wells at Shortlands. All the area ended up with was a sewage works somewhat upstream of much of its urban area; not deliberately, as the Elmers End sewage works was sited to be downstream of Croydon which had the wealth to build it. Wealth built on the trade, by canal and by rail, running through, but straight past, Penge and Anerley.

Apart from ridding waste water of most microbes, the sewage works also filtered out tiny amounts of trace metals, metals which, over a century, accumulated in the soil which was used for this filtration. They accumulated so much that when, a century on, the sewage works was made redundant by economies of scale across Greater London, they were considered sufficiently poisonous to scupper housing plans which both Bromley and Croydon felt would be advantageous to generating more housing tax. This left no option but to convert the area into even more open parkland – a silver lining in several ways.

Pollution's silver lining: the presence of heavy metals saved our South Norwood country park from being transformed into a housing development. **(RM)**

Above: *Muirhead Ltd, the largest local employer during much of the twentieth century.* (PV)

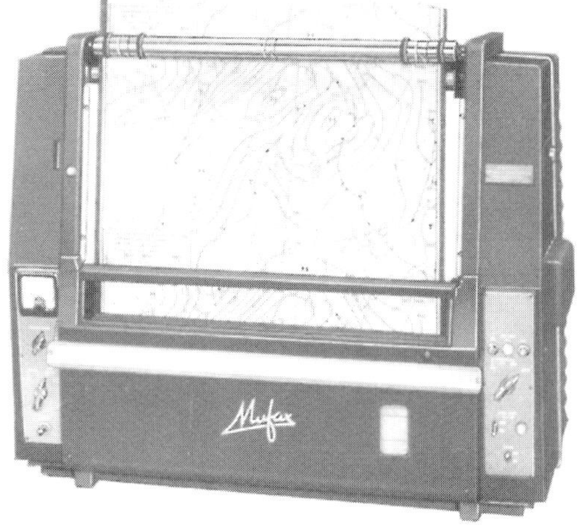

Left: *Muirhead picture receivers replaced meteorologists on every North-Atlantic ship by 1965.* (PV)

Industry Brings Electricity

An even greater bonanza for Penge and Anerley was the coming of Muirhead Ltd. Although today it is located in the heart of Penge, in Oakfield Road, it was founded in Elmers End, close by the station. As a manufacturer of precision electrical components it needed more than anything a good supply of electticity for its workforce, and so it built its own power station, which was kept in working order until the early 1960s. In its heyday the company employed over 2,500 people, from engineers to accountants, from chippies to charwomen. Its team invented stabilisers for ships and the fax machine. Yet it would be 15 years before it brought the merits of electricity to the eyes of the burghers of Beckenham who built the first local power station in Churchfields Road, on a site long since made redundant by the inception of the national grid in the 1940s. It closed around 1955 and the site today is a refuse transfer station.

The Fax Machine & Muirhead Ltd

Now being rapidly replaced by the internet's e-mail, the fax machine led to a major communication revolution in the 1960s, for industry and administration alike. Oddly enough it was an invention brought about by the customer rather than the supplier. There was a successful provincial daily newspaper in the north, the *Manchester Guardian*, which by the 1950s found itself selling more copies in London than in the North. However, the journey time and cost of delivering it to London meant that it had to be put to bed rather earlier each night than its rivals. Thus it planned to set up an additional printing works in London. The paper's directors discreetly approached Muirhead Ltd to ask if it would ever be possible to transmit an entire page of newsprint over the wires, as it were, for quick printing and distribution from a London base. Muirhead's intrepid engineers, hot from devising no end of specialist products (its 1953 catalogue listed several hundred, from Wheatstone bridges to Weston cadmium cells), did not hesitate in addressing this new challenge. They came up with the world's first facsimile machines, about the size of a large washing machine. A pair of these, one transmitting over telephone wires from Manchester, one receiving in London, could transmit an entire page in 28 minutes. It was set to revolutionise the world on a major scale. The *Manchester Guardian* immediately ordered twenty-five sets of these machines and set about obtaining suitable premises at each end. Muirhead Ltd raced ahead perfecting their machines and turning out more than sufficient for what was already seen as a big breakthrough.

However, not everyone saw the fax machine in this light. The printing unions dominated Fleet Street. Even proofreaders were paid nearly as much as directors and their chapel determined to which son a retiring member's job would be allocated. They could see a threat to their very livelihoods here, a fear that would lead to major riots 20 years later. 'Over our dead bodies,' they said, 'will such automation come to Fleet Street.' The owners capitulated. The first Muirhead Ltd knew about all this was the paper's chief buying officer phoning to ask, 'If you were to stop all further work on these machines, today, how much would we owe you?' It was a bombshell right out of the blue. The fleet of shiny new machines, the greatest thing the company had delivered since its torpedo-aiming mechanical computers of the 1930s, faced mothballing. The managing director, Mr John Foll, anticipated Norman Tebbit's famous dictum by 20 years and 'got on his bike'. He toured the world trying to sell a surplus set of machines to someone able to use them. Not until he reached Japan was he successful. Here, in Osaka, was a provincial newspaper selling more copies in Tokyo than in its home base. The rest is history.

Every large ship on the North Atlantic employed a meteorologist on board to receive radioed weather data, construct weather maps, predict where the worst weather was to be expected, and advise the captain to adjust course accordingly. With the Met Office being persuaded to broadcast up-to-date, detailed and accurate weather maps by facsimile machines using longwave radio, manning levels on board could be significantly reduced.

Sainsbury's updated its product prices every day and at noon each day an armada of motorcyclists would deliver these to each of its 400 London branches. Now a single typewriter-sized machine at each branch could do this far faster and more reliably.

Should a prisoner escape jail, his or her photo could be in every patrol car on the beat within minutes. Except that nearly all UK forces were too strapped for cash to buy a fax and it was left to the German police forces, and others all over the world, to keep Penge and Anerley workers busy.

The family of the firm which had founded the fax was no longer interested in its management and brought in a chairman with a City reputation, Sir Raymond Harrison. The company divisionalised, which meant that smaller units were made more accountable. The charismatic, dynamic Peter Gough, who had joined the firm as an apprentice in 1938, was made managing director 18 years later and the company's fortunes soared. Wages and the size of its workforce followed suit.

It wasn't all honey and roses, though. As a family firm Muirhead Ltd had sponsored a wide range of sports and welfare services throughout the twentieth century, and owned a 23-acre sports centre in Eden Park. But with the advent of popular TV and mass holidays in the sun, such paternal provisions were less urgent. The firm primarily had to compete with those more focused on the core activities. So it was an honour as well as an exception and a surprise when Sir Raymond asked to be allowed to attend the sports club AGM. But he'd come with a bombshell for the enthusiasts present, particularly the soccer team which had recruited far and wide to provide a southern league maestro of a team. Announcing that the site would be sold for several millions, Sir Raymond softened the blow by adding that each of the 15 separate clubs could apply for whatever funds they needed to relocate elsewhere. Loudest in its protest, orchestrated by all these clubs, was the dynamic and forward-looking soccer team. Yet equally resolute was Sir Raymond, who merely remarked he was in place to look after the firm and its workers. When he asked how many workers were in the club's first team, there was only silence – there were none.

Fire Brigades

The district has been served by several fire services over the years. The first was the private brigade provided by the Crystal Palace Company and operating from a fine if incongruous little brick building in front of the Palace. Sadly this was not able to save the North Transept in 1866 when it was gutted, so the decision was taken not to rebuild.

According to the *Beckenham Journal*, now the *Kentish Times*, in 1878 the Fire Department of the Metropolitan Board of Works declined to establish a fire station in 'Penge Hamlet' but would establish telegraphic communications between Penge Police Station and Sydenham Fire Station.

In June 1880 fire gutted three wooden houses in Penge Square. Engines from the Palace and from Beckenham attended, the families survived the fire but were left homeless and penniless. The *Journal* doesn't seem to report on what had become of them. Yet a wooden fire station was built in 1901 on the site of the former Penge Empire across the road from where Woolworth's now stands.

Penge Urban District Council's 1936 official guide records:

> *The Council's highways depot, fire station and ambulance station are housed in an admirably planned and well-furnished building in Croydon Road, opened in 1906.*

It was situated between Evelina Road and Franklin

Road. In 1941 responsibility for fire prevention was transferred to Kent County Council and in 1947 the station was closed and cover provided from Beckenham. Chris Doran's researches found this created quite a furore which rumbled on for several years. It seems that, in exchange, most if not all of Beckenham's ambulances went to the Croydon Road depot. So Penge complained about poor fire cover, Beckenham about poor ambulance cover.

Clearly, society must have been both more strenuous and more informal at the end of the nineteenth century; not only were early fire pumps brought to fires on hand-held carts, but training in pulling such carts seems to have included racing them as a spectator sport around the stadium in front of the Palace, even to the extent of wrecking them and going back to pick up the pieces.

Not until the early-twentieth century were diesel-engined machines made available, but even these had to be filled from natural water sources like the boating lake at the Palace.

Slowly, better education regarding the risks of fire, the introduction of less flammable soft furnishing, smoke alarms in houses, sprinkler systems in commercial buildings and the general decline in smoking, all contributed to a reduction in the number of fires and their severity, more than compensating for an increase in the number of electrical appliances, higher intensity of building generally and less supervision of children.

With the formation of the Greater London Council (GLC) in 1965, the fire and ambulance services were formed into London-wide organisations, which gradually became centralised. The Penge firemen and their machines were brought under the umbrella of Beckenham Station. A simple brick-and-steel cube, it stands as a poor comparison with that of its Croydon Road predecessor.

Above left: *The district's second public fire station, Croydon Road.* (LHC)
Above right: *Beckenham Fire Station, now serving Penge and Anerley from Beckenham Road.* (RM)
This image: *A nineteenth-century Crystal Palace fire engine – drawn by hand!* (ER)

An early-twentieth-century Penge fire engine, filling up from the boating lake. **(EP)**

Engine of Urban District Council Fire Brigade, after the opening of the fire station in Croydon Road in 1906.

Below: *Chariots of fire!* (ER)

An 1823 view across Penge Common, from Fox Hill. (TB)

The site of the proposed Crystal Palace, c.1852. (LHC)

Twelve

PLEASURES & PASTIMES

Since men first argued about living to work or working to live, holidays have increasingly been seen as an important goal in life. Interests and hobbies and sports for all, especially since the Second World War, have become the norm. Tumbling air fares extended holidays from the visually-stimulating England to the sun-tingling of warmer climes. Leisure and pleasure became the new gods.

Which other London locality can boast over a third of its area as green? Never mind the numerous smaller parks, Crystal Palace Park alone is larger than either Penge or Anerley's built-up areas. It is not just green but has been the home, from time to time, of the world's largest exhibition centre of its time, a National Sports Stadium, the world's largest collection of full-size dinosaurs, Formula Four motor racing, a zoo and a dry ski slope – not to mention 100 other diverse activities. A maze, model-car racing, a fishing lake, a boating lake, botanical gardens, geological displays, a museum, cafés, arboretums and avenues, an Olympic-size swimming pool, a miniature railway, aerobics classes, a children's playground, a fairground, soccer and cricket pitches and lots more besides – all can be found here.

Of course before the Palace's arrival the place was rustically rural if not incomparably idyllic. As the pictures *opposite* show, the site before construction was a blend of rural occupations and natural beauty.

It would be interesting to speculate how planning permission for the first Palace, never mind the second one, might have been granted if today's laws had applied then. But life moves on. Other, greater, injustices existed in those times, not necessarily caught in these views but certainly of the squalor described in works like those of Charles Dickens. Equally, the three depictions of Penge Lane, *below*, apparently drawn in 1843, appear simply light years from anything there today, including of course the historic Watermen's cottages in the same road (see Chapter One). Even the inscriptions upon these paintings, 'W Richards, from nature upon stone,' seems to speak volumes regarding the 'canvas' upon which they were etched.

Despite the rural tranquillity and enduring nature which such scenes evoke, one can nevertheless ask why so few people were able to take advantage of living here in those days. The canal had arrived in 1809, the Enclosure Acts in 1827 and the railway in 1839. One can imagine that farming only supported a meagre number of workers in the area, transport even less, and that trade with incoming commuters from 'the City' was still highly embryonic. Change on a major scale was to occur in three waves; first the 1851–4 arrival of the Palace and with it droves of City gents, followed by those who served them; next the 1877 dastardly murder and the subsequent flight of the discerning gentry; and thirdly the post-war modernisation of the place, perhaps beginning with the mock-art-decor Haysleigh and Wheathill Houses of the 1960s, in Croydon Road, and still continuing to this day.

In 2001–2 all the notorious high-rise flats of the Groves Estate were finally demolished and far more 'pleasant' low-rise alternatives were erected in their place. With much other improvement, this new era might well have been capped off appropriately with the reconstruction of a second, new, proposed Crystal Palace. But once again, things went seriously wrong.

Three of the six Penge Lane (now Newlands Park) cottages shown on the 1871 Ordnance Survey map. (LHC)

The Penge Empire Theatre, c.1905.

The Odeon was first a Co-op, a Coral Bingo Hall in 1985, more recently a DIY store and now the Moon and Stars public house. (LHC)

The under-used and forbidding National Sports Centre, 1985. (LHC)

Early 1960s modernisation: Haysleigh House, Croydon Road. (LHC)

The Penge Empire

From at least the 1920s to the '50s there stood opposite Woolworth's, in the centre of the High Street, a most flamboyantly Victorian theatre called the Penge Empire. Externally it was a huge red-brick rococo-style edifice. After the First World War Queen Mary commissioned a spectacular show there to entertain the troops returning home, or merely billeted in Penge on the way back to further parts of the country. So ever afterwards, recalls Ron Whellan (see Chapter Ten) it advertised itself as 'The Penge Empire by Royal Appointment'. According to Ron Peskett, that ardent supporter, follower and reporter of Crystal Palace Football Club, the Empire even attracted such world-renowned comedians as Ted Ray. He recalled him telling a story of his first appearance at the Empire. He thought he was doing quite well until 'the entire audience walked out as if one man. Then down came the curtain.' Astounded, Ted Ray demanded to be told what was going on. 'I can't be that bad,' he insisted, only to be rebuked with the riposte, 'Sorry mate, they've gone to watch a better show. The Crystal Palace is burning down.'

But wars took their toll everywhere and soon after the Second World War it became impossible to sustain such extravagant entertainment. The place bowed to changes in public demand and in 1950 it became the district's third cinema, after the King's Hall and the Odeon. It also changed its name to The Essoldo, a curious appellation, many felt, but as Simon Finch explained:

> *It was owned by a Soloman Sheckman. His wife was called Ester and his daughter Dorothy. So the cinema's name became an acronym of parts of all their first names.*

Inside it sported a giant organ which rose magically as if from the depths of an orchestra pit before film shows, complete with organist playing as it rose into view. The very name Essoldo conjured up deep excitement. Penge's oldest purpose-built cinema, however, must have been the King's Hall, perhaps named after the not-too-far-away King's Hall Road. Brian Vernon's son Paul recollects seeing his first films there, such as 'Snow White and the Seven Dwarfs' and 'The Wizard of Oz', before it became just another Gaumont in 1955. Four decades on, the new Weatherspoon pub nearby harped back to those days with life-size figures of the characters from 'The Wizard of Oz' as its central interior decorations.

The Odeon, also in the High Street, opened in 1938 seating a massive 2,110. It was converted into a three-screen cinema in 1974 but closed following increasing competition from television in 1981. One source, Michael Webb, says that it was demolished in 1985. Another, LHC's photographic record, says it was a bingo hall in 1985. Thus ended an era of three cinemas in the district, disappearing as they did throughout neighbouring areas as well. It was not until the 1990s that a considerable recovery proved possible, though for this district that must now wait, what with the rejection of the second Crystal Palace.

The Spectre of the New Palace

The protesters were jubilant. 'Multiplex plan is buried,' proclaimed the headline in the *Croydon Guardian*. 'Four-year campaign ends in celebrations as contract is terminated.' What the national newspaper, the *Guardian*, called 'a staggeringly impressive campaign' had succeeded.

Peter Colvin, Chairman of the Crystal Palace Campaign, said:

> *Bromley's capitulation was a victory of the local community, a tribute to the tens of thousands of people who stood together against aggression and greed. I want Crystal Palace to stand as a symbol of what can be achieved when ordinary people unite.*

Malcolm Wicks, MP for Croydon North, said

Bromley Council now had the necessary breathing space for consultation and suggested a design competition, saying:

We need an architecturally fine building in keeping with the site, perhaps containing a museum or an art gallery, but we need to address a whole spectrum of interests to make the new building a focal point everyone is proud of.

Simon Allison, the prospective parliamentary candidate for the Conservatives, said he thought the announcement would mean a significant weight off the minds of Upper Norwood residents, adding that losing the predicted economic benefits of the development would be outweighed by other benefits relating to the appearance of the park and congestion at the Upper Norwood triangle, already bad enough. Bromley Council said, in a cross-party statement, they were disappointed that they had to take this step, continuing:

It'll mean the hundreds of jobs the development would have generated will not now be realised, despite the fact that none of the legal challenges against the Council's actions in granting planning permission for the development have been upheld.

The leader of the Liberal Democrats in Bromley, Chris Maines (the LDs then controlling the Council along with Labour), said:

London & Regional Properties Ltd have lost a development that would have been a prestigious building and would have brought them a tremendous amount of kudos.

But what protesters? What plans? Why were all these people saying all these things?

To begin at the beginning. Some might have felt that when responsibility for it passed from the GLC to Bromley in 1986 a bright new day had dawned for Crystal Palace Park. A local borough council would surely know what was best for the future of a prime green-belt site? But even though Bromley prided itself, on its very logo, as being 'Bromley, the green borough', there were those who were not quite so sure that while it was the obvious authority to inherit overall responsibility for the site, the Council would necessarily bring that criterion to bear on any future development they might consider for it. The doubters should have been convinced by the clause in the Crystal Palace Act of 1990 which stated that any building erected on the site should reflect 'the spirit and style' of Paxton's original, and that glass and steel would be the prime materials in any such development. But were they? For what was meant by 'the spirit and style' of Paxton's original? Was it contained in the strategy agreed in 1995 by Bromley Council, called Restoring the Vision, encompassing as it did four key projects – developing the Crystal Palace site; restoring the Park; modernising the National Sports Centre and building a new concert-bowl? Was it in the proposal by London & Regional, submitted in the spring of 1997, which included a 20-screen multiples cinema, with attendant car parking (1,200 cars, on the roof of the development), restaurants and bowling alleys and the like? Not in the opinion of the Crystal Palace Campaign. Overnight it seemed, a rash of window posters appeared in houses and shops in the district, some with a portrait of Paxton, who was already allegedly pleading with the populace to 'Say "No" to the plans for my Park.'

Some are still to be seen in 2002, although they do appear a bit turned up at the corners, and the occupiers of the properties have clearly left. Was it before or after they knew the successful outcome of their campaign? But what was the reason for the protest? Surely it was a good thing to bring new life to a neglected part of south-east London? Weren't employment prospects – particularly for young people, at a local level, without needing to commute to town daily – not a good thing?

'Not in our Back Yard'

'Not in our back yard,' said the Campaign – in effect, if not in so many words. Strain on already overcrowded roads was one factor (which any 'local' will tell you is a legitimate 'gripe' whenever there is any kind of event happening at 'the Palace', be it fireworks, open-air concerts, veteran car rallies, sports events or what you will). Noise was another (which again locals will complain of, particularly in the summer). Pollution was a third (and again the by now weary locals will tell you that is already a nuisance, again particularly in the summer – they will point to overflowing rubbish bins as evidence). And those were only three of the objections.

The Council itself predicted the project would double the number of visitors to the area from two million to four million a year – and this in an area where there was no branch of the Underground system, and overground train services were already inadequate. And while reading the rest of this chapter it is perhaps worth noting that a 'hung' council controlled Bromley's affairs: the Liberals only retained power in a coalition with Labour. Maybe if they had enjoyed a workable majority at least their actions might have been seen to have been justified. As it was, they were in a precarious position throughout. At that time it was said that more than 500 residents had written to the Deputy Prime Minister of the day, John Prescott, who was also Minister for the Environment, Transport and the Regions, demanding that a public local inquiry be held. One local resident probably spoke for many when he said that the proposal was 'gut-wrenchingly ugly'.

Another said: 'The design has been variously described as a huge shed, an airport terminal, a public convenience and a sci-fi nightmare.'

> *The huge influx of extra visitors will make our narrow Victorian roads unbearable. Council officers are already talking about the need for one-way systems, parking restrictions and even residents' parking permits, which we have never had before...*

said a third protester.

But amongst the influential voices which called for Bromley Council to reconsider the proposals for the £55-million (later estimated at £75m-) complex was Tarsem Flora, Chairman of the Croydon District RIBA (Royal Institute of British Architects). He was a founding member of the architectural panel set up to advise the Council on the choice of scheme for the project. Amongst his criticisms of the scheme were those that although the design seemed modern, it was in fact quite stale; that it offered no focal point for the park; that it has an ill-thought-out car park, on the roof, with ramps leading to it which, he said 'tend to strangle the building at both ends', continuing: 'The sheer size and scale of these two lack the quality one expects from buildings of this nature.'

The Crystal Palace Campaign welcomed such a powerful influence, adding to Mr Flora's assertion that plans to improve transport links with a new £600,000 bus terminal and more frequent services would be insufficient to deal with the needs of the four million visitors a year. Also among the Campaign's complaints were that while Bromley had consulted its own residents, those of Croydon, Lambeth, Lewisham and Southwark, all right alongside, had been neglected.

Bromley Council countermanded this by saying that there was plenty of opportunity for people to put something into the design. The competition to find the winning developers had been widely advertised. L&RP had been chosen from more than 200 applications 'for their design, mix of leisure uses and arrangements for financial funding. Overall they offered the best value for the project.'

At a public meeting held in July 1997 – one of several – a majority of 500 votes to nine urged the Council to reject the plans as unsuitable for an historically important place badly served by public transport. In spite of initial rumblings from the populace at the far north-eastern reach of the borough, and those from residents in the neighbouring boroughs – the district has always suffered by being at the junction of so many boroughs – Bromley issued planning permission.

Only a week later illegal squatters began to occupy the site. 'Save our Trees' became the battle cry as they chained themselves to these doughty arboreal occupants of the locality. Though whether they were professional protesters, who climbed abroad any local case which appealed to them, before moving to another, has yet to be proved. Certainly they were not slow in claiming their State benefits from the local Post Office and causing a nuisance in the locality. That, of course, is part of the price to be paid. 'Swampy', one of their leaders, hotfoot from protesting against Manchester Airport's planned enlargement, appeared on television. Again. The matter was referred to the High Court and leave was refused for a judicial review.

Was defeat round the corner? Not a bit of it! On 2 September 1998 the Court of Appeal granted the campaign a judicial review of the outline planning permission, restricting it to the matter of the complying of the development's 'style' with the 1990 Act.

But such a style is open to interpretation. 'Was it,' as journalist Rowan Moore commented rhetorically in London's *Evening Standard* (19 September 2000):

> *... contained in the fairytale name that evokes both Cinderella's glass slipper and Prince Charming's home? Is it that of a rather average football club, or an area of genteel suburbia* [what does he mean by 'genteel'?], *or a TV-masted hilltop in SE19 from which you get awe-inspiring views of the capital? Or is it the adventurous spirit of the Great Exhibition of 1851 and the magnificent structure Joseph Paxton built to house it, which was unsurpassed until the arrival in our own time of the glorious Dome? Or the coarsened modification of Paxton's structure that was put up in Sydenham after 1851?*

But then this did follow several years of similar anti campaigning by the local press. Never perhaps did so much depend for so many on the interpretation by so few of one six-letter word – spirit.

The protest spread to Leicester Square, where another of L&RP's multiplex cinemas became the scene of concerted effort to prevent this latest development from being erected. What the customers of the cinema thought of the leaflets pushed into their hands was not generally known.

In the meantime the Court of Appeal had dismissed the judicial review, finding that Bromley had taken proper account of the terms of the 1990 Act, having borne in mind the style and relevant parking issues when outline planning permission had been granted. But had they taken account of the congestion and other aspects of the proposal? Not in the mind of the Campaign which redoubled its efforts and its pleas for funds to continue its efforts.

On 21 January 1999 the Campaign lodged an appeal with the House of Lords, which was refused on 22 June. During June 1999 Diane Barker, a single mother living in Anerley Hill, lodged an application for a judicial review of the permission granted on 5 May, being granted legal aid, to enable her to do so. This was set aside by the High Court on 29 November, delaying it until the following March

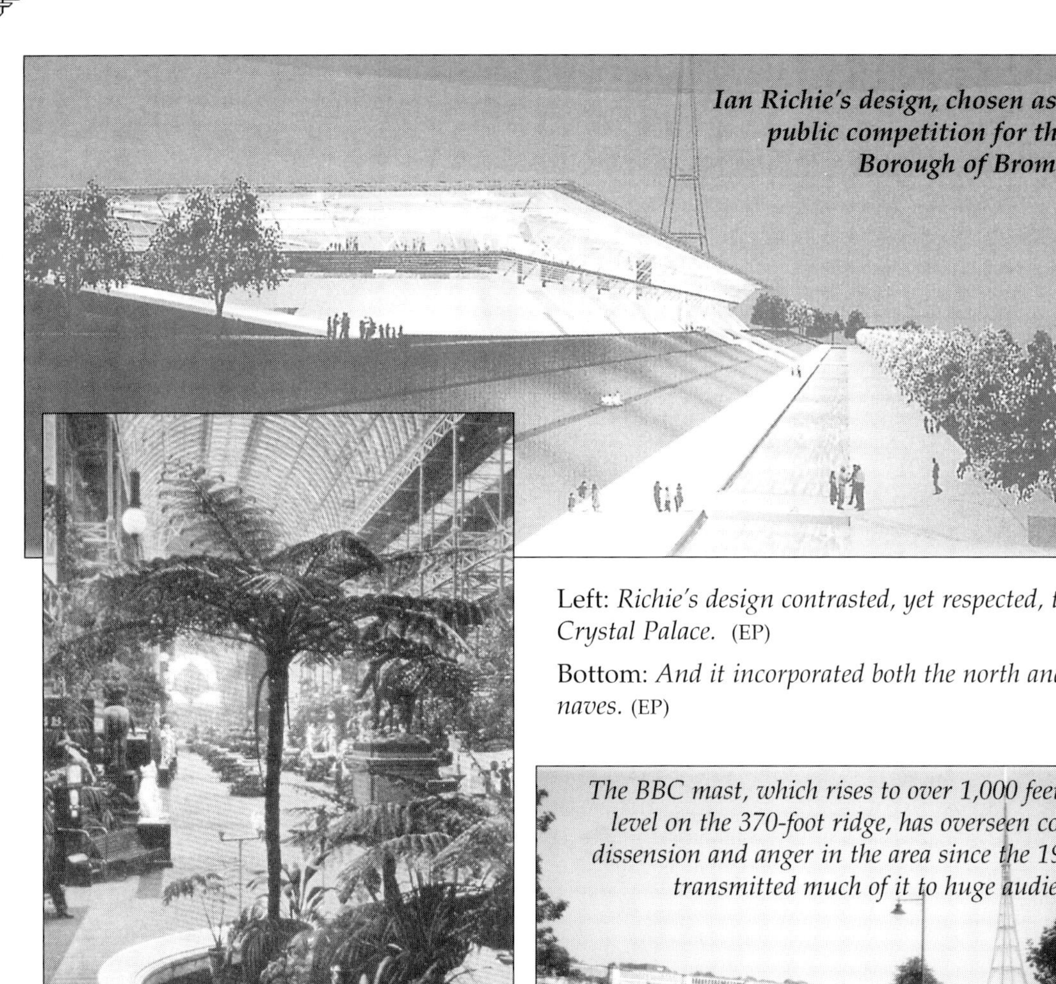

Ian Richie's design, chosen as part of a public competition for the London Borough of Bromley. **(LBB)**

Left: *Richie's design contrasted, yet respected, the original Crystal Palace.* (EP)

Bottom: *And it incorporated both the north and south naves.* (EP)

The BBC mast, which rises to over 1,000 feet above sea level on the 370-foot ridge, has overseen considerable dissension and anger in the area since the 1960s – and transmitted much of it to huge audiences. (PA)

since it was thought that it would take longer than had been allowed. The review was granted in the following March, but was restricted to issues around the detailed planning permission. But on 3 April 2000 the High Court dismissed the judicial review, finding the planning permission to have been granted lawfully. The tug-of-war became more and more acrimonious; neither side seemed willing to give way.

Bromley said, for instance, that:

This latest victory is a significant one, it clarifies beyond any doubt that the way Bromley had dealt with this planning matter has been correct all along... The development will bring much needed jobs to an area of high unemployment. It will also inject over £50 million into the economy and add to the range of leisure and recreational opportunities in the Park.

Another scheme had been submitted by Agenda 21 Architects (according to *The Architects' Journal*, 9 March 2000) featuring a six-screen cinema located nearer the National Sports Centre site (see Chapter Fifteen for details and developments).

By now there were two factors in the campaign (spelt, NB, with a lower-case 'c'); the one being the future of the 'top site', where Bromley had granted L&RP planning permission, and that of the Park proper. So far as the latter was concerned, the Court of Appeal refused Diane Barker's written application for leave to appeal, on 18 December 2000, though it subsequently gave her leave to appeal to an oral hearing. It would later rule unanimously in favour of Bromley the following November.

An unexpected and perhaps little-known development occurred when the powers of Section 1 of the Wildlife and Countryside Act 1981 were invoked. This says that it is an offence to 'damage or destroy the nest of any wild bird while in use or being built.' The nesting season lasts from 1 March to 31 August. Bromley was forced to announce that, 'In respect of people's concerns,' and in view of the Wildlife Act, 'we will not be felling trees at this time.' The trees were reprieved – for the time being at least.

But the climax came on 11 May 2001 with the announcement by Bromley that it had terminated the agreement with L&RP to develop the site due to the company's failure to complete the lease within the prescribed period.

In the summer of 2001 the Crystal Palace Campaign published a blueprint for a charitable trust, the Crystal Palace Trust, to consist of representatives of the five boroughs around the park, and local residents. The Trust would work with Bromley in raising funds, consulting local opinion and guiding regeneration generally. Having consulted widely on the idea of the Trust, both among the community representatives and the politicians, they found these to be broadly supportive.

At that point they had not put the idea to Bromley; they were only hopeful that the Council would agree. At the same time as making this announcement, the Campaign spoke of, 'the wonderful response to our consultation questionnaire; over 2,000 people having taken the trouble to complete it.' Schoolchildren had been consulted and many schools had cooperated.

The European Commission announced in August 2001 that it was intending to pursue infringement proceedings against the UK Government in view of Bromley Council's refusal to conduct an environmental assessment of the proposal submitted by L&RP. Its environmental commissioner, Margot Wallstrom, regretted that:

... the Commission has to remind member states to safeguard the important environmental rights of the public to receive environmental information and be consulted on the possible environmental impacts of projects... These rights are a tangible expression of a community that is close to the citizen.

Furthermore, because of the stand taken by the campaign, the Commission was to challenge the whole structure of UK planning decision-making, which excludes the possibility of environmental assessment at the detailed planning stage. In making all this known to its members and to the public in general, the Campaign said it hoped, 'this ruling will give greater protection to green space threatened elsewhere.'

Finding a Solution

Following all this campaigning, and as a result of an agreement failing to materialise, a new proposal was put forward. On 10 September 2001 a 'Crystal Palace Consortium comprising experts in planning, architecture, financial strategies and project development' announced 'an exciting new concept for the largely neglected tree-lined ridge at Crystal Palace.' The Consortium said in its media release that it was 'keen to offer an alternative strategy that has widespread community support.' The proposal centred on:

... the restoration of the unique and beautiful Grade II listed subway that once brought Victorian and Edwardian visitors from the high-level railway station, under the road, to Paxton's magnificent Crystal Palace.

The subway, which was originally built by Italian cathedral bricklayers in 1865, was said by now to be 'in a state of advanced neglect'. Indeed, local historian Alan Warwick wrote in his 1972 book, *The Phoenix Suburb*, that the subway was similar to '... some Pharaoh's tomb...' He went on to proclaim, 'Perhaps in time it will be brought back into use, when the present horrid desolation will be replaced by something worthy of its history.'

The new proposal focused on the restoration of the subway, in order to make it suitable for a variety of purposes. A relocated Crystal Palace Museum would find a home there, together with a coffee shop and a wine bar. Its large entrance court 'would become a venue for live performances and the visual arts'; the western entrance balcony would provide restaurant facilities. It was hoped the area would emerge as a:

> *suitably styled development not compromising the overall integrity of the tree-lined ridge but sufficient to provide a number of community-based and educational facilities* [which] *would become a focal point for the area.*

A world-class butterfly house, science centre and much more were also detailed.

John Payne, the Consortium's spokesman, stated that it was essential to make the park a safe, exciting and beautiful place to visit. He saw its development as a means of generating civic pride.

Bromley Council was not convinced:

> *This scheme appears to impact on the site of the former Crystal Palace. Until the future use of that site has been determined, it would be premature to consider uses for the subway and surrounding area.*

Bromley had already proposed to downgrade the site in its revised unitary development plan, which would make any new planning application easier to approve. This included classifying the site 'disused land' instead of 'Metropolitan open land'. Bromley was asked to justify this decision by London's new Mayor, Ken Livingstone, who had already spoken publicly against the L&RP scheme. A further turn of the screw came from Croydon's Labour MP, Geraint Davies and Labour peer Lord Warner of (nearby) Brockley, who introduced private members' bills calling for the Crystal Palace Park to be transferred to the Greater London Authority.

So the future of the 'top site' is not a particularly gentle stroll towards a sun-filled upland. A new campaign may be just around the corner. And that the site's future is uncertain is perhaps the only certain thing that can be said about it.

CLUBS & ORGANISATIONS

Penge, Anerley and Crystal Palace are together a district not just rich in local clubs, societies and associations, but increasingly growing in the list of voluntary organisations; always a sound indicator of an established community.

Some, like Rotary and the Women's Institute, go back nearly a century; others, like the Scouts and the Guides, have many groups in the district. Like all voluntary groups, they wax and wane, set new traditions and standards, and have much to hand on to new members.

With rising 'street crime', there is a demand for effective youth leadership, clubs and facilities. As part of the millennium celebrations and local regeneration funding schemes, a fine modern youth provision, Youth Action 2000, has opened in Anerley Station Road. It took over a disused pub, The Railway, and equipped it with nine bedsits, a coffee shop and other facilities.

Some local clubs have quite a small membership and members are often given large roles, as is the case at the Anerley Writers Circle. At the other end of the spectrum, The Crystal Palace Foundation has over 600 members, while the Norwood Society has 300 members.

There are also informal clubs: the neighbourhood groups, the churchgoers, the soccer fans and those that frequent the pub on a regular basis. Yet despite all these organisations, many people still feel isolated, alienated or lonely.

Formerly the Railway, now Youth Action 2000, Anerley Station Road. (PA)

Street Parties

Street parties provide a most welcome break to the routine of life, and the more special the occasion, the more special the event. Those held in Anerley Vale, off Anerley Road, are typical. The earliest recallable by local residents is the Silver Jubilee of George V and his wife Queen Mary in May 1935. The Vale may have only held 42 houses, but that didn't stop over 100 locals sitting down to the Anerley Vale's street party for the children. Often weeks of preparations went into such an event, with photography now making it all the more memorable.

The people may have been extremely poor by modern standards, with many not having running water or inside toilets, but the street was swept spick and span, the occasional gas-lit street lamps were dressed overall with spiralled red, white and blue crêpe paper, bunting was strewn across the road between every single house, and large flags shoehorned in wherever possible.

Mrs June Burrows, née Ridout, recalls:

It didn't matter how poor we were. My mother made that large Union Flag in the middle of the picture from odd bits of material we'd saved up from wherever.

Mr Tripp senior and his son, local builders, were called upon to organise the entire event, making it a most memorable occasion for so many.

Come VE Day, in May 1945, all the carefully saved decorations were once again wheeled out, this time quite spontaneously. Mr Tripp was naturally expected to coordinate matters, and with emphasis again on the children, street races were the central attraction. The Tripps even constructed an elaborate dias, complete with canopy above and loudspeaker system in front. Stage performances were invited from members of the community, no doubt forerunners to the modern karaoke craze. Everywhere Mums and Dads would greet each other with the by-now-famous Churchillian Victory sign.

Left: *Anerley Vale street-party rejoicings for King George V's Silver Jubilee, 1935. Organiser Mr Tripp is seen in the centre, top-hatted and made up as a minstrel; his son, to his right, is standing wearing a bowler hat.* (JBs)

Right: *Anerley Vale dressed for the 1935 Silver Jubilee of King George V with homemade Union Flags, maypoles and bunting.* (JBs)

Victory souvenir day, Anerley Vale, May 1945. The organiser Mr Tripp, senior, sits among the children in the front row; his son stands out to the right in the back row. Others recognised by June Burrows are her sister, Hazel Ridout, the families Beasley, Ewen, Levey, Arnold, Little (including Joyce), Purbrick and Rita Stockford. June herself was absent, having travelled to Whitehall to see the procession, where she fainted and was taken to hospital! (JBs)

Thirteen

Stability & Change

The Good Old Times

Many folk so often talk of 'the good old times'. As a cliché it has a pedigree going back a good long way. A description of local John Gwyer's background, penned in 1895, includes reference to the old times in ironic terms:

John Gwyer

His father died of smallpox when James was only a month old, so that his poor mother was left to struggle and provide for her four children the best she could, and they were often greatly pinched by poverty and anxiety. These were the so-called good old times; good fosooth in what, save ignorance, poverty and vice, especially among the working classes, with all wages much lower than at present, and all kinds of provisions at fabulous prices, bread three times as dear as now, meat much dearer, tea such a luxury that few could indulge in it, six, seven and eight shillings a pound, while sugar fetched about 6d. per lb, and clothing and everything of that nature was at an equally dear rate.

Apart from having to convert old pence into new and in due course no doubt into ecus, and then pounds into kilograms, similar sentiments could have been expressed by every generation imaginable. It would seem that the only rational definition of the 'good old days' must have been the age in which the speaker was a teenager and learning about the world around him or her – involving a kind of yearning for what seemed, at least in comparison with what had happened since, the only time of stability in the speaker's experience.

Architecture: A Force for Change or Stability

Good architecture points the way to the future; just look at the vast amount of splendour in Central London, inspiring those who see it, and earning billions in tourism; or even many fine examples right here in Penge, in Anerley and in Crystal Palace. Perhaps the toughest question is, 'What does one mean by 'good' architecture – the maisonettes of Croydon Road (1998), the town houses of Anerley Road (2001), the latest ones in Croydon Road (2002)?' There has always been the narrowest of lines between 'modern' architecture and poor architecture. All too often utility reigns supreme, little concern is shown for the future, and survival for just the shortest time ahead takes overriding consideration. What can a planning committee do when asked to approve a mediocre construction, be it a single residence, industrial plant or office block, when their officers advise after speaking to the applicant, indeed often after lengthy negotiations, that the choice is between this and a continuing eyesore?

The Information Age

The Information Age has and is making its mark here on Penge, Anerley and Crystal Palace as anywhere. Its origins can be traced to the mobiles popularised in the late 1990s, the internet from the mid 1990s, computer games from the 1980s and back to the personal computers of 1978. That was when local housewife and part-time bookkeeper Anne Isted, also a first-aid instructor for Scouts in Penge, was doing very nicely looking after the books for a local architect with clients in Oakfield Road, a Maple Road contract office cleaner and a jobbing builder and decorator busy on some Avenue Road conversions. She was only doing the bought ledger for the latter in those days. He, Mr Winterbottom, found his business expanding faster than his clerks could keep count of the money passing through his hands.

'You seem to do the bought ledger pretty fast these days, could you take on the wages ledger as well?' he asked. She made it clear she was already overloaded as it was. 'Well,' he added, 'what if we

Above left: *The White House, Penge High Street, one of the oldest residences in the district, now the local dentist's.* (LBB)

Above right: *Belvedere, in Belvedere Road; representative of prestigious design.* (PA)

Left: *Modern maisonettes, Croydon Road, Penge, 1998, complete with avante-garde attriums.* (PA)

Below: *The Old Bank, corner of Anerley Road and Anerley Park.* (PA)

Above: *The fine old Thicket Tavern, Anerley Road.* (PA)

Left: *The respectable homes in Avington Grove; typical of an earlier heyday.* (PA)

Below left: *At the start of the twenty-first century, mobile phone shops are as prolific as greengrocers once were.* (PA)

Right: *Town houses, Croydon Road, Anerley, 2002.* (RM)

The Royal Hotel, top of Anerley Hill, where Queen Victoria stayed on several occasions. It has since been replaced by The Occasional Half public house. On the left is the Crystal Palace South Tower. (EP)

computerise them?' She put this to her husband, a consulting engineer at the time partially involved with computerisation, who advised, 'It'd cost £4,500 for a complete system. Ask him if he'll give you a three-year interest-free loan from his business, and I'll help you get it running.' It was a brave move for all three parties involved, but, with their spirits firmly focused, they soon got a good system working so efficiently that Anne was quickly taking on other business, which led to a computer retailer asking first if she'd take on his payroll work, and then act as a part-time consultant showing others how to do it. Before one could say 'Jack Robinson' she was automating the payroll of more than ten local businesses. However, more work was the last thing she needed, but as this consultancy work paid twice her former rate it didn't take her long to find three assistants, train them up on the payroll program and focus solely on the consultancy and training herself.

It was a story repeating itself everywhere; computer games at a lower level, major waterworks, hotel bookings and airport control on a larger scale, right up to the cell-networking mobiles which caused Penginians and others to have to change their phone numbers thrice in a decade, as mobiles rapidly spread countrywide, Europewide and nearly worldwide.

Where once the greengrocer dominated high streets, at the time of going to press mobiles were proliferating, it not being uncommon to see three such shops adjacent to each other.

Breaking the Rules

There are many who think we have too many laws and that an obvious sign of a civilised society is one with less rather than more laws. They argue that self-discipline is superior to imposed discipline and that this should be encouraged to the highest degree, as indeed it invariably is within a family.

Much has been made, mostly by government, of introducing identity cards as a way of making life safer, especially after dusk, for the more vulnerable members of our community. Equally vociferous are the voices arguing about this being an impingement upon personal liberty. It is difficult to weigh up one argument against the other and it may well be that a compromise will be reached; the cards could be issued on a voluntary basis and if favours were bestowed upon people who had one, eventually most people would accept them. The intrusion is countered by recalling they caused little if any difficulty during the Second World War. Indeed, they were even issued here until 1952.

But where do you draw the line? Society is constantly evolving, and as such its laws must be adapted to cope with the community's changing needs.

Mrs Longhurst, now retired, still vividly recalls the time she was encouraged to get rid of one outdated law, rule or custom. She was the highly regarded children's librarian at Beckenham in the 1950s when she noticed something strange. No sooner was their copy of *Treasure Island* placed on the 'returned books' shelf, than within a quarter of an hour it was borrowed again. It never had time to be sorted onto its proper shelf. In those days it was felt that the right and proper use of taxpayers' money was to have only a single copy of each book; any extra copies would of course only be at the expense of not buying some other and no doubt deserving book; and in any case, libraries were always sensitive to the criticism that they were doing both bookshops and authors out of a living by their mere existence.

But Mrs Longhurst felt that she had an overwhelming duty to her customers, the library users. She put it to her chief librarian that maybe it wouldn't do any harm to just stock a couple of copies of this most laudable and popular book. But old habits and tradition die hard, and a polite way of saying no was readily found. Later she was discussing this with her immediate boss, the deputy librarian, and realised she might have made a minor administrative blunder by not channelling her request through him. Anyway, for whatever reason, he hit upon the simplest of ruses to help her meet her aim. 'If *Treasure Island* is so popular, it must be rather dog-eared and dirty by now?' She agreed, as was her inclination anyway, and he continued. 'Well, have it withdrawn and replaced with a new copy, okay? Now, when's your day off? If that withdrawn copy accidentally finds itself back on the shelves, will anyone ever notice?' 'I suppose not,' she had to admit. 'But then there's the little question of two identical books having the same access number.' This was a major obstacle, and neither of them could see a way round this dilemma. The deputy eventually admitted, 'Well, if it's happened accidentally, they'll both have the same number, and if they're always out on loan as you claim, no one will ever be able to notice, will they?' The scheme succeeded, except that there still wasn't either copy on the shelves for more than a few minutes, so, in the course of time, she arranged for a third and fourth copy to infiltrate the 'returned books' shelf.

By now several of the staff were in on the arrangement, and the deputy felt obliged to find a suitable moment for the chief librarian to be in the loop too. He was to give a speech to a convocation of chief librarians and sought ideas from his deputy to spice it up a little. He agreed to a modest experiment of stocking up to ten copies, if demand really warranted it; after all there were the beginnings of a newish culture to treat visitors to the library not just as users but as customers. In no time all ten copies were bought and still none ever graced the shelves for long before being snapped up. Eventually, Mrs Longhurst recalled, it took a stock of about 40 copies before a single one could be expected to find its way onto its proper shelf and remain there for more than a day or two. And by then they'd devised a modification to the system of access numbering to cater for this anyway.

Citizens' Advice Bureau in Avenue Road; where next? **(RM)**

Citizens' Advice Bureau

While it's everyone's earnest desire to keep as clear of 'the law' as possible – both being stopped by a policeman or having to appear in court, there has been, since 1968, a most useful halfway house in Penge, the Citizens' Advice Bureau. Staffed entirely by trained volunteers, and not really known about by the vast majority of Penginians, it still tends to get overloaded. Go there most times, except to queue up before opening times, and you're likely to be given an appointment to come back later; though if you're lucky, that would be only a few hours hence.

The Penge Bureau deals with both enquiries about, and disputes between couples, spouses, between neighbours, between tenants and landlords, between employees and employers, and between individuals and the State. It offers advice to either side of any uncertainty or dispute and maintains total confidentialities for all who come to seek help. It even has a sort of hissing-sound loudspeaker system throughout its offices to make it well nigh impossible for anyone to overhear anyone else's conversations.

But – and it's a big but – its services could easily be doubled. Apart from the inconvenience of its part-time nature, it is little known about, advertises its services almost never and is located at one extreme end, the Beckenham end, of the district. Either its premises should be doubled in size, for which, most fortuitously, there is ample space, or, maybe preferably, it should open a further branch at the Anerley end of town.

The Onslaught of Change

The service offered by the Citizens' Advice Bureau only covers the more serious aspects of things that go wrong with one's life from time to time. There may well be a far larger need for a different sort of service altogether, one which might focus more on reducing the ordinary stresses and strains, fears and phobias, concerns and uncertainties of life. Although this may seem an eccentric view, the history of this district and the people who live in it reveals that life is dripping with worry, anxiety, nerves and sheer anger about what's going on – or not going on. There was a time, maybe in those mythical 'good old days', when grandparents were hallowed sources of help, advice, reassurance and even wisdom – but all too rarely nowadays. Yesterday's advice and ways of doing things may be less and less appropriate in today's ever-somersaulting world and yet older people do have more and more time on their hands, do find themselves sidelined, and do fear loneliness creeping up on them, so slowly that it is often unnoticed. Something substantially different, something new, will soon be needed, something which, like the canal, the railways, the Palace and its planned replacement, will probably be scoffed at violently. We hate change, we hate it on a large scale, we hate it if it's proposed by others. And we hate it most of all if it's proposed without full discussion with ourselves.

What is needed is a less formal network of things than might once have been provided by wise old grandparents or by the highly focused 'How can I help you' approach of the Citizens' Advice Bureau.

Many youngsters are already nibbling at the edges of the potential solution with their hi-tech devices; their mobile phones, their text-messaging and their internet chat rooms and so on. The era of networking is upon us. Personal computers and the Internet yesterday, email and web-surfing today, WAP (wireless application protocols) technology and comprehensive networking tomorrow. WAP will enable us to summon help simply by pressing a button. We will be able to access information about where we are, which will enable emergency services, friends or anyone nearby, to reach us quickly should that be necessary. We will also be able to find the right bus or nearest minicab. The service may even help us cope with long-term challenges such as finding a new and suitable partner, when singles clubs, dating agencies and personal contacts have not been effective. Of course the changes needed to bring about such things will take several years. Years to work out how the hardware can best be provided and how the software can best be developed. It will also be some time before society as a whole is ready to access information in this way.

But such changes are coming; a dozen or so of the world's largest companies, plus a number of smaller local ones such as our very own Muirhead-Vatric, have already invested over £60,000,000,000 in WAP technology from 1997 to 2002 alone, paving the ways for such provision.

Fourteen

Recent Revivals

I once imagined that the most beautiful thing about the patch I'd been brought up on was my very familiarity with it. Then after travelling, I realised there was a myriad of ways in which any place could be improved. The challenge was how best to do it. Making things better is often a choice between concerns of the moment and launching far-sighted projects, of which few can see the ultimate benefit.

Crystal Palace was not only the setting for the biggest exhibition in the world, it was also a playground as big as either Penge or Anerley themselves. Today, few if any of London's 950 districts are so well endowed. Although the entire park fell into disrepair after the 1936 fire, by the early 1950s the LCC launched many a project to revive public interest again. As well as the Formula Four race track already mentioned, there was an outdoor concert bowl where audiences of several thousand could experience Tchaikovsky's 1812 to fireworks. An off-street driver-training centre included a large skid pan.

Clearing the Slums

Headings tend to raise hackles. 'What slums?' many will say with justifiable indignation. Slums are relative; today's ideal homes, having served their purpose, become tomorrow's slums; yesterday's high-rise skyscrapers become today's ghettos. Many slums were swept away in Penge in the 1960s and '70s. Sometimes they looked as if they were being swept away too fast, too drastically, too uncaringly. The extensive Groves Estate's nine streets – all called Groves – certainly look much smarter, but you have to live there, belong there, be involved there, to realise the anger and bitterness which was not swept away. That could take generations longer.

There's always so much more to be done, of course. Brian Wright's splendid book, *Penge Papers*, notoriously described how joggers and dog-walkers fought for supremacy in one particular part of Bett's Park renowned for its canine-derivative problems! Today, a quarter of a century on, such satire and cynicism is fast becoming a thing of the past.

Neighbours, colleagues and fellow drinkers point to the piles of rubbish in so many corners, the graffiti on so many walls and the vandalism everywhere else, not to mention the drugs, burglary and violence which we're so scared of. And they all shrug their heads in forlorn shame. But then each generation has always left some things for the next one to focus on. Until recently it was not difficult to spot half-a-dozen abandoned or burnt-out cars by Weighton Road or large stretches of Croydon Road and Anerley Hill being used as car lots for old bangers. Everyone – from a bright little schoolgirl who rips her new shoe on jagged steel, to Councillor Gaster, who in September 2000 reported that Bromley Council investigates 800 reportedly abandoned vehicles a month (of which 200 are removed) – is despairing of the situation. With the collapse of the price of waste paper, from £25 to £1.50 a tonne, recycling became less attractice. Plastic bags, wrappers and milk bottles create a vast amount of environmental pollution. Some 25 CCTVs were being installed around Penge, Anerley and Crystal Palace. And all that was in just one month. A recent survey by the author showed that in Penge and Anerley each night over three times as many cars were garaged on the public highway than off it, a sort of crude alternative to speed humps. In some streets barely any off-street provision has been made, parked cars are nose to tail along both sides, delivery and other vehicles double park to totally block the thoroughfare and car owners are forced to walk rather than risk losing their parking slot.

In the same month, there were six accidents at a single junction. At least this prompted Bromley to paint yellow lines at the corner in question, though not until a year after a motorcyclist was killed there. He was an off-duty policeman.

Speed humps, or 'sleeping policemen' as they're affectionately known, are becoming a countrywide scourge – ruining cars and shortening their lifespans, seemingly doubling their scrapping rate. It is as if half the community, failing to train its children in PSE (Personal and Social Education), is happy to slow everyone down to a more compatible speed. Unclogging the streets of cars, not in use for 90 per cent of the day, seems quite out of the question, until, that is, one gets to the outer, leafier, suburbs – like most of the rest of Bromley, calling itself 'the' green London borough.

Bromley's Response

Bromley
THE LONDON BOROUGH

Bromley is helping Penge and Anerley towards a better future via something Brussels calls a single regeneration scheme. This really does sound 'Brusselsinian' but it simply means a conduit for channelling capital funding of a one-off and socially-benefiting nature to help the slightly down-at-the-heels bits of town pull themselves up more easily to a better level of life. In the 1980s this worked wonders for all sorts of neglected corners of Europe; in the '90s it helped pretty well every former coal-mining part of Britain to join the twentieth century; and now it was our turn to leap headlong into the twenty-first century.

Bromley's SRB (single regeneration budget) for us hinged on bringing in some £150m of investment for cleaning up, rebuilding, training, job-creation and crime-reduction measures to the locality. It was to bring private, lottery, local-authority and central-government monies together to help generate a concerted and supportive action. And to avoid any them-and-us feeling, all was co-ordinated by Mr Mike Ellis, the Business Co-ordinator and Town Manager in an office in the heart of town, at 134 Anerley Road.

What was this budget supposed to deliver? According to the July 2000 plan, its 'outputs' were:

- *1,000 new jobs*
- *2,000 existing jobs protected and 8,000 new construction jobs*
- *2,500 people gaining qualifications*
- *40,000 training weeks delivered*
- *230 people entering self-employment*
- *120 new businesses set up*
- *120 commercial buildings having their security upgraded*

As the regeneration area map showed, this uniquely involved the co-operation of nine local authority wards in no less than five separate boroughs, not to mention having a significant area of influence in 37 wards across these five local authorities. However, of the 50 or so projects within this £150m scheme, one item was dominant over all the others, namely the rebuilding of a Crystal Palace on the site of the old one, a site untouched save by insects and fly-tippers for over 40 years. It would use £58m of the money, pretty well all of it from the private sector. Bromley invited design, construction and operation bids on the open market and a scheme chosen by a local panel with local architects, English Heritage and planners on it.

They chose, and gave outline planning permission for, the scheme proposed by a firm called London & Regional Properties plc (LRP). It was said to be a third the size of the previous palace, but still

looked rather large. It was to contain a large number of restaurants and cinema screens and a roof car park, no doubt sporting spectacular vistas and views, weather permitting. Inside it was to be designed with considerable flexibility to cater for changing public tastes and fashions over the decades to come. But, as we have already seen in Chapter Twelve, the locals – supported by the press – rebelled vociferously against the scheme. (Recall that the local press also played a pivotal role in the Penge murder case – see Chapter Three.) As the regeneration map shows, the nearest residents were primarily in Lambeth, Southwark and Lewisham, all long-held Labour strongholds; while Bromley, the promoter of the project, was always a Tory stronghold. It was also a time when the country at large had had enough of Tory rule nationally and was bringing in the first Labour Government for nearly 20 years. Or it might have been an eddy current of this last change. The Tories had abolished Labour Ken Livingstone's GLC; Crystal Palace Park which had been under his control, had been given to Bromley who'd resurrected these plans on this long-desolate site. Labour had vowed to bring it back something like the GLC, but Ken had fallen out with the Labour PM, Tony Blair, had stood as an independent, and had won. He went on to court further public support by siding with the local residents against Conservative Bromley. Bromley also changed its colours, for the first time in living memory, albeit to the middle-way of the Liberal Democrats, if only briefly.

Police officers on parade in the now rebuilt S. Norwood High Street. The first sergeant in the second row is A.F. Wixey, father of Mrs Brenda Brent of Abbotts Way, Beckenham. (BB)

The Norwood Triangle Campaign

Other significant players included John Price, founder and treasurer of the Norwood Triangle Campaign, architect Tarsem Flora and Diane Barker. And although their actions failed in law, by 2001 LRP seemed to have lost interest and failed to continue with their agreement with Bromley to progress the project. Bromley has spent several millions of pounds on safeguarding and securing the site, on occasion employing 1,000 police officers and now has nothing to show for its troubles, and the campaigners, having found a common cause around which to rally and meld strong passions, may have stopped the project but remain concerned that the planning permission is still in place.

Change invites negative reactions, and here, especially right at the top, in more senses than one, reaction against change occurred on a massive scale comparable with the 15 years of protest against the Heathrow Terminal 5 or against the lengthening of Manchester's airport. Not only did the project run into local opposition vastly greater and fiercer than could ever have been imagined from the outset, and more time and money were expended than anyone could have foreseen, but its repercussions will affect the neighbourhood for decades to come. Or, if the Harriet Staunton case was anything to go by, for centuries to come.

Yet both sides did learn lessons from the past. The Bromley Tories, having lost control of the council in May 1998, worked assiduously to repair matters and regained control again in June 2001. Likewise, the Norwood Triangle pressure group did learn a key lesson from this turmoil; one cannot be entirely negative. Not only did they raise six-figure sums for legal fees, but they also engaged to draw up an environmentally more sensitive scheme the very architect first chosen by Bromley to guide them in the original selection panel, Mr Tarsem Flora. Of course when there's work to be done, damage to be repaired or new projects to be launched, ideas rain down thick and fast. Ideas become two-a-penny; it is action, or funding to finance action, which really matters. And indeed, just as the 1851 Crystal Palace design competition raised 20 bids, the 1990 Bromley one generated quite a few too, so the aftermath of this latest debacle gave rise to a plethora of ideas. But Flora's was the only one to drum up any significant support – crucially, even from the local press.

The Agenda 21 International Scheme

Flora's scheme was developed through his architectural practice, Agenda 21 International. The practice took its name from the important resolution on sustainability and energy conservation agreed by nearly all of the 178 governments present at the 1992 Earth Conference in Rio de Janeiro. The most startling aspect of the scheme is that it was largely underground *(see overleaf)*. That alone would commend it to the increasing siren voices who argue that the park already has vastly more concrete in it than anything remotely wishing to call itself a park. The trouble with all politicians is that they love to leave behind a legacy of note, a memorial to posterity – and what better than a vast array of constructions. The last thing Crystal Palace Park needs is another few tens of thousands of tonnes of concrete. Perhaps an underground complex could be expected to generate at least a modicum of support and, indeed, the outline plans do depict considerable dexterity of thought, vision in appeal and glamour in execution. Sadly, however, as many a great tunnelling engineer has found to his cost, underground works are inevitably the most expensive; unless financial backing can be found on a large scale, schemes like this stand little chance of taking off.

The Italian-built Renaissance-style long-abandoned Crystal Palace Park Road, which, if extended, Flora has proposed could house Britain's finest butterfly collection, currently at Ham but looking for a new home. (PA)

More modest parts of the regeneration scheme took off; £5m plus has been spent on restoring the 37 dinosaurs and landscaping with 185,000 flowers, shrubs and trees. £4m was spent on refurbishing the gloriously oversized yet wondrous Crystal Palace Station. A bus terminal with incredibly deep foundations was completed, albeit for 11 routes and 1,100 buses a day. £1.1m was allocated to making the often gridlocked Norwood Triangle a one-way system. Grants were provided to replace 40 dilapidated shop fronts, contributing to a face-lift for the entire area. The number of vacant shops was reduced from 120 to under 60. A training centre offering courses for subjects from IT skills to childcare, from administration to veterinary nursing was opened. Arts, youth, medical, housing, ex-offender, crime, drugs and law centres, and CCTV – all made up just a soupçon of the 50-plus projects and ongoing schemes.

Is That It?

One is reminded of Bob Geldof's famous remark on returning from supervising the spending of tens of millions he'd raised to help with some of the world's worst starvation in Africa. He asked simply, in one of the shortest speeches ever given, 'Is that it?'

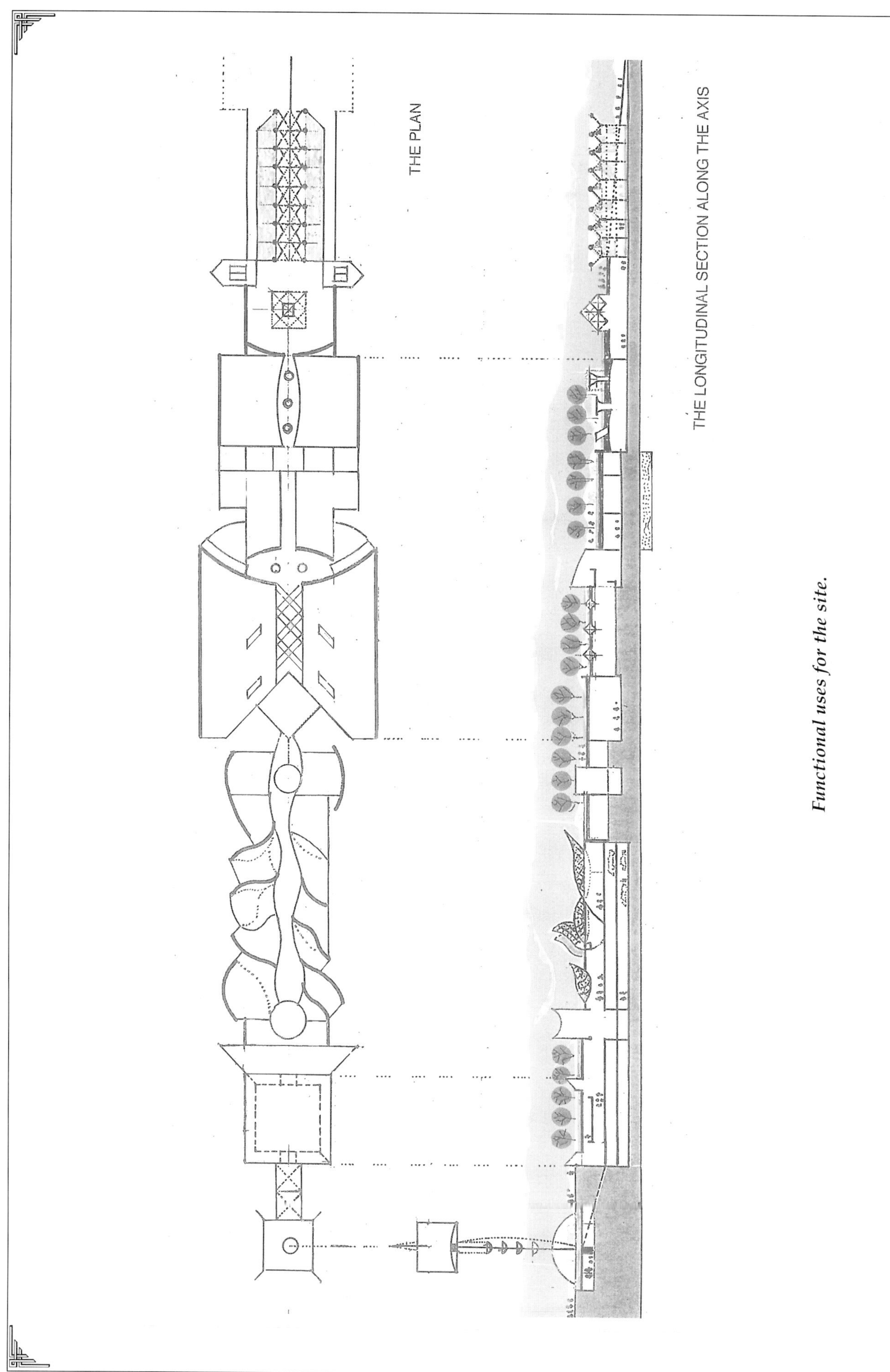

Functional uses for the site.

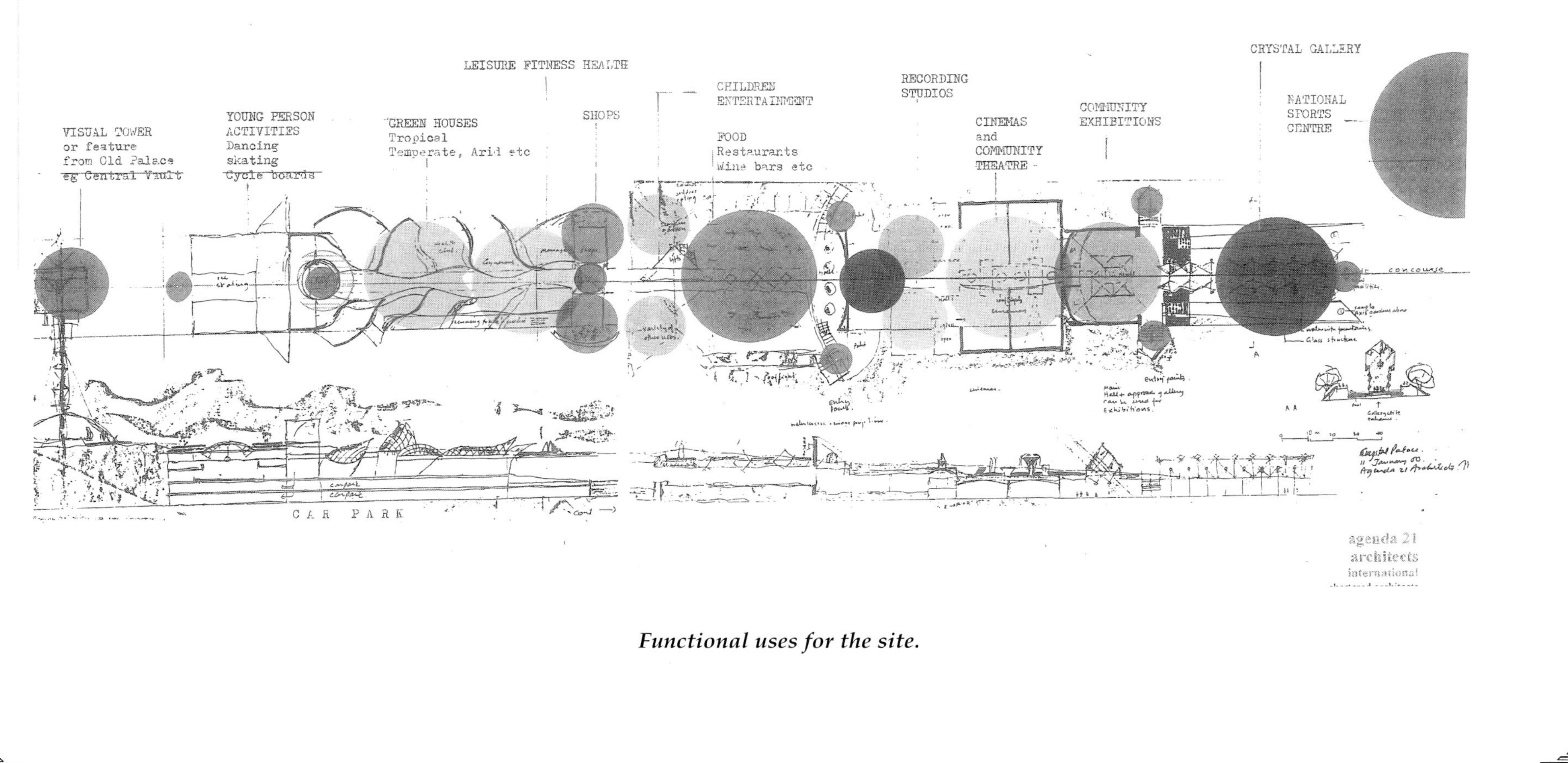

Functional uses for the site.

Most arguments, some say nine out of ten, are not the result of firmly-held but differing beliefs, but more of misunderstandings. Was the Palace replacement £6m fiasco a misunderstanding? Certainly Bromley put out much publicity, from its taking over of the site in 1986, via its being granted permission to proceed in its 1990 Crystal Palace Act and its 1994–6 public competition for a viable scheme. The Act authorised 'a building that should reflect the spirit and style of Paxton's original and should be predominantly made of glass and steel.'

Certainly, despite political changes in the running of the council, the leaders of all three parties were mostly united in the major steps Bromley took in bringing the scheme forward over a 15-year period.

Were there other agendas, unfinished business and/or anger spilling over from earlier issues, being enacted out in this particular project, maybe in an opportunist manner? Perhaps. Until societies learn to become communities, issues constantly get swept aside. Democracies may have been around for 1,000 years, a class-wide franchise for 200 years and a bi-gender franchise for nearly a century, but even that leaves many a score to settle – scores on which the press works assiduously, day after day. If occasionally they also find it necessary to look after their own interests, say twice in a century, they should not be judged more harshly than others.

Mention has been made of Penge and Anerley being launched in the first place by transport: the Crooked Billet lured Kentish travellers to pause for refreshment; the Croydon Canal was built to get its produce to London more reliably; the railway company was required to build Anerley Road; and the rich merchants of the City found that they could commute from the better atmosphere here, first by rail, and then by metalled road. To this day such emphasis on transport continues apace. Since the 1970s the district's car ownership has almost doubled. In the 1980s low-cost back-street repair garages followed suit. Penginians were never slow in spotting a business opportunity.

But not by any means do all reap the benefits of car ownership. So in the 1990s, after bus deregulation, privatisation and passes for old and young, bus routes doubled. Transport is what economists call a sensitive leading indicator of economic trends. So when in the nineteenth century Britain in general and London in particular invested heavily in transport, its economic growth multiplied. The greater the distance one can commute, both to work and to pleasure locations, the better the chances one has of finding providers of such facilities that match one's talents, needs and desires. Thanks to the affluence on which much of the district was founded, many roads are wide, laid out on a generous grid, and have coped well with the phenomenal growth in traffic. On this basis, the future of Penge and Anerley is well assured.

Smartening Up

New housing, developing education, improved transport facilities, street beautification, park enhancements available all night and ever increasing transport facilities are but a selection of improvements to have been undertaken in the district in the last years of the twentieth century. Pedestrianisation of the shopping centres, cycle routes, modern sports and leisure facilities, new types of shops, pubs and restaurants are others. Yet these are but transient changes; in reality they are only markers, encouragements and pointers towards what could and would be possible in the future.

It is now up to us, the residents, voters and taxpayers, to discuss, decide and determine what's to be put on the agenda for the generations to come.

Even small two-up, two-down nineteenth-century Maple Road cottages are now modernised and put on the market for a hitherto unimaginable £249,000. (PA)

Fifteen

Facing the Future

When Paxton's Palace builders had nearly finished, he got 2,000 of them to volunteer as Army labourers for the Crimea. It is not known how many returned. At the end of the First World War, Penge would have to record the loss of 410 good Penginians on the memorial at our Recreation Grounds – not to mention the thousands disabled or severely injured. A generation on we had to add a further plaque to their progeny. Yet another plaque commemorates those who kept the home fires burning in Penge. And today, as we worry about what we can do about Ulster, Bosnia, Burundi, Rwanda, Sri Lanka, Afghanistan and beyond, we wonder where will it all end.

But if on these pages we have noted no end of local disasters and catastrophes, we have also charted no end of progress, so much so that the woods are not easily seen through the trees. Most Penginians most of the time are naturally more concerned with 'doorstep matters'; like 'how long will my job last or how can I make the money go a little further?', 'what am I going to do about the noisy neighbour or broken-down gizmo?', or 'what to do about the children and self-discipline?' There are two great strands of progress here, so enormously large we often can't see them. First, ironing out little hiccups, we all get richer by the decade, and sometimes by the year. That's got to be the first big story of the country, including Penge and Anerley, since the last world war, if not longer. We have half the unemployment of a generation ago, even if holding on to a job seems twice as tough. Twice as many homes have central heating and three times more people own their own home. We have four times the level of car ownership than a generation ago and we send five times as many of our children to university. Second, we are becoming more tolerant of each other's vast number of unique points; gender, colour, size, creed, class, IQ, sensitivity and even age. Of course some get richer, and some get more civilised, some faster than others. It has always been thus and for many nothing happens fast enough. In the last two decades of the twentieth century two new things have come on the scene to hasten such changes. One is soft, the other hard. The hard one is computerisation. It is everywhere: PCs, mobiles, videos, CD players, the internet, playstations – many children are not so much taught tables as computer literacy. The soft one is our enormous affluence compared with bygone times. Some have even claimed that there is no homelessness any more in Britain today, except self-made homelessness. This is sometimes difficult to believe when a district is surrounded by others more affluent still, and countless TV programmes bombard us all the time with scenes of ever more riches. Homes which a few generations ago had seven to 11 members are replaced by the famous post-war family of 2.4 children. Penge and Anerley homes by 1991 had an average occupancy of just 2.2 people per household and only 25 per cent of households had children in them at all.

Of course it's not Utopia and never will be; there have always been downsides – short-lived partnerships, single-parent families, abuse of all sorts, too many unemployed and far too few visions of better prospects. Too often everyone in the working half of the labour force is doing the work of two, while the other half looks on in amazement. In the opening chapter we saw how public transport rocketed the population upwards spectacularly in a great big ogee curve. In Chapter Three we saw how it all fell apart following that most dastardly murder of Harriet Staunton. In Chapter Two we saw further ups and downs; first in the Palace itself, second the football club of the same name, third the spectacular pleasure gardens of the park, and now, most recently, in Chapters Twelve and Fourteen, with the various plans for renewing the 'top site'. We've also seen that London itself is a collection of 950 villages, growing into some 100 towns, growing some more to merge into suburbs and form 33 boroughs. But what is it that made some villages absorb others? What left Penge an urban district council after 1935 when its neighbour, Beckenham, was 'elevated' to borough status, and left so until both were subsumed into the London Borough of Bromley in 1965? There are as many answers to such questions as there are people available to answer them, yet a few recurring strands are uttered over and over. Power struggles, many of them friendly and diplomatic, are mentioned. Fortune and flukes, both positive and negative, are being cited. Some strands will reflect greed or pride and others demonstrate great altruism. Penginians often have good cause to complain to, and about, the local and the national authorities above. Sometimes they pat them on the back. More occasionally still, Penginians roll up their sleeves and do something to really help and support this or that initiative being promoted by the authorities. Maybe Penginians feel that by just contributing to taxation, they were giving more than enough approval to the powers above. Income tax, council tax and, more recently, value-added tax, applied every time they spent in the shops.

But who looks at things through the eyes of 'authority'? Whoever considers the burdens of being in some way 'in charge'? Whoever says to themselves 'What can I do to help?' Of course there are countless thousands who go beyond 'the call of duty', especially obvious in times of greatest disaster. There are many unsung heroes who put themselves out for the community, people like Potato Joe, John Paxton, Charles Darwin and countless others – Cllr Chris Gaster, writer Brian Wright, architect Tarsem Flora, resident Annie Fernando – who knows, it is often difficult and dangerous to mention the living at the time of going to press; only the long and posthumous eye of history might spot the real saints.

Then there are those who see through the mists of time what might work a little more clearly, who understand something about the directions in which our chosen leaders – both elected and appointed – are trying to take us and go out of their way to support them. If this happens but rarely, then such support is all the more noticed by these authorities when it does occur. Who knows why some suburbs seem to do rather better than others? From time immemorial, urban renewal has been a constant challenge for both council members and officers. One can be forgiven for imagining that with rising standards local authorities would have more funds available, but it is rarely so. Of the wealth we earn, Westminster constantly strives to reduce the portion taxed and spent by the State. New ways have to be found to generate new jobs, preferably local jobs.

For instance, in 2002, Bromley is trying to have the Crystal Palace rebuilt again for leisure activities, creating construction and operating jobs, not to mention considerable leisure opportunities. But accepting change on such a large scale can be tortuous. In one way our district is fortunate; it jumped straight from the agricultural age to the service-industry age – the Information Age, as it is likely to be called. Largely bypassing the industrial age, it lacks large derelict sites needing clearance and renewal, but it does have more than its share of unattractive urban spots. Low-cost schemes can make a large difference here.

There's a dearth of facilities for teenagers in Anerley – coffee bars, video shops, music centres and the like. The youth centre replacing the former Railway pub by Anerley Station in 2001 is a fine example. With one of the lowest car-ownership areas of London, this district could well do with such facilities, and planning committees could do much to release perfectly suitable premises for these.

As we saw in Chapter Six, there are no secondary schools in Anerley and also few adult-education facilities, bar the ones in Kingsdale Road on the Beckenham edge of the district and at the Hawthorne Centre. But that is no excuse for not encouraging the hidden demand for things like bookkeeping, arts and crafts, car maintenance, creative writing, English, music, painting, singing for non-singers and small-scale gardening (indoor, bonsai and window-box), etc.

As we have seen, public transport has always proved a catalyst for further development and improvement. The Croydon Tramlink is planned to extend to the Palace. But will it happen? – only if there is concerted local support, not an endless series of objections and protests. Where the Crystal Palace Loop line crosses Croydon Road a new railway halt could readily be shoehorned in, stimulating the local population's ability to reach London jobs.

One thing there's no shortage of in Penge and Anerley is children; all that is needed is more crêche, nursery and child-minding places – plus the whole panoply of facilities, opportunities and stimulation to help them reach forward as previous generations have so much benefited from.

During a recent survey in Penge High Street, passers-by were asked what their visions for the district's future held. Among suggestions were the following: proper High-Street parking, coffee bars in Anerley, street trees renewed, Anerley adult education, railway halt at Croydon Road, child-caring facilities, tramlink to Crystal Palace, modern shops and offices, business park, road safety training centre, arts centre, a mixed secondary school, Crystal Palace rebuilt, pedestrian shopping centre above High Street, kart racing, canal restored, a helipad and a theatre.

Just as other deprived or neglected areas qualify for tax incentives for job-creation initiatives, more could be done to encourage experimental retail and office businesses. Often only some low-cost inspiration is lacking. Some no doubt imagine much of the above to be sheer daydream; it's either not wanted, too expensive or controversial, or else just wouldn't work. If these are your reactions, flick through these pages again. Remember what brought affluence to Penge and Anerley in the first place – the world's greatest exhibition hall, highest fountains and greatest show of life-size prehistoric animals. Remember too what brought the place to its knees for a century – just one dastardly deed – and then imagine the vast potential the place holds today. What little miracle might you support here next?

For those who were brought up with any knowledge at all of the biblical stories, recall the one about the talents. History will not judge us by who was given the most talents (Matt.xxv, 14–30), but by how well we used those limited talents. Happy hunting!

Subscribers

Tricia A. Abbott, Crystal Palace, London
Leslie Lewis Allen, Clacton-On-Sea
Louise Bacon, Lower Sydenham
Basil N. Baker, Anerley, London
Stephen G. Baker, Brixton
Mr and Mrs J. Ball, Sydenham, London
Mr David Barber, Sydenham, London
Mrs Barbara Barry
Phil Barstow, Maple Road, Penge
Linda Bartlett, Ascot, Royal Berkshire
Rose Bateman, Anerley, SE20
Eileen Beavis, Penge, London
Keith A. Bernhardt, Beckenham, Kent
Rick Biddle, Wallington, Surrey
Grazyna Maria Bielecki, Crystal Palace, London
John Blundell, Orpington
Ellen Boucher MA, East Oakley, Basingstoke
Christine M.R. Bowdery, Anerley, London
A.J.C. Breck, Penge. AFS/NFS
Mr A.J.C. Breck, Tankerton, Kent
Mr P. Breck, Penge, London
Brenda Brent (née Wixey), Beckenham, Kent
John W. Brown, Local History Publications
H.E. Brown, Radlett, Hertfordshire
Carol Browne (née Boyce), Upper Norwood, London
The Brushett family, Penge
Geoff and Janet Bunn
June Burrows (née Ridout)
Mr Frederick C. Burton, Crystal Palace, London
Kevin Carleton-Reeves, Crystal Palace, London
Nigel Lees and Marc Carlton, Penge, London
Alan and Sheila Carpenter, Anerley, London
Andrew Cleary, Crystal Palace, London
Professor Alice Coleman, Dulwich, London
Elenore Collins, Halstead, Kent/late of Norwood
Mike Conrad FCSD, FRSA
Sandy and Harry Constantine, Sydenham, London
Mrs Lesley Elizabeth Cook
Mr Alan S. Cooling, Upper Norwood, London
J.R. Copland
George A. Cornish, Penge, London
Dennis W. Costidell,
Raymond and Ruth Cousins, Dulwich
Alice Coyle, Upper Norwood, London
Frank Cribbens, St Johns Church and School
John and Valerie Crutchlow, Rushden, Hertfordshire
Clive A.R. Dalgliesh, Penge, London
James A. Daly, Penge, London
Peter Davey, Crystal Palace
Anne Davey, Sydenham Hill
Michael and Margrete Davies, Crystal Palace
M. Deighan, Upper Norwood, London
Mr P.R. Dennison, Kenley, Surrey
John Douglas, Anerley, SE20
Mark Anthony Dowd, Anerley, London
Margaret Durrant, Penge, London
Mark-Antony Dutton, Crystal Palace
Dennis and Mary Ede, formerly of Upper Norwood
John K. Emery, Penge, London
Mr and Mrs Neal T. Etchells
S.J. Farage, Croydon, Surrey
Anthony James Fryer, Anerley, London
Mrs Dorothy Garland (née Piercey), Croydon, Surrey
Rosaleen Gaynor, Penge, London
John Gent, Croydon
Lee J. Gibson, Anerley, London
Gary R. Giles, Penge, London
Robyn M.M. Gillett, Penge, London
Mrs Pat Gillett, Yeovil, Somerset
William E. Glover, Penge, London
Revd Tony Graham

Mr Michael R. Green, Penge, London
Roy and Eileen Green, Rollesby, Norfolk/late of West Norwood
Nick Grimsdale, Anerley, London
John W. Grimstone, Norbury, London
Audrey V.R. Hammond, Crystal Palace, London
H. and D. Harding, Herefordshire
James Hardy, Beckenham, Kent
Miss Gladys Harper, Anerley, London
Rev. Mary Hawes, Crystal Palace, London
Mrs Julia S. Heard, Upper Norwood, London
Miss V. Herrington
Pete Herron, Crystal Palace, London
Gary F. Hewitt, Dulwich, London
Brian J. Higgott, Upper Norwood, London
Myron G. Hill Jr, Washington DC
Jack Hilton, Penge, London
Douglas C. Hoare, Sleaford, Lincolnshire
Martin John Hoare, Crystal Palace, SE19
Geoffrey F. Holder, Penge, London
The Hollingsworth family, Oakfield Road, Penge
Wendy L. Holt, Addiscombe, Surrey
Colin Hood, Beckenham, Kent
Donald C. Hookway, Penge, London
Cliff and Stephanie Hope, Anerley, London
Alfred John Hopkins, Penge, London
Janet C. Howard, Scotland/formerly Crystal Palace
Eddie E. Howarth, Penge, London
Peter and Beryl Hubbard, East Grinstead, West Sussex
Mrs Glynis Hunt (née Byrne)
Stanley K. Hunter, Glasgow, Scotland
Frank A. and Rita A. Jackson, Penge, London
Mr Cyril Janes, Crystal Palace, London
Kenneth A.G. Jeffries, Dulwich, London
Fiona and Nick Jenkins, Penge, London
Lawrence T. Jenkins, Penge, London
R.S. Jones, Anerley, SE20
Paul M. Kay, Penge, London
Professor and Mrs A.V. Kelly, Upper Norwood, London
A.K. Khandwala (JP, Ret'd), Bromley PSD
Malcolm E. King, West Norwood, London
L.C. Leach
Jacqui and David Lemmon, Beckenham
Mr Peter Lepino, Great Bookham, Surrey
Michael and Lynette Letts, Penge, London
Mr J.M. Lockton
Don Madgwick, Thornton Heath
Dr Peter Main, Crystal Palace, London
Damian and Jan Mann, Stone Cross, East Sussex
Patrick Edward Manning Esq., Penge, London
Tom Manthorpe, born 1928, Thicket Road
Susan O. Marsh, Crystal Palace, London
Otis and Ann Martin
Margaret L. Martin, Anerley, London
The Mary Ellis Theatre School of Dance and Drama, Anerley, London
Mr P.J. McSharry, Penge, London
Esme A. Meads, Penge, London
Beryl Mealing, Upper Norwood, London
Jack Merrifield, East Grinstead, West Sussex
Jean M. Miles, Penge, SE20
Douglas Miller, Station Cottage, Penge West Station
Jorge J. Miralles Vernon and Christina A Miralles Vernon
Michael, Dianne and Scott Morgan, Upper Norwood, London
Philip and Karen Morris, Upper Norwood, London
Bernard J. Morris, Upper Norwood, SE9
Jeffrey N. Moss, Newdigate, Surrey
Mr Raymond D. Muggeridge
Katherine Negus, Anerley, London
Alan Nelhams, Edgware, Middlesex
Dr Margaret Nelson (née Rayner), Dungannon, Co. Tyrone
Jean Nicholson (née Goldthorp), Beckenham
James M. Nicolson, Vauxhall, London
Wayne Obee, Anerley
Master Daniel J.B. Osborne, Crystal Palace, London
Alan M. Owens, Sydenham, London
Mr Yashvantkumar M. and Mrs Diptz Y. Patel, Penge, London
Marjorie V. Payne, Westfield, East Sussex
Mrs Linda S. Phelps, Penge, London
Margaret V. Phelps, Penge, London
Dr Geoffrey Phillips, Caterham
Mr and Mrs B.E. Price, Bridge Row, Croydon, Surrey
Jane D. Pulley, Dulwich, London
Monica Pyle, Anerley, London
N. Randall, Penge, London
John Reed Family, Reed's Dairy, Penge, London
Graham Reeves
Sheila Richardson, Croydon, Surrey
Terry Risk, Sydenham, London
Moira and Dick Robinson, Dulwich, London
Matt Robinson and Owen Courtney, Crystal Palace
Mrs Angie V. Roche, Upper Norwood, London
Marcos Rodrigues, Penge, London
Barbara A. Rosamond, Anerley, London

Bernard Rosefeld, New York, USA
Chris Rothwell, Sutton Coldfield, West Midlands
Sarah 'N' Tony F., Upper Norwood
Amy Saunders, Penge, London
Matt Sawyer, Penge, London
Adrian F. Sawyers, Upper Norwood, London
Mary Scanlan, Penge, London
George P. Scott, Croydon, Surrey
Ivan and Morris Sewter, Alkmaar and Beckenham
Mrs Doreen Sharkie, Penge, London
Peter F. Simpson, Battersea, London
The Skinner Family, late of Penge
Joseph William Richard Slaby
Julian E. Smalley, Crystal Palace, London
Martin, Lucie and Denney Smith, Crystal Palace
Jean and Jack Smith, Sydenham, London
Walter C. Smith, Penge
Kenneth E. Snow
Lilian M. Sopp, Sydenham, London
Mrs M. Spaughton
Raymond J. Speller, Penge, London
Iris Spice, West Wickham, Kent
Sally J. Stanton, Crystal Palace, London
Miss Hazel Stapley, Anerley, London
Melinda C. Steffens, Crystal Palace, London
Martin and Dorothy Stevens, Penge, London
Deirdre Stevens, Crystal Palace
Doreen M. Stewart, Sydenham, London
W.A. Stirland, Anerley, London
Johanna Sullivan, Anerley, London
Jasper M. Swarray, Penge, London
Teresa Symes, Upper Norwood, London
Jean and Philip Taylor, Sydenham, London
Mrs V. Tippett, Sydenham
Mrs Eileen M. Tiveen
Alan Tiveen, Chesham, Buckinghamshire
Carlton Townsend, Brisbane
Rev. Dr John C. Travell
Trevor Tween, Luton, Bedfordshire
Susan M. Vincent, Anerley, SE20
Joan E. Viner, Sydenham, London
Susan A. Walker, Beckenham, Kent
Scott Walker, Anerley
Barnaby J. Walker, Anerley, London
Peter Walker, Croydon, Surrey
John F.W. Walling, Newton Abbot, Devon
John Wickenden, Anerley, London
Malcolm G. Wildeman, Penge, London
Tracy M. Wileman, Anerley, London
Mr and Mrs O.R. Williams-Ellis, Crystal Palace
Steve Williamson and Lucile Combes, Gipsy Hill
Peggy Irene Willis, Penge
Mr A. Wilson, Sydenham, London
Mrs Margaret D. Wilson, Sydenham, London
G.D.M. Wilson BA
Derek W. Wood, Anerley, London
Evelyn A. Woosnam, Orpington, Kent
Mrs O.B. Wylie, Penge, London
Mrs Marian Young, Beckenham, Kent
Barbara Zuckriegl, Penge, London

Gentrification of the area from the early 1850s; a rare view showing one of the orginal Paxton water towers which were replaced within months by Brunel's, and the North Transept, which burnt down in 1866. (LHC)

Titles from the Series

The Book of Addiscombe • Various
The Book of Addiscombe, Vol. II • Various
The Book of Bampton • Caroline Seward
The Book of Barnstaple • Avril Stone
Book of Bickington • Stuart Hands
Blandford Forum: A Millennium Portrait • Various
The Book of Bridestowe • R. Cann
The Book of Brixham • Frank Pearce
The Book of Buckland Monachorum & Yelverton • Hemery
The Book of Carshalton • Stella Wilks
The Parish Book of Cerne Abbas • Vale & Vale
The Book of Chagford • Ian Rice
The Book of Chittlehamholt with Warkleigh & Satterleigh • Richard Lethbridge
The Book of Chittlehampton • Various
The Book of Colney Heath • Bryan Lilley
The Book of Constantine • Moore & Trethowan
The Book of Cornwood & Lutton • Various
The Book of Creech St Michael • June Small
The Book of Cullompton • Various
The Book of Dawlish • Frank Pearce
The Book of Dulverton, Brushford, Bury & Exebridge • Various
The Book of Dunster • Hilary Binding
The Ellacombe Book • Sydney R. Langmead
The Book of Exmouth • W.H. Pascoe
The Book of Grampound with Creed • Bane & Oliver
The Book of Hayling Island & Langstone • Rogers
The Book of Helston • Jenkin with Carter
The Book of Hemyock • Clist & Dracott
The Book of Hethersett • Various
The Book of High Bickington • Avril Stone
The Book of Ilsington • Dick Wills
The Book of Lamerton • Ann Cole & Friends
Lanner, A Cornish Mining Parish • Scharron Schwartz & Roger Parker
The Book of Leigh & Bransford • Various
The Book of Litcham with Lexham & Mileham • Various
The Book of Loddiswell • Various
The Book of Lulworth • Rodney Legg
The Book of Lustleigh • Joe Crowdy
The Book of Manaton • Various
The Book of Markyate • Richard Hogg
The Book of Mawnan • Various
The Book of Meavy • Pauline Hemery
The Book of Minehead with Alcombe • Binding & Stevens
The Book of Morchard Bishop • Jeff Kingaby
The Book of Newdigate • John Callcut
The Book of Northlew with Ashbury • Various
The Book of North Newton • Robins & Robins
The Book of North Tawton • Various
The Book of Okehampton • Radford & Radford
The Book of Paignton • Frank Pearce
The Book of Penge, Anerley & Crystal Palace • Various
The Book of Peter Tavy with Cudlipptown • Various
The Book of Pimperne • Jean Coull
The Book of Plymtree • Tony Eames
The Book of Porlock • Denis Corner
Postbridge – The Heart of Dartmoor • Reg Bellamy
The Book of Priddy • Various
The Book of Rattery • Various
The Book of Silverton • Various
The Book of South Molton • Various
The Book of South Stoke • Various
South Tawton & South Zeal with Sticklepath • Radfords
The Book of Sparkwell with Hemerdon & Lee Mill • Pam James
The Book of Staverton • Pete Lavis
The Book of Stithians • Various
The Book of Studland • Rodney Legg
The Book of Swanage • Rodney Legg
The Book of Torbay • Frank Pearce
Uncle Tom Cobley & All: Widecombe-in-the-Moor • Stephen Woods
The Book of Watchet • Compiled by David Banks
The Book of West Huntspill • Various
Widecombe-in-the-Moor • Stephen Woods
The Book of Williton • Michael Williams
Woodbury: The Twentieth Century Revisited • Roger Stokes
The Book of Woolmer Green • Various

Forthcoming

The Book of Bakewell • Various
The Book of Barnstaple, Vol. II • Avril Stone
The Book of Brampford • Various
The Book of Breage & Gurmoe • Stephen Polglase
The Book of the Bedwyns • Various
The Book of Bideford • Peter Christie
The Book of Bridport • Rodney Legg
The Book of Buckfastleigh • Sandra Coleman
The Book of Carharrack • Various
The Book of Castleton • Geoff Hill
The Book of Edale • Gordon Miller
The Book of Kingskerswell • Various
The Book of Lostwithiel • Barbara Frasier
The Book of Lydford • Barbara Weeks
The Book of Lyme Regis • Rodney Legg
The Book of Nether Stowey • Various
The Book of Nynehead • Various
The Book of Princetown • Dr Gardner-Thorpe
The Book of St Day • Various
The Book of Sampford Courtenay with Honeychurch • Stephanie Pouya
The Book of Sculthorpe • Garry Windeler
The Book of Sherborne • Rodney Legg
The Book of Southbourne • Rodney Legg
The Book of Tavistock • Gerry Woodcock
The Book of Thorley • Various
The Book of Tiverton • Mike Sampson
The Book of West Lavington • Various
The Book of Witheridge • Various
The Book of Withycombe • Chris Boyles

For details of any of the above titles or if you are interested in writing your own history, please contact: Commissioning Editor Community Histories, Halsgrove House, Lower Moor Way, Tiverton Business Park, Tiverton, Devon EX16 6SS, England; email: naomic@halsgrove.com

In order to include as many historic photographs as possible in this volume, a printed index is not included. However, the Community History Series is indexed by Genuki. For further information and indexes to volumes in the series, please visit: http://www.cs.ncl.uk/genuki/DEV/indexingproject.html